FAKES,
FRAUDS,
AND
FLIMFLAMMERY

FAKES,
FRAUDS,
AND
FLIMFLAMMERY

Even More of the World's Most Outrageous Scams

ANDREAS SCHROEDER

M&S

Canadian Cataloguing in Publication Data
Schroeder, Andreas, 1946–
    Fakes, frauds, and flimflammery

Includes bibliographical references.
ISBN 0-7710-7954-0

1. Fraud – Anecdotes.   2. Swindlers and swindling – Anecdotes.
3. Impostors and imposture – Anecdotes.   I . Title.

HV6691.S334 1999   364.16'3   C98-932563-6

We acknowledge the financial support of the Government of Canada through the Book Publishing Industry Development Program for our publishing activities. We further acknowledge the support of the Canada Council for the Arts and the Ontario Arts Council for our publishing program.

Typeset in Bembo by M&S, Toronto
Printed and bound in Canada

McClelland & Stewart Inc.
The Canadian Publishers
481 University Avenue
Toronto, Ontario
M5G 2E9

1 2 3 4 5   03 02 01 00 99

Dedicated, as always, to the irrepressible crew
that concocts and produces
"The Basic Black Show":

Arthur Black, Host
Chris Straw, Executive Producer (Vancouver)
John Stinchcombe, Producer (Toronto)
Rosemary Allenbach, Producer (Vancouver)

and to
Mike Chandler, of Halifax, Nova Scotia,
whose suggestion (Fakes, Frauds, and Flimflammery)
won the "Basic Black" competition to
name this book

Contents

Preface

————◆————

"A series," to paraphrase the noted French epigrammatist François de la Rochefoucauld, "invariably occurs when its author loses all sense of shame."

Guilty as charged.

Shameless barely begins to describe this series.

What began as a single collection of some of the world's most outrageous scams and hoaxes, broadcast on CBC-Radio's "Basic Black" and published under the title *Scams, Scandals, and Skulduggery*, proved so successful that a second volume seemed called for. That collection, *Cheats, Charlatans, and Chicanery*, promptly outsold its predecessor and seemed itself to beg further issue. "We're on a roll!" my publisher telephoned happily from Toronto. "They're absolutely insatiable out there! Even the

Lithuanians have bought translation rights. Can you have a third collection ready by next spring?"

I whined something about all this getting in the way of the volumes of great and deathless literature I was also trying to write.

"Deathless schmeathless," my publisher boomed. "This is your pension, you idiot! Is there enough material in your files for a third collection?"

I had to admit that a decade's worth of research into the shenanigans of some of the world's most ingenious rogues and rascals had actually produced enough material for a dozen more books.

"Well there you go," he crowed triumphantly. "You love this stuff! And you love writing about it! So get cracking, and send me another manuscript by Christmas!"

Such are the true motivations that engender a series.

Like their predecessors, the stories in *Fakes, Frauds, and Flimflammery* were first broadcast on "Basic Black," though each has been re-researched and rewritten to anywhere from four to eight times its original broadcast length. Also like their predecessors, the stories featured are those that received the greatest listener response. You could call the book "The Best of 'Basic Black' Scams, Volume III."

Three caveats applied to the first two volumes, and they apply to this one as well. Since these stories range over a period of several centuries, I sometimes found the relative size of their thefts and frauds, expressed in original dollars, difficult to compare. To solve this problem, I have adjusted all their dollar amounts to 1999 values, using the Statistics Canada historical price index as a rough guide. This should give today's reader a more meaningful sense of the true financial impact of each fraud, both in terms of the size of the crime, and of the law-enforcement costs it engendered.

Second, readers should appreciate that stories of this kind are, inevitably, reconstructions. Each story really happened, but sources often differ on many details. In choosing which to include and which to ignore, I freely admit to the motivations of a storyteller rather than those of a scholar or historian.

Finally, I have also taken the liberty of occasionally dramatizing scenes for which I had only the descriptive facts, and quoting, paraphrasing, or even inventing dialogue where I felt it did not misrepresent those facts. Since most of these stories were originally reported by persons who were not themselves participants in them, it seems safe to assume that any dialogue quoted in such texts was itself concocted by similar means.

Andreas Schroeder
Mission, B.C.

Acknowledgements

———◆———

Once again, the creation of this book owes a considerable debt to the kindness of librarians. My thanks to the staff of the Vancouver Public Library, the University of British Columbia Library, the Burnaby Public Library, the New Westminster Public Library, the Mission branch of the Fraser Valley Regional Library, and the library of the University College of the Fraser Valley.

I'm also grateful to the many "Basic Black" listeners who contributed leads and suggestions for the contents of this book.

Special thanks to my editor, Pat Kennedy, and my copy-editor, Peter Buck, whose help I never think I need at the beginning, but whose vigilance and expertise I'm always hugely grateful for by the end.

And thanks to my family, Sharon, Sabrina, Vanessa, and Tante Gertraut, for their patience and forbearance when deadlines loomed.

The Ladies Sock It to the Franc

*Two Gender Skirmishes in the World of
French High Finance*

1. The Thérèse Humbert Hornswoggle

Thérèse Aurignac was having a lot of trouble getting used to the indignities of being a servant girl.

Though life had never been easy for the daughter of the town drunk in Bauzelles, France, she had never been treated like trash before. But her father's death on January 5, 1874, when Thérèse was sixteen, had left the family penniless, forcing everyone – her mother, her two brothers, and her younger sister – into private service in nearby Toulouse. It hadn't taken Thérèse very long in service to realize that, without beauty, money, or connections, her prospects for even a modest future were quite hopeless.

For as long as she could remember, her father had assured her this wouldn't happen. Whenever his drinking had cost him yet another job, or his debts had forced the family to subsist yet again on rice and beans, he would invariably remind them of the estate they would inherit the day after his death.

They'd all grown up with this story: how, as a rebellious young man, René d'Aurignac had been kicked out of his noble family's home and sent into the world to sink or swim – with only the assurance that, after his death, his children would be welcomed back into the bosom of the d'Aurignac family with all their inheritance rights reinstated.

All the documents to this effect were locked in an old brass-studded oak chest in his bedroom.

After René's funeral, the whole family had huddled around the chest, watching as Thérèse's brothers attacked the lock. Though none of them had ever been truly convinced of their father's claims, some desperate part of them urgently wanted it to be true. The lock was so badly rusted, it took an axe and a hammer to smash it off.

Inside was nothing but an ordinary brick.

Thérèse remained furious about it. Not so much at her father's betrayal, but at her own gullibility. Since she'd inherited her father's guile and imagination, she should have known better. Meanwhile, she was losing jobs as regularly as he had, refusing to be pushed around. Perhaps there'd been some truth after all to his guff about the noble blood in her veins.

And then, on March 2, 1881, everything changed.

That morning, through the door of the third-class rail carriage she'd taken to visit an aunt in Paris, Thérèse saw an American tourist in the adjoining first-class carriage fall out of his seat in exactly the same way she remembered an uncle falling during a heart attack he'd suffered in his parlour. She rushed through the door and lifted his head, shifting him onto his side and opening his shirt exactly as the doctor had done in her uncle's case. Then she gently massaged his temples. She stayed with him until the train reached the Gare du Nord, then hailed a carriage and helped him to the nearby Hôpital Lariboisière. As he was being carried into a treatment room, he stopped the orderly and haltingly asked Thérèse if she'd be willing to wait until he came out.

She said she would.

She spent the next three days caring for him in his luxurious rooms at the Grande Métropolitain, bathing his face and chest with cool water, helping him drink his medicines, and feeding him soups from the hotel restaurant. He was immensely grateful, utterly charming, and in his thoughtfulness, appreciation, and concern, very much the father she'd always wanted.

In his broken French he had told her he was Robert Henry Crawford, an industrialist from Chicago, come to Paris to transact some business, which he had fortunately concluded two days previously. He had been returning from a hiking trip to Chantilly – perhaps too ambitious an undertaking for a man of his seventy-five years – and had planned to spend several days resting up before returning to New York by ship.

It was an itinerary he still hoped, with her help, to manage.

Thérèse assured him she would do what she could.

At Le Havre three days later, still shaky but considerably improved, he kissed her gallantly on both cheeks, squeezed her arm affectionately, and pushed an envelope firmly into her hands. He refused to take no for an answer.

On the train back to Toulouse, she tore it open.

It contained 250,000 francs ($24,000)* – twice as much as she earned in an entire year.

Thérèse used the money to buy her mother a linen shop.

But there was more to come. Two years later a letter arrived from the Paris law firm of Sauvignon and Hébert, informing Thérèse Aurignac that she had been named in the will of a recently deceased American industrialist, Robert Crawford, bequeathing her certain sums and securities, the effecting of which would require her personal attendance in Paris.

For Thérèse, now twenty-one, still unmarried and with no better prospects than when she'd gone into service, this was an absolute godsend. Not only had Robert Crawford left her the astonishing sum of $240 million in bonds and securities, but the bequest came with two intriguing conditions:

(1) that the bequest be held in trust by the law firm of Sauvignon and Hébert until Thérèse Aurignac reached the age of thirty, and

(2) that the bequest plus accrued interest be paid to Thérèse Aurignac at or after age thirty, only if or when Thérèse Aurignac married.

News of this extraordinary inheritance travelled quickly, and it wasn't long before Thérèse was being swarmed by eager suitors. Many a girl might have lost her head in such circumstances, but Thérèse was strong-willed and strong-minded, and not about to waste this once-in-a-lifetime opportunity. Within a year she had chosen and agreed to marry Frédéric Humbert, a lawyer and the

---

* For consistency, all dollar amounts have been adjusted to 1999 values.

son of the rich and widely connected mayor of Toulouse, Gustave Humbert.

Frédéric was quite unlike his ambitious father. He preferred solitude and contemplation to the rough and tumble of French law and politics. He was quite happy to play second fiddle to the decisive Thérèse. While unimpressed by his new daughter-in-law's looks and manners, Mayor Humbert soon came to appreciate her for exactly the opportunism and enterprise he'd always hoped to find in his son.

The newlyweds moved to Paris and immediately began making their mark, borrowing and spending on the strength of their future prospects. Thérèse chose a luxurious $5-million mansion on the fashionable avenue de la Grand Armée, which she had stripped and refurbished in expensive silks and hardwoods. She added a huge solarium and a three-storey glass rotunda. She expanded the stables and added a lush bowling green.

Word of the Crawford bequest had long ago swept through Paris's financial community, so there was no shortage of bankers willing, indeed eager, to lend her any funds she required. Thérèse was just as enthusiastic about accepting them. After she'd finished her Paris home, she purchased a country estate and a 110-foot yacht with full crew. Then she bought several million dollars' worth of clothes and jewellery.

Frédéric didn't get involved in any of this. He had the carpenters add a modest artist's studio to the rear of their Paris mansion and spent most of his time there, quietly painting and reading.

By 1885, Thérèse Humbert was cutting a wide swath through Paris society. Her salon was fast becoming the most interesting meeting place in town, attracting artists, writers, actors, lawyers, and the city's most cultured businessmen.

Despite her poor education and brusque manner, there was something undeniably fascinating about this reedy-voiced, plain-spoken woman. Her very presence seemed to induce people to drop their pretensions and affectations. Businessmen in particular enjoyed her hardheaded opinions and perspectives. They liked the way she took a greater interest in money than merely the spending of it.

Having provided for her most basic personal needs, Thérèse began borrowing heavily to invest in real estate and art. She bought houses, estates, office buildings, and warehouses. She acquired El Grecos, Velázquezes, Daumiers, and even Toulouse-Lautrecs. She invested in half a dozen art galleries, whose owners promptly developed an unabashed predilection for Frédéric's watercolours (if they knew what was good for them). She bought shares in several Parisian utilities.

Then, in 1886, a front-page story in *Le Matin* trumpeted the news that the famous Robert Crawford will – the very basis of Thérèse Humbert's fast-growing business empire – had been challenged in the Supreme Court of the United States.

The plaintiffs were two nephews of her benefactor, Robert and Henry Crawford. They announced they had found a second will, apparently undated, naming them and Thérèse Aurignac as its *three* beneficiaries. Their lawyers thus claimed a share of the Crawford estate, and challenged Thérèse's right to its interest – and even its in-trust possession.

Nobody was surprised at Thérèse Humbert's reaction. Her first move was to march straight into the offices of Sauvignon and Hébert and demand the immediate handover of all Crawford estate securities. Next, she had a large, steel fireproof safe installed in the bedroom of her Paris mansion. Finally, she obliged Charles Sauvignon himself to attend and initial a formal, itemized list of all Crawford securities deposited into her safe, after which the safe was closed, locked, and sealed. The securities were thus safely beyond reach of the Crawford nephews and the safe would never, Thérèse swore, be opened until their challenge had been successfully beaten back. All this was done in the presence of a roomful of witnesses, including reporters from all of Paris's major financial newspapers.

The story soaked up more ink throughout France than the death of a president.

Next, Thérèse hired a battalion of lawyers and went on the warpath. The Crawford nephews, reportedly, did the same. In the fall of 1887 the two combatants went head to head for the first time in a Paris courtroom, where Thérèse Humbert and her lawyers countersued with a vengeance.

Luckily for Thérèse, the challenge to the Crawford will did little to alarm her growing consortium of lenders. In fact, the large cluster of lawyers now crowded around the will and its legal disposition seemed to give it an added credibility. A few of her more sharp-pencilled bankers upped their interest charges by a point or two, but, in the main, life went on as before. By the spring of 1889 her aggregate loans had grown to more than $100 million dollars, with several banks carrying Humbert paper to the tune of $12 million to $15 million each.

On the other hand, what was a $100-million debt against securities of $240 million, plus compounding interest?

Besides, the banks were earning premium interest rates on Thérèse's loans.

And in any case, Thérèse Humbert wasn't sitting idle during these legal wranglings. In the spring of 1890 she and her two brothers, Émile and Romain, founded an ambitious insurance company, which quickly captured the lion's share of France's lucrative life-annuities market. Like all Humbert enterprises, the

Rente Viagère enjoyed excellent newspaper coverage and reported impressive profits during the next half-dozen years.

Whatever business she undertook, "La Grande Thérèse" seemed invariably to thrive.

This was no less true on the social and political front. As her financial empire grew, her father-in-law, Gustave Humbert, rose to become France's minister of justice, then leader of the senate. This did Thérèse no harm at all. Her powerful connections soon included many of France's most influential politicians and judges. When one of France's most coveted symbols of influence – a premier box at the Théâtre de l'Opéra – became available following the death of its former holder, Baron Haussmann, in 1887, Thérèse Humbert was chosen from among hundreds of France's aristocratic applicants. (She rewarded the theatre board's good judgement by donating more than half a million dollars to the maintenance and refurbishing of the venerable opera house.)

It was only on the legal front that Thérèse's magic touch didn't seem to be working. Despite herculean efforts, her army of legal beagles couldn't make any significant headway. Every case they won was appealed; every case they lost they were instructed to appeal. Robert and Henry Crawford seemed to have endless resources and an indefatigable resolve. So did Thérèse Humbert. In the face of this, the interest of France's financial newspapers began to flag. Though the outcome held considerable interest for their readers, the space they were willing to give to this endless trench warfare dwindled steadily.

As Thérèse Humbert's thirtieth birthday came and went, Crawford's will seemed no closer to being probated than when it had first been announced.

In some ways, it hardly seemed to matter. Thérèse was repaying her loans on time – at least for the most part – and whenever there was a delay, she always had a good explanation. Everyone knew her legal bills were staggering, and no banker in his right mind would have suggested she skimp on good legal help in a matter of such importance. In comparison, the millions she spent on clothes and jewellery and parties on the Riviera were considered trifles. Her receptions at her Paris mansion were now the highlight of the city's social season; even the president was known to dine with the Humberts now and again. Such advantages, from a business perspective, were cheap at twice the price.

But you can't satisfy everyone, and one such malcontent was Monsieur Jules Bizat, an official of the Bank of France. Nosy by both inclination and profession, Bizat had heard certain rumours that led him to inquire, at one of Thérèse Humbert's receptions, exactly where the Rente Viagère invested its clients' contributions.

Thérèse assured him that they were all invested in good, safe French treasury bonds. The next day Jules Bizat checked at the French treasury but found no record of the Rente Viagère holding such bonds. That seemed curious, and Bizat mentioned it to several of his banker friends who held Humbert paper.

One of these bankers, a Monsieur Delatte of Lyons, was about to visit the United States. He asked Thérèse at a business luncheon exactly where these remarkably litigious Crawford nephews lived. She told him a suburb of Boston. While in New York, Delatte made a side trip to Boston and searched for a Robert or Henry Crawford. He found no trace of them – not in Boston, nor in Crawford's home town, Chicago, either.

In a telegram to a colleague in Paris who had also lent Thérèse money, Delatte described his futile search. He wondered whether a more thorough investigation was called for. He suggested his colleague make some discreet additional inquiries.

Delatte's colleague didn't believe in discreet. He simply called on Thérèse Humbert at her Paris mansion and showed her the telegram.

Thérèse just laughed.

The Crawfords lived in Boston, Georgia, she explained. It was a small family seat in Thomas County. The Crawfords had lived there for more than a hundred years.

Delatte's colleague felt like a fool.

(Delatte himself never returned to take up the issue. In an unrelated incident he was murdered in New York City by thugs, who dumped his body into the East River.)

The great spoked wheels of the Thérèse Humbert business empire ground steadily on.

By 1901 Thérèse's debts had grown to more than $212 million – fast approaching the point where they would exceed the value of her entire holdings. It was a point Thérèse's bankers were eyeing anxiously – to the extent of finally overcoming their normal reticence and opening their Humbert records to one another.

How could a business empire as profitable as hers continue to require such vast amounts of debt capital?

True, she had never been one to stint herself; by now her personal residences numbered twelve, and the number of her employees exceeded fourteen hundred. As well, the interest she had been paying on her debts for the past two decades amounted to some $135 million.

And then, of course, there were her never-ending legal expenses.

The Humbert–Crawford court battle had by now been grinding on for an eyebrow-raising fifteen years.

As with the rest of Thérèse Humbert's business empire, her legal battles had been generating rumours, too. Some lawyers were saying it was Thérèse's own unreasonable demands and delaying tactics that accounted for much of the wasted time and money. Some went even further, claiming she had actually won the case on several occasions, but had always, at the last minute, ordered her lawyers to withdraw a suit or countersuit, forcing them to start all over again.

Of course, that didn't make any sense. Why would anyone in her right mind deliberately avoid winning a court case that was costing her $6 million a year?

Thérèse Humbert's debts kept rising.

By now, none of her lenders were willing to advance her any further funds against the Crawford will, and many had begun to demand houses or office buildings as collateral. Old loans up for renewal were no longer automatically rolled over.

And absolutely no one was prepared, as in the past, to accept "when the Crawford will is probated" as a loan's maturity date.

Meanwhile, Jules Bizat was still snooping around the Rente Viagère. He was becoming more and more certain that there was something fishy about this company, but was reluctant to do anything drastic, because his own father-in-law had a lot of money invested with Thérèse Humbert. That, when you came right down to it, was now almost every major moneylender's problem in Paris: anything that might cause an abrupt meltdown of the Humbert empire could well cost them all a lot more money than if they just hung on for the ride.

But how long could this ride go on?

Many of his banker friends, Bizat discovered, were having similar thoughts.

Finally, some of the more alarmed lenders decided to consult with France's prime minister, Maître Waldeck-Rousseau, who was also one of the country's top jurists.

Waldeck-Rousseau didn't know much about Thérèse's financial affairs, but what he knew of her legal manoeuvrings had already made him suspicious. From his jurist's perspective, the Crawford nephews had had a very thin case, which should have been lost or thrown out years ago. He shared the view of a growing number of lawyers that Thérèse Humbert indeed seemed to be wilfully trying to *avoid* winning her case.

He also found it odd that no one seemed ever to have met or seen these Crawford nephews – or Robert Crawford himself, before his death.

He agreed with Bizat that precipitous action might prove counter-productive, but suggested a little "journalistic heat" to drive a few more facts out of the woodwork. He promised to contact a writer friend of his, one Émile Zola, who might be prevailed upon to do the dirty.

Zola's provocative articles in *Le Matin* several months later had exactly the effect Bizat had been hoping for. Thérèse Humbert was offended, but took his jabs with comparative equanimity. Her chief counsel, however – one Maître du Bruit – was incensed.

He threatened mayhem and prosecution. He claimed slander and irreparable damage to his honour. He became so infuriated that he offered, without consulting Thérèse, to take upon himself the responsibility of opening her safe and permitting her creditors to examine its contents to their own satisfaction, to prove once and for all that there was nothing irregular about the Crawford will. After that, he announced, he intended to prosecute his slanderers to within an inch of their lives.

Stunned, Thérèse reminded du Bruit that their lawsuit with

the Crawford nephews had not yet been resolved, and that opening the safe could seriously jeopardize the very resolution for which they had spent the past fifteen years fighting. She also reminded him that the contents of the safe had been attested to among witnesses by a Paris lawyer in good standing; what purpose could it serve to open it now?

In fact, this wasn't the first time Thérèse had had to confront calls for the safe to be opened, but in the past her father-in-law, then minister of justice, had always helped her deflect them. His death the previous year had cost her that protection, and rumours that the current prime minister was in agreement with Maître du Bruit now closed off all other avenues of escape. Thérèse even tried to convince poor Frédéric to goad some of his legal friends into action, but Frédéric merely retreated further into his studio. This wasn't his speed, and anyway, his friends all wanted to see the inside of Thérèse's safe, too.

In the interim, du Bruit had done his homework and was able to demonstrate that certain clauses in French inheritance law actually did provide for the exceptional breaking open of officially sealed documents, where public, official circumstances made such an act necessary. He assured Thérèse that, if they invoked these clauses, any attempt by the Crawfords to proclaim the inheritance forfeit would be denied.

On May 7, 1902, two days before the safe was scheduled to be opened, a mysterious fire broke out in the Humbert mansion, consuming a large part of the building's west wing – the wing in which Thérèse's bedroom and the safe were located. While the safe proved fireproof and was unharmed, the bedroom was totally destroyed. The fire gave Thérèse such a case of jangled nerves that she packed her bags and left for one of her country estates, leaving Maître du Bruit to handle the opening of the safe.

On May 9, du Bruit, armed with a court order and surrounded by a crush of bankers, lawyers, and reporters, had workmen attack the scorched and peeling safe – Thérèse had forgotten
to give him the key. The safe proved so solid and impregnable
that the workmen sweated for more than an hour with axes and
hammers before they were able to force the door.

What fell out when the last hinge had been smashed off was
not a brick exactly, but not much more than a brick. All they
found was a few virtually worthless securities, several francs, an
empty jewellery case, a copper coin, and a brass button.

A warrant was sworn out for the immediate arrest of Thérèse
and Frédéric Humbert, and Émile and Romain Aurignac. All
four proved to have flown the coop. They were found four
months later, hiding out in a boarding house in Madrid.

Despite the opinion of the banking profession – or perhaps
precisely because of it – Thérèse Humbert became a folk hero
overnight. As she had once conquered the moneyed aristo-
cracy, she now conquered France's blue-collar class. She had
always been one of them, after all. They admired the way she
had solved her lack of wealth, her lack of prospects. They
loved the clever way she had overcome her lack of beauty, her
spinsterhood.

And they absolutely adored the way she'd stuck it to the
banks. There was no love lost in nineteenth-century France
between its blue-collar workers and its bankers. Thérèse
Humbert had simply done to the bankers, in reality, what most
workers did to them in their hearts every day of the week.

The ensuing trial, on May 9, 1903, mostly confirmed what
everyone already suspected. While there may actually have been
a Robert Crawford, or someone like him – where would
Thérèse Aurignac have got her initial $24,000 after all? – the

subsequent will had been pure invention. So were the Crawford nephews, whose persistent court challenges had been intended merely to ensure that the real contents of the safe were never revealed.

As for the Rente Viagère, Jules Bizat's nose had been right; the company had never invested a penny of its clients' contributions. In classic Ponzi-scheme tradition, most of its money had simply flowed directly through to Thérèse and her brothers.

In final total, this simple servant girl had bilked France's most sophisticated lenders and investors out of more than $340 million.

It took the jury less than twenty-four hours to find all the accused guilty. Their sentences, however, were surprisingly lenient. Thérèse and Frédéric received five years in prison (Frédéric cited as a passive but informed accomplice), Romain three, and Émile two. The crowd outside the courthouse cheered and booed by turns; the rock-throwing and speech-making continued through most of the night.

Later commentators speculated that the reason for the court's lenient sentences had more to do with avoiding a potentially embarrassing appeal than reflecting the defendants' huge popularity. It was hard to believe, they said, that such an enormously complex fraud could have been carried out without the help of a lot of well-placed lawyers, politicians, and bureaucrats. Considerable suspicion fell on the late Gustave Humbert, of course, but there were undoubtedly many others.

Thérèse's willingness to accept her sentence without comment, and to emigrate to the United States after her release in 1908, may have saved a lot more careers than she had ruined.

She died in Chicago in 1918.

2. The Marthe Hanau Humbug

If there was one thing Marthe Hanau truly loved, it was high finance.

She delighted in the tactical challenges of a big business deal. She thrilled to the roller-coaster ecstasy and despair of the Paris stock market. She was fascinated by the intrigue, thrust, and parry of French corporate enterprise.

From an early age she had perched on her industrialist father's knee and watched him play the big money game. She'd pestered him to let her add up balance sheets, record market investments, keep the ledger books. As a teenager she'd implored him to let her try her hand at some small equity plays, risk a little venture capital.

Daddy was charmed, but not convinced. High finance wasn't for girls – or women, for that matter. He found it amusing that Marthe was clever with numbers – would even admit, when confronted by her flashing eyes and furious anger, that she was occasionally better at them than he was – but that didn't change the point. The point was that, 1890s or not, women were meant to marry, have babies, and raise families. They had no business in the boardrooms of the nation. That's the way it was, because that's the way it had always been.

Sometimes Marthe just wanted to whack her dad with a ledger book.

Since he refused to change his mind, Marthe got married at age sixteen and set out to show him. Her husband was a small businessman without much capital, but within two years she had invented a beauty cream, built a factory to manufacture it, and was marketing it successfully all over France. By 1914 her company was employing more than a hundred workers, and business was booming. Marthe took to leaving copies of her company's balance sheets conspicuously on her father's desk.

Then the First World War broke out, and all her male employees were sent to the trenches. Her female employees were ordered into the armament factories. Marthe's business collapsed.

"I told you women shouldn't be running businesses," her father said. "It may work for a while, but never for long. You're trying to fit a square peg into a round hole."

Sometimes Marthe just wanted to tear his head off.

With labour impossible to come by and capital tight, Marthe tried hanging out her shingle as a financial adviser. She had an excellent grasp of the stock market, and could read a balance sheet better than anyone she knew. But corporate executives were reluctant to consult a woman, and she had trouble just meeting her overhead. Even her husband didn't seem to think much of this new idea – though he knew better than to say so.

"How come you're not leaving your balance sheets on my desk any more?" her father joshed. He was now manufacturing bayonet mountings and doing a roaring business.

Sometimes Marthe just wanted to throttle him with his own cravat.

Shortly after Armistice, somebody told Marthe about a small business weekly, the *Gazette du France et des Nations*. It was in difficulties and available for a song. Marthe looked it over and decided it was simply being mismanaged. So she scraped together every sou – even borrowing from her father, though she almost choked on it – and bought the journal. She fired the manager, hired a new editor, and began taking business journalists to lunch.

So far, the *Gazette* had restricted itself to reportage and general commentary about developments in French financial circles, but Marthe saw the opportunity for more direct involvement, essentially an extension of what she'd been trying to do as a financial consultant. The *Gazette* began to run columns offering financial advice, news about what was hot and what was not in the stock, bond, and other securities markets. It also developed – at a time when French business journals tended to take rather uncompromising sides in most financial and political issues – a reputation for looking at both sides of such questions.

It wasn't long before the *Gazette* was making quite a name for itself as a lively, well-informed, free-thinking financial newspaper.

It wasn't long, either, before Marthe was once again dropping impressive-looking balance sheets on her father's desk.

But while Hanau was happy enough to dine out on her new publication's success, she was at heart a businesswoman, not a journalist. It didn't take her long to realize that the profit potential in merely performing midwife services between investors and corporations was the most limited of the three roles.

She didn't see why that had to be so.

Her first move to redress this imbalance was simply to take her own advice. She invested her paper's profits in the companies she was recommending.

This improved her balance sheet, but while investigating a company to determine its rating, she often decided she could run it more profitably herself. She began buying majority interests in the companies her paper recommended.

(French financial law required that majority shareholders make such conflicts of interest public, but Marthe couldn't see much point in burdening her readers with such trivialities.)

It wasn't long before the benefits of Marthe's wider-ranging approach became self-evident. She found companies that struck her as undervalued, bought a majority of their stock at this undervalued price, then recommended them to her readers as good buys. When her readers followed her advice, share prices went up, and everybody was happy.

Especially Marthe.

Then she tried a further refinement. Buying companies, she realized, was a lot more expensive than simply founding them – especially if they didn't require a lot of expensive manufacturing or production equipment. So she began to found inexpensive "service" companies with vague names like Gerrard Enterprises or Chapdelaine Consulting, which didn't really produce anything – except, of course, shares. Recommending these shares to her readers produced quick profits for them (as the rapidly rising share prices attracted wider market attention) and an almost 100-per-cent profit for her.

Much better.

And everybody was still happy.

By now Marthe was making so much money she hardly knew what to do with it, but one thing that struck her as an important use for her funds was solidifying her position. One financial journal among many is a voice crying in the wilderness, but a lot of journals speaking as one is a chorus. She began to buy more financial journals.

This was a little trickier, because it meant relinquishing some of her former control. With the *Gazette*, it had been easy to write its various advisory columns herself under a variety of pseudonyms, but with more journals, this became impossible. It became necessary to hire the sorts of journalists who would write what they were told and keep their mouths shut – for a generous bonus, of course. Marthe Hanau's journals quickly became known in financial writers' circles for their lavish rates of pay and reduced leg-work.

So now Marthe, her reader-investors, her companies, *and* her writers were happy.

It's hard to imagine how much more happiness might have been possible – or even wise. The square peg was obviously fitting quite snugly into the round hole. By 1923 Marthe owned so many financial journals that she actually had to order some of her writers to disagree with each other and offer conflicting recommendations, just to maintain appearances. (This didn't cost her any money because she always made certain to own *both* companies being recommended.)

On the other hand, the comparatively unanimous opinions of her many journals had begun to give the normally volatile French stock market a welcome respite. Lack of turmoil in financial markets invariably translates into confidence, and confidence translates into profits. And Marthe's profits were becoming astounding.

Her assets at this point were estimated to be in the $750-million to $900-million range.

But Marthe Hanau was insatiable.

For a while, she toyed with the idea of capping her publishing empire with a couple of national dailies. That would have given her yet another layer of influence over the nation's politics and high finance – which, in market terms, would certainly have given her profits yet another major boost. But buying or launching a national daily involves enormous risks and a huge outlay of capital, and she was no more a newspaper-woman than a journalist.

Besides, there was another, far less risky and expensive, solution available.

French daily newspapers, she discovered, didn't generate their own financial information. They simply subcontracted it to organizations known as financial press agencies. In effect, this meant the dailies simply sold the space in their financial sections (their *bulletins financiers*) to the highest bidder – an agency that hired its own financial columnists and reporters and provided the dailies with a predetermined amount of financial news. Nobody seemed to care whether such agencies had any untoward connections with the corporations whose shares they recommended, or whose operations they reported on (read: promoted).

It was an arrangement that would make a modern-day investor's hair stand on end.

In other words, an arrangement custom-designed for Marthe Hanau.

At the time, most dailies in France subcontracted their *bulletins financiers* to a press agency known as the Agence Havas. Marthe decided to challenge this industry giant by first picking off its smaller, provincial customers and then moving in on the larger dailies. She did this by operating her new financial press agency, Agence Interpresse, at a loss, subsidizing it with the profits she made on the stock-speculation end.

The effect was promptly salutary. Since she didn't have to run Agence Interpresse at a profit, Marthe captured more and more of the *bulletins financiers* in France's many dailies. In effect, she was gaining the benefits of "owning" the financial sections of these dailies without having to buy, found, or operate the dailies themselves. The dailies, meanwhile, were pleased because she was paying them a lot more for their space than they'd earned in the past from Agence Havas.

And Marthe had found yet another megaphone through which to trumpet her cooked stock information.

By 1927 Marthe Hanau's intricately spun web of business journals and companies extended beyond France into Germany, Spain, Belgium, and Austria. Few people knew the full extent of this web, since she always kept her own involvement as secret as possible. Most of her journals and companies were registered to middlemen, so most people had to assume that her lavish lifestyle and posh residences were the result of her extraordinarily – even stupendously – profitable *Gazette du France et des Nations*.

For Marthe Hanau certainly lived lavishly. It hadn't taken her at all long to get used to being obscenely rich. As one of France's first billionaires, she spent money like the proverbial drunken sailor, on mansions, horses, yachts, cars. She especially loved expensive cars, owning an absurdly large fleet of Rolls-Royces, Hispano-Suizas, Mercedes-Benzes, and even a custom-built steamer costing more than $350,000. She also surrounded herself with so many young women, on whom she showered so many expensive gifts, that rumours began to abound about the exact nature of the lady's sexual proclivities.

Hanau couldn't have cared less.

Of course, running a billion-dollar empire in secrecy required a lot of help. To pay for such help – which was often enormously expensive – Hanau set up what she called her "Reptile Fund." This bribe fund pumped millions into the French economy, and was especially popular among France's accountants, lawyers, and politicians. In fact, most people who worked for Marthe Hanau received salaries that were quite generous by the standards of the day. It made for a lot of discreet and loyal employees.

With so many contented people working for the vast Hanau empire, one might have concluded that there were hardly any unhappy people left in France. The country's investors were certainly doing well. Its reporters and journalists were enjoying fat paycheques. Many of its politicians, civil servants, inspectors, and lawyers were basking in unprecedented "reptilian" prosperity. Even Hanau's father, whose bayonet-manufacturing business had collapsed after the war and who'd had to borrow money from Marthe to tide him over several unfortunate business decisions, was flourishing again.

He'd finally seen the light and invested his entire portfolio in Hanau companies.

There was, admittedly, the Agence Havas. Various Havas principals had taken their agency's losses very hard, and had sent reporters to investigate their upstart competition. These reporters hadn't yet uncovered much hard evidence, but they'd encountered an awful lot of rumours.

The country's bankers had begun to eavesdrop, too. A decade's worth of growth in the stock market had convinced a lot of investors to leverage huge stock purchases with bank loans, which were making the bankers nervous. They tried to confer with various politicians, but the results were curiously mixed. Some politicians were prepared to discuss the issue, and some even pronounced themselves alarmed, but an astonishing number seemed completely incapable of understanding the problem. This became known in political circles as "having a reptilian ear."

In the end, it was Havas which rang the first public alarm bells. In the few dailies it had left, its reporters launched a determined anti-Hanau campaign that was at first merely entertaining, but eventually began to draw blood. Though the evidence was soft and also frustratingly intricate – well beyond the comprehension of most ordinary newspaper readers – the overall message was this: if you've invested in any of a growing list of companies associated with Marthe Hanau and her Agence Interpresse, your money is in danger. Better get out.

It took more than a year of relentless Havas pounding to make any serious dents in Hanau's empire, but by then the public prosecutor's office had also become involved – Havas reporters had begun to file a welter of formal complaints. A run on the companies listed in Havas's reports had begun, and share prices were dropping. By December 1928, Marthe Hanau and the Havas accusations were the main item on the agenda of an anxious, confidential government cabinet meeting, chaired by French premier André Tardies himself.

Exactly what was discussed and who said what was never revealed, of course, but one can make fairly good deductions from what transpired. Premier Tardies called on Marthe Hanau personally for a confidential chat, during which he asked her informally, but with some urgency, to wind up her business affairs as quickly and quietly as the size of her empire allowed. He asked her to do this, moreover, in a manner that wouldn't spook the market.

That was, by any measure, a devastating demand.

The only way a person in Hanau's position could wind up her business affairs "in a manner that wouldn't spook the market" was to buy back all the millions of shares that had been issued by her vast array of companies over the past thirteen years – currently valued at several *billions* of dollars.

Hanau didn't have billions of dollars. She owned companies *valued* at billions of dollars, but their share values wouldn't be worth a red cent to her if she had to buy them back. Besides, maintaining the lifestyle to which she'd become happily accustomed was costing her about $360 million a year.

And then there was her father's likely reaction to consider.

She told Premier Tardies to get stuffed.

Hanau's hardball tactics weren't entirely reckless. Over the past thirteen years, she had progressed from being a participant in the French stock market to virtually *being* the French stock market. If they pulled her down now, she'd pull them all down with her. And if Tardies thought that an empty threat, she dared him to go ahead and try.

When the premier reported Hanau's reply – not mincing any words – his cabinet colleagues were outraged. They might have been prepared to compromise on some aspects of the arrangement, but this was outright blackmail. It was simply too much to swallow.

Warrants were sworn out for the arrest of Marthe Hanau, her husband, her editor at the *Gazette*, and several other associates.

The next day the French stock market took its biggest dive in seventy-eight years.

The crash, which cost French investors well over $4 billion, only increased Marthe Hanau's fame. And as so often happened in such cases, the public's anger ended up directed at the messengers, not the culprits. Everybody had been making money until the government decided to meddle.

That was the essence of Hanau's pre-trial defence, but the judge seemed disinclined to buy it. When he refused to allow her counter-experts to challenge the government's forensic accountants, and also refused her bail, she went on a hunger strike in protest. When her lawyers tried to dissuade her, she threw them out of her cell.

Half-a-dozen warders at St. Lazare prison tried repeatedly to feed Hanau by force. She resisted them successfully for eleven days. Then she was transferred to the Hôpital Cochin in Neuilly, where a dozen male nurses had no better luck. When she suddenly accepted some coffee with milk on the twenty-second day, they thought they had broken her resolve, but they discovered their mistake at 9:30 that night. Hanau had twisted several bedsheets into a rope and escaped through her hospital-room window.

The note she left behind read, "Disgusted with the violence to which I have been subjected, I am leaving."

She didn't try a genuine escape. She simply took a taxi back to St. Lazare prison. The warder at the gate was utterly non-plussed. The French public was delighted. The newspapers praised her determination and pluck.

The judge knew a successful public-relations ploy when he saw one, and released her on bail.

During her trial, which began on February 20, 1931, the government's greatest problem was keeping the names of Hanau's "Reptiles" out of the press. As a result, much of the prosecution's evidence couldn't be used. During the following six weeks, it was sometimes hard to tell who was on trial, Marthe Hanau, or half of France's accountants, lawyers, reporters, and politicians. When the judge eventually found Hanau guilty but sentenced her to only two years' imprisonment – much of which she'd already served at St. Lazare – nobody was overly surprised. (Her husband received eighteen months, her editor was levied a small fine, and her associates all got off scot-free.)

By the end of 1931, everyone who'd been arrested in con-nection with Hanau's financial débâcle had been paroled and was back on the job – including Hanau. Though the collapse of her companies had reportedly left her without a sou, she'd somehow managed to scrounge enough money to buy a small, almost-bankrupt financial journal called *Forces*, and had already hired her old *Gazette* editor to run the publication for her.

Officials in France's financial markets and its public prosecutor's office watched in horror as the whole disastrous madness seemed to be beginning again.

This time, however, they didn't wait to let Hanau get a solid foothold. Only months after her return to the market she was arrested again, on a charge of having published information gained from confidential government documents. (The documents, it turned out, were police reports about herself!) In the spirited scuffle that erupted when police agents showed up at *Forces* to confiscate the offending issue and arrest Hanau, her leg was broken.

Once again, the public cheered for Hanau and booed the authorities.

This time, however, she lost the toss. Sentenced to three months for receiving a stolen document, she appealed, but her appeal was rejected. She tried to flee the country, but was caught at the Belgian border and returned to custody.

Back in St. Lazare prison, it must have dawned on her that, while she might win some of the battles, they would never let her win the war.

Three weeks later Hanau was found dead in her St. Lazare cell. On the floor lay a roll of cotton wool that had contained smuggled sleeping pills. There was also a note with the partly obliterated message: "You shall not (indecipherable). I shall always be mistress of my fate."

Around the World in Eighty Megahertz

Donald Crowhurst and the Sunday Times
Golden Globe Yacht Race

As far back as anyone could remember, Donald Crowhurst had been a loose cannon.

He was fearless and reckless, and given to bursts of dare-devilry. As a child in the 1940s, he'd loved to climb a nearby water tower during windstorms, dancing carelessly around its narrow catwalk.

As an adult he'd hurtled across the hills and moors of southwest England like a demented racing driver, smashing up three cars by the age of twenty-six.

He'd been kicked out of the Royal Air Force after a three-year stretch of repeated disciplinary offences, including tearing blind drunk through a sleeping barracks on a big-bore motorcycle. A brief stint in the army, where he studied electronics and set a regimental record for drunken binges, had ended the same way.

Yet Crowhurst had charm enough for two. He took a genuine interest in people, regardless of class or wealth. He was impetuous and witty and generous and clever, and a lot of fun to be around. He could make you feel as if you were the most interesting person in the world.

But by the mid-1960s Crowhurst had flunked out of three careers and was about to wreck a fourth. Electron Utilization, a company he'd founded after being fired from several similar electronics firms, was on the verge of bankruptcy.

As always, the problem had little to do with Crowhurst's abilities. He had a brilliant grasp of electronic design and engineering, but he simply had no stomach for the daily grind. He thrived on new ideas and inventions, but the details bored him. When a challenge became stale, he lost traction.

When Crowhurst got bored, he looked for distractions. He'd already run for municipal councillor and won. He'd taken up amateur acting and played a role in several local productions. This time he decided to take up sailing.

Meanwhile, the dozen employees in his electronics factory dwindled to six, then to two, then to one assembler working part-time. His main financial backer became alarmed and asked to examine the books.

Crowhurst stopped coming to the office, and ignored his mail.

Then, on May 29, 1967, the newspapers trumpeted the news that Francis Chichester, a sixty-five-year-old yachtsman from Plymouth, had just completed an astonishing, single-handed, 119-day one-stop circumnavigation of the world. He would be sailing his *Gipsy Moth IV* back into Plymouth harbour in a few days.

The welcome that awaited Chichester was tumultuous. Thousands of local small craft formed a vast armada to escort him into the harbour. More than three hundred thousand people on shore cheered, waved flags, and celebrated his accomplishment. British television abandoned its regular programming to cover the event. The Queen arrived to knight him.

Chichester's financial rewards were nothing to sneer at either. His log-cum-diary book, entitled *Gipsy Moth Circles the World*, became a runaway bestseller. Every company whose equipment he'd used aboard the *Gipsy Moth IV* clamoured for his endorsements. His television and lecture fees soared, and his book appeared in more than a dozen languages. His small map and guidebook business quadrupled in size.

The more Crowhurst thought about it, the more he became convinced that such a splendid haul would solve an awful lot of his problems.

His money problems. His reputation as a sprinter rather than a long-distance runner. Even his lack of a career.

Not to mention his increasingly battered sense of self-worth.

Besides, what had Chichester really accomplished that was so different from what yachtsmen had been doing with some regularity since Canadian Joshua Slocum had single-handed his way around the globe between 1895 and 1898? The only difference was that Chichester had done it faster, and with only one stop.

Which, come to think of it, made the next challenge obvious: a single-handed circumnavigation of the world in *less than* 119 days, *with no stops at all*.

Unbeknownst to Crowhurst, the London *Sunday Times* (which had sponsored Chichester's voyage) had already come to the same conclusion. In fact, a committee of its editors had already been meeting for several weeks, to draft the rules and work out the logistics. The result, announced with much fanfare on March 17, 1968, was the London *Sunday Times* Golden Globe Race, a solo, non-stop, around-the-world yacht race with a purse of $50,000[*] for the fastest voyage and a "Golden Globe" trophy for the first boat back in its home port. (The two awards were necessary because competitors were permitted to enter the race any time between June 1 and October 31 of 1968, and to start the race from their own home port.)

The announcement flushed an impressive group of sailing veterans out of the woodwork. First to declare himself was the British ex-naval submarine commander Bill Leslie King, whose specially built turtle-backed yacht, *Galway Blazer II*, looked disconcertingly like a submarine. Next was the well-known British yachtsman Robin Knox-Johnston in his thirty-two-foot Bermudan ketch *Suhaili*. Third was a legendary yachtsman from France, Bernard Moitessier, who held the current record for the longest non-stop voyage by a small sailing vessel – 14,216 miles – and who planned to use a welded steel yacht named *Joshua*.

There followed professional adventurers John Ridgway and Chay Blyth, already known to the sailing fraternity as the first men to have rowed across the Atlantic (together) in 1966; the seasoned French yachtsman Loick Fougeron in another steel-hulled ketch; British naval commander Nigel Tetley, who would be using a large trimaran of the Victress class; Australian dentist Bill Howell in a small catamaran; and Alex Carozzo, the "Chichester of Italy," in a newly built sixty-six-foot ketch.

And – on impulse, as usual – a man totally unknown in yachting circles, a man whom the newspapers and yachting press took to calling "the mystery entrant," because they couldn't

---

[*] For consistency, all dollar amounts have been adjusted to 1999 values.

seem to find out the first thing about him – British electronics engineer Donald Crowhurst.

✦

To call Crowhurst's entry into this high-profile yacht race impetuous was putting it mildly. Not only was he a novice sailor, he didn't even own a boat.

Nor did he have any realistic expectations of being able to build, buy, or borrow one. When his friends first read the story in the *Devon News*, they were simply flabbergasted. What kind of a stunt was Crowhurst pulling this time? Though, Crowhurst being Crowhurst, one never knew for *certain* that it was just a stunt.

One thing *was* certain: since he'd announced his entry, Crowhurst was transformed. Recharged with purpose, he rushed around like a man possessed, making long lists, telephoning anyone and everyone, trying to nail down the million and one things that would have to be done before his voyage could become a reality. He was exhilarated and panicked by turns; he filled boxes and dumped them, drafted letters and scrapped them, mapped routes and erased them.

Finally, as much out of sympathy as comradeship, a clutch of his friends pitched in and began to help him bring some order to the chaos.

Crowhurst's scheme to solve his largest problem – finding a boat – wasn't altogether uninspired. Having heard that the *Gipsy Moth IV* was to be embedded in concrete at Greenwich, England, as a public monument to Chichester's achievement, Crowhurst wrote to the town clerk to argue that, first, it would be shortsighted to immobilize a perfectly seaworthy vessel in this way, and, second, it would make a lot more sense to lend her to the very enterprise her own most recent voyage had engendered – namely, the London *Sunday Times* Golden Globe Race. He, Donald Crowhurst, was prepared to sail her to a further triumph, and to donate the entire proceeds from winning this race to Greenwich.

Lord Dulverton, the owner of the *Gipsy Moth IV*, wasn't interested. The Cutty Sark Society, which was responsible for converting the yacht into a monument, wasn't either. Its chairman, Frank Carr, reminded Crowhurst that Chichester had dumped all over the boat in his diary, criticizing her many design and construction flaws.

Crowhurst refused to be put off. Attempting an end-run around Dulverton and Carr, he sent the same letter to every major newspaper and yachting magazine in England; most editors and readers readily agreed with him. It led to a loud and occasionally nasty war of words that changed no one's opinion and didn't get Crowhurst a boat – but it certainly got him a reputation. He was no longer "the mystery entrant."

Undeterred, Crowhurst plunged his hand back into the hat and tried again. This time he pulled out the name of Stanley Best, the financial backer who had been trying to dump his investment in Crowhurst's electronics company. One might have thought that Best would be the last person on earth to back this most hare-brained of Crowhurst's schemes. That was certainly Best's own opinion. But somehow, after a series of impassioned telephone calls and meetings, Best emerged willing to finance the building and outfitting of a forty-one-foot Victress-class trimaran to the tune of $60,000.

Best's wife told him he was totally, hopelessly crazy.

Best couldn't have agreed more.

At this news, however, Crowhurst's friends' doubts vanished. If Crowhurst was capable of this, he was capable of anything.

Everyone threw themselves into his project with renewed vigour. The Crowhurst home became a headquarters, a design centre, a think-tank, a warehouse, a barracks, and an assembly plant. In view of the job's urgency, several local shipyards teamed up to build and outfit the boat. She would be a trimaran not unlike Nigel Tetley's, but with a flush deck and an ingenious Crowhurst-designed anti-capsizing mechanism. (A trimaran's primary advantage is its speed; its main weakness is its obstinate refusal to right itself after capsizing.)

This challenge alone bordered on the preposterous. Crowhurst's vessel would have to be built, launched, tested, tuned up, and fully provisioned in a mere five months – a process for which any reasonable yachtsman would have budgeted twelve to eighteen months. But Crowhurst just grinned. "The impossible we could do in *three* months," he quipped. "This being the ridiculous, we'll take the full five. But we'll be ready by October 31."

And somehow, by some miracle, they were. Despite endless arguments about design and materials, despite leaking hatches and various faulty installations, despite mixed-up sails and a shake-down cruise on which so many things went wrong that it took almost two weeks instead of the planned three days to return to home port – not to mention costs that ballooned to a whopping $120,000 – the newly minted *Teignmouth Electron*, her cabin still chaotic with uninstalled nautical equipment and her paint barely dry, was towed out over the Teignmouth harbour bar at 4:52 p.m. on October 31, 1968, entering the *Sunday Times* globe-girdling yacht race with barely seven hours to spare.

She was the tenth and last contestant to enter the race.

For the first week, things did not go well. In a November 2 radio message to Rodney Hallworth, Crowhurst's press agent (a former crime reporter for the *Daily Mail*), Crowhurst reported that his self-steering gear had begun shedding parts. On November 3, he reported that his port-bow float was filling with water. Bailing it out, repairing the leak, and fixing a host of other mechanical and electrical problems were proving exhausting and depressing. Headwinds and steering-gear problems were keeping his progress down to a mere seventy-five miles per day. On November 5, he radioed that his generator had failed, and that his batteries were running down. Shortly after, Hallworth lost radio contact completely.

On November 16, Hallworth's radio crackled back to life with a message from Crowhurst that he'd managed to fix his generator, and had reached the coast of Portugal. He was now heading for the island of Madeira. Hallworth was relieved, but Crowhurst's scorekeepers in Teignmouth were extremely disappointed. Crowhurst was now managing less than fifty miles per day, less than every other competitor at this stage of the race.

But Crowhurst seemed unfazed by his poor performance. His message to his wife, Clare, and his backer, Stanley Best, two days later was a laconic *All's well*.

Ironically, in a sense it was. Unbeknownst to Crowhurst, his chances of winning the race, despite his lacklustre performance, had already improved considerably – if only because his rivals' luck had turned even worse than his own. Ridgway, Blyth, and Howell had dropped out of the race with a variety of mechanical problems. Alex Carozzo had developed a stomach ulcer and had thrown in the towel near Lisbon. Bill King's *Galway Blazer II* had been de-masted and was being towed into Cape Town after a roll in a south Atlantic storm. Loick Fougeron had capsized in the Roaring Forties and had quit the race as well. Knox-Johnston had also capsized but was hanging on, limping through the Tasman Sea with his self-steering gear smashed and his sails in tatters. Only Nigel Tetley and Bernard Moitessier were so far undamaged, and making good (but not spectacular) time.

So, simply by virtue of not yet having been sunk or rolled, Donald Crowhurst had already risen to fourth place.

He didn't reply when Hallworth radioed this news to him on November 19. But on November 21 Stanley Best received a radio-telephone call in which Crowhurst announced that his generator was acting up again, and there might be more radio silences. He seemed to be somewhere south of the Cayman Islands.

And then, on December 1, Hallworth received his first cheerful radio telegram from the *Teignmouth Electron*: TUNING TRIALS OVER. RACE BEGINS!

Crowhurst had finally reached the end of the prevailing Westerlies and could now stop sailing to windward (at which trimarans balk), running instead with the Northeast Trades at his back (at which trimarans excel) straight down the middle of the Atlantic. Directly ahead lay a more than thousand-mile sail with a following wind, all the way to Cape Town and the Cape of Good Hope.

The results weren't long in coming. On December 10 Crowhurst radioed happily that he'd just finished an entire week of 145 to 174 miles per day, capped by one stupendous burst of 243 miles in a single twenty-four-hour period. He slowed again in the doldrums, but snapped his pace right back up after crossing the equator. On December 14 he cabled cheerfully: OFF BRAZIL. AVERAGING 170 MILES DAILY. STRONG SOUTHWEST TRADE WIND. By December 20 he was approaching Tristan da Cunha Island in the Roaring Forties, and by Christmas Eve, in a short radio-telephone call to Clare, he reported his imminent rounding of the Cape of Good Hope. He was still spanking along at a steady 170-plus miles per day.

Rodney Hallworth was ecstatic. So were England's and Europe's betting shops. Crowhurst's extraordinary performance was finally making this competition into a horse race, and both the mainstream and the yachting press were becoming pumped. Under the headline CROWHURST SPEED WORLD RECORD?, the *Sunday Times* reported: "Donald Crowhurst, last man out in the *Sunday Times* round-the-world yacht race, covered a breathtaking and possibly record-breaking 243 miles in his 41-foot trimaran *Teignmouth Electron* last Sunday. The achievement is even more remarkable in the light of the very poor speeds in the first three weeks of his voyage; he took longer to reach the Cape Verdes than any other competitor. . . ."

Hallworth, meanwhile, sent Crowhurst the latest standings: KNOX–JOHNSTON LEADS. MOITESSIER BEYOND TASMANIA. TETLEY EASTERN INDIAN. YOUR AVERAGE DAILY 30 MILES HIGHER. SUNDAY TIMES RECKONS WINNER HOME APRIL NINE. THIS YOUR TARGET. PLEASE GIVE WEEKLY POSITIONS AND MILEAGE. CHEERS RODNEY.

Crowhurst's odds kept improving until January 1969, when he cabled news of renewed generator problems: 100 SOUTHEAST GOUGH 1086 GENERATOR HATCH SEALED. TRANSMISSIONS WHEN POSSIBLE ESPECIALLY 80 EAST 140 WEST. In a message sent the same day, he reported even more worrisome details to Stanley Best: REGRET FLOAT FRAME SMASHED. SKIN SPLIT DECK JOINTS PARTING. REPAIRS. NOT HOLDING SPEED SO HORN AUTUMN ILLFOUND.

By January 21 Crowhurst was off the air again.

For the next three weeks, Cape Town Radio relayed Best's and Hallworth's increasingly anxious queries again and again towards the co-ordinates reported in Crowhurst's January 19 transmission, but neither received an acknowledgement.

At first, Crowhurst's pit crew in Teignmouth wasn't unduly alarmed. So far, Crowhurst had always been able to fix his generator eventually. As long as it didn't hamper his sailing, it was a small price to pay. But Hallworth had contracted with several newspapers to send them regular reports, and dead air made for flat stories. True, he could imagine a good deal of what Crowhurst was experiencing, and that, increasingly, became the source for his ongoing dispatches, but as time went on, his stories became ever more speculative.

As he waited more and more impatiently for hard news, Hallworth extrapolated Crowhurst's progress by repositioning the big red pin symbolizing the *Teignmouth Electron* another 170 miles farther eastward every day. The pin moved steadily through the Indian and Southern oceans, but there were no corroborating radio messages from Crowhurst. It moved past Australia to New Zealand, through the Tasman Sea, and still there was no definitive word. By March 15 it had moved all the way into the Pacific, and Hallworth's regular updates to the *Daily Mail* and the *Sunday Times* began being rejected as "largely conjecture." Commentators began using words like "uncertain status" and "possible demise." Crowhurst's odds in the betting shops began to drop.

News of the other three competitors, meanwhile, was similarly problematic. After a four-month radio silence, Robin Knox-Johnston was feared out of contention or even dead. Bernard Moitessier had been making excellent time, but on April 2 the *Sunday Times* received a long letter from him, mailed from Tahiti, explaining that he had enjoyed his passage through the Roaring Forties so much that he'd decided to drop out of the race and remain in the southern latitudes. That left only Nigel Tetley, who had rounded Cape Horn on March 20 and entered the final lap for home.

Then, on April 6, a tanker spotted Knox-Johnston in the mid-Atlantic, battered but indefatigable, ahead of Nigel Tetley but sailing so slowly that he was really only in contention for the Golden Globe (first boat back in home port) award.

Shoving their slide-rules and quadrants back into their pockets, the press and the gamblers touted Knox-Johnston for the Golden Globe and Tetley for the $50,000 fastest-time purse.

Crowhurst's odds dropped even lower.

But three days later, on April 9, almost eleven weeks after Crowhurst had lapsed into radio silence, a faint signal from the *Teignmouth Electron* reached a radio station in Buenos Aires, where it was deciphered and forwarded as HEADING DIGGER RAMREZ.

This brought everyone right back out of their seats and the slide-rules back onto the table. Diego Ramrez was a tiny island just southwest of Cape Horn, which meant that Crowhurst was not only alive and still in contention, but belting along at a remarkable rate – even faster than Hallworth's optimistic red pin! At his speed of approximately 178 miles per day, there was now an increasing chance that Crowhurst might actually beat Tetley for the fastest-time award.

The betting shops promptly sent their chalk-boys scurrying back up the ladders. Knox-Johnston's odds went down, Crowhurst's went up. Nigel Tetley's remained level.

Ecstatic, Hallworth cabled Crowhurst on April 12: YOURE ONLY TWO WEEKS BEHIND TETLEY. PHOTO FINISH WILL MAKE GREAT NEWS. ROBIN DUE ONE TO TWO WEEKS. RODNEY.

Crowhurst took his time replying, but when he did he confirmed his rounding of the Horn on April 18. 201 DAYS

AFTER DEPARTING LIZARD. FIRST SIGHT LAND FALKLANDS, he wired. HAZY AUTUMN EVENING WOODSMOKE ON WIND . . .

By golly, Hallworth decided, the perfect title for Crowhurst's future memoir of the race. *Woodsmoke on Wind.*

Nigel Tetley's supporters, meanwhile, were in a state of near-panic. They'd already been celebrating their man's imminent fastest-time victory when Crowhurst's reappearance had knocked it all into a cocked hat. Radio messages flashed back and forth. Everybody had a different opinion on what might be the best strategy. Though Tetley was still ahead, his yacht was in rough shape and making slower time than Crowhurst's. With five thousand miles still to go, the outcome was anybody's guess.

Finally, Tetley decided to take the chance. He began to sail at utmost speed, straining his equipment to the maximum, squeezing another fifteen to twenty-five daily miles out of his boat. His floats were leaking worse than Crowhurst's – he'd had to drill holes in his forward compartments to let water *out* – and their fibreglass skins were peeling away like onion curls, but he pounded on relentlessly.

On April 22, the spotlight briefly left the duelling trimarans to celebrate Robin Knox-Johnston's arrival back in Falmouth, England: he had circumnavigated the world single-handed in 313 days and arrived home first. Newspapers throughout the world headlined the achievement, the BBC made a dutiful amount of fuss – even Tetley and Crowhurst cabled their congratulations – but there was no avoiding the fact that the most significant contest, the one that would undoubtedly put Knox-Johnston's achievement into the shadows, was still being slugged out in the mid-Atlantic.

Like Tetley, Crowhurst was also struggling with a continuous string of mechanical breakdowns. On May 12 he complained of SIX BROKEN FRAMES. TWO FOOT SPLIT STARBOARD FLOAT

TOPSIDES, but assured Hallworth that he was keeping up the pressure. After a week of extraordinary speed, in which his daily mileages almost matched the record-breaking performances of his outbound leg, he reported FOUR DAYS LOST UNUSUAL NORTHEASTERLY GALE, and then, unhappily, OVERTAKE TETLEY ONLY BY LUCK NOW. He became snappish and defensive when one of his boatbuilders wired some suggestions about loosening a strut; his reply was uncharacteristically long and bitchy. It took two apologetic radiograms to calm him down.

By the middle of May, with Tetley approaching the Canary Islands and Crowhurst just off Rio de Janeiro, the word around the betting shops was that Tetley would beat Crowhurst to the finish line, but Crowhurst would win the fastest-time race, since Tetley had started almost a month before him.

Over in Teignmouth, the excitement was reaching a fever pitch. Hallworth had already booked the town's largest convention hall and was preparing the biggest, noisiest celebration in Teignmouth's history. Naturally, as Crowhurst's agent, he was also negotiating television and radio documentary rights with the BBC, book contracts with a variety of publishers, a lecture tour throughout Europe and North America, and a welter of commercial endorsements. TEIGNMOUTH AGOG AT YOUR WONDERS, he cabled Crowhurst excitedly. WHOLE TOWN PLANNING HUGE WELCOME. RODNEY.

Crowhurst seemed resolved to be contrary. METHS PETROL LOW, he radioed. FLOUR RICE MILDEWED. WATER FOUL. CHEESE INTERESTING.

And then, just after midnight on May 21, disaster struck.

Sailing under full press through a storm near the Azores, still trying desperately to beat Donald Crowhurst's elapsed time,

Nigel Tetley's already cracked port float bow finally broke away and smashed into his trimaran's centre hull.

The damage, some of it below the waterline, proved lethal. As water poured into his main cabin, Tetley had just enough time to radio an SOS with his position, untie his rubber liferaft, and abandon ship.

His yacht sank within minutes before his eyes.

He was rescued the next morning by a British destroyer.

Crowhurst's reaction, when he heard the news two days later, was restricted to a radio message to Tetley's wife: EVELYN TETLEY. SYMPATHISE DAVY JONES DIRTY TRICK. REJOICE MASTER SALVAGED. CROWHURST.

The world's media went absolutely wild. After seven months and twenty-six thousand miles in a hastily built boat that had never been properly finished or provisioned, Donald Crowhurst, a mere weekend sailor from a nondescript little town in southwest England, had beaten a group of the world's most eminent and experienced yachtsmen for one of the world's most prestigious yachting trophies.

To receive it, all he had to do now was loaf the remaining four thousand miles to his home port of Teignmouth, tie up his boat, and let fame and riches fall into his lap.

It was a Horatio Alger story to beat all Horatio Alger stories.

Hallworth cabled that more than a hundred thousand people were expected to attend the hero's welcome he had planned for Crowhurst. There would be rallies, feasts, and celebrations lasting for at least a week. An international tour was in the cards, meetings with royalty, interviews with top-drawer journalists, hundreds of feature articles – the whole ball of wax. Best of all, money was no longer a problem. Hallworth's phone was ringing off the hook with corporations frantic for endorsements.

Crowhurst's company, Electron Utilization, was as good as back in the black!

Crowhurst's laconic reply was simply a litany of his ongoing mechanical troubles. His floats (like Tetley's) had been deteriorating, taking on increasing amounts of water, requiring increasing amounts of bailing. His self-steering gear was now completely out of whack, requiring such large corrections that he often found himself having to backtrack after naps. Most frustrating of all, his Marconi transmitter was continually cutting out during radio transmissions; he suspected a malfunctioning converter. Could somebody call the manufacturer and ask for advice?

Marconi's advice was to use the transmitter as little as possible. Malfunctioning converters tended to self-destruct without much warning during use, they said. The transmitter probably wouldn't be serviceable very much longer.

Marconi's assessment was apparently correct. Crowhurst stopped answering his radio messages on June 1, 1969.

His progress, however, could be deduced from a variety of sightings by tankers and freighters, since he had now crossed the equator and entered the more crowded shipping lanes in the North Atlantic. He was sailing more and more slowly, sometimes making only twenty miles a day. Observers reported no sign of his mainsail; he seemed to be using only his mizzenmast.

Hallworth, on the other hand, was under full canvas. He was now in such demand that he'd had to rent an extra office and hire more staff, install another telephone line. Offers and requests were pouring in: demands for interviews by the hundreds; a request to have Crowhurst present the Duke of Edinburgh Awards on behalf of Prince Philip; the Post Office, offering to use a special Crowhurst franking mark during the week of his arrival, and to hang autographed commemorative *Devon News* covers in all its branches. A sculptor eager to donate a special trophy featuring a "symbolic hull in aluminium alloy extrusion, and translucent sail in acrylic sheet."

Hallworth had already printed up ten thousand postcards featuring Crowhurst's photograph, and was sending them all over the world on behalf of the Teignmouth Chamber of Commerce. They read: "Greetings from Teignmouth, the Devon resort chosen by Donald Crowhurst for his triumphant around-the-world yacht race."

The BBC, which had provided Crowhurst with a 16mm camera and tape recorder, was desperate to get started on a Crowhurst documentary. It requested permission from the *Sunday Times* to send a helicopter to rendezvous with the *Teignmouth Electron* off the Scilly Isles, to pick up whatever film and tape Crowhurst had exposed and recorded. The *Sunday Times* refused.

The *Teignmouth Electron* was now crossing the Sargasso Sea, that mysterious expanse of eerily heaving seaweed in the North Atlantic, centred roughly on the Tropic of Cancer. She seemed to have slowed to less than five miles per day. But the Sargasso was known for its placid weather; being becalmed in it wasn't unusual. Though Hallworth and Stanley Best sent out periodic messages tactfully urging Crowhurst to crack on a bit more sail – there were, after all, millions of people waiting – his continued radio silence made it impossible to know whether he was receiving their messages or not.

And then, on the evening of July 10, two policemen arrived at the Crowhurst home to bring Clare some disquieting news. At 7:50 that morning the Royal Mail vessel *Picardy*, en route from

London to the Caribbean, had swerved to miss a trimaran apparently adrift in the Sargasso Sea, some 1,800 miles southwest of England. The *Picardy*'s master, Captain Richard Box, had sounded his foghorn three times, but no one had appeared on deck. On boarding the *Teignmouth Electron* (which the *Picardy*'s crew had immediately recognized from media coverage), they had found her still seaworthy, her liferaft still lashed to her deck, her galley still provisioned with food and water, and no obvious sign of wave or storm damage.

Yet there was no sign of Donald Crowhurst.

Perplexed, Box had alerted the British navy and radioed the U.S. Air Force for assistance. During a day-long sea and air search of the area, which failed to turn up either Crowhurst or any further clues, Box had had time to examine the *Teignmouth Electron*'s logbooks, whose final entry on June 29 suggested that the trimaran had already been ghosting along on her own for almost two weeks.

Was Crowhurst dead?

Or had he decided for some mysterious reason to disappear?

Or was this just another Crowhurst publicity stunt?

As days turned into weeks and there were no sightings or reports of Crowhurst's whereabouts, the media made the relatively easy switch from covering a spectacular triumph to reporting a heartrending tragedy. On the evidence, Donald Crowhurst appeared to be dead – either from misadventure or suicide.

The *Sunday Times* promptly established an appeal fund for the Crowhurst family, and Robin Knox-Johnston generously donated his entire $50,000 purse, which now fell to him by default as the only participant who had completed the race. Cheques and messages of condolence poured in, as the media described the plight of Crowhurst's widow and their four young children. In a gesture of respect and sympathy, the Golden Globe celebrations were called off.

Trying further to ease the Crowhurst family's financial burden, Rodney Hallworth offered Crowhurst's three logbooks – which only Captain Box had seen so far – for sale to Britain's newspapers. After a brisk auction that pitted the *Daily Express* against the *Sunday Times*, the *Sunday Times* topped the bidding at $40,000. But when two *Times* journalists and Hallworth met Captain Box to take receipt of the logs, Box took Hallworth aside and urged him, for the sake of the Crowhurst family, to tear the final three pages out of the third book. Those pages, he explained, made it very clear that Crowhurst had lost his mind and committed suicide.

Hallworth agreed and tore out the pages. His intention was to show them in confidence to the *Sunday Times* editor on some more convenient occasion.

But what the three men discovered, after spending the following day reading Crowhurst's logbooks, proved a great deal more explosive than Crowhurst's suicide.

What the logbooks showed was that Donald Crowhurst *hadn't sailed around the world at all.*

In fact, *he hadn't even left the Atlantic Ocean.*

All he had done was sail far enough into the Atlantic to avoid the major shipping lanes, and then *pretended* to sail the rest of the way by filing false positions in his radio reports, or feigning radio problems when false reporting wasn't possible.

This news, released on July 27, stunned the world's yachting community and unleashed a media tidal wave even bigger than that for Crowhurst's apparent death the week before. At first it engendered a lot more questions than answers. How had such an extraordinary fraud been possible? Had anyone else been involved?

And how did all this tie into Donald Crowhurst's apparent suicide?

Fortunately for investigators, Crowhurst had kept three log-books – one honest, one fake, and one filled with all the data and calculations he would have needed to make the fake one more convincing if challenged.

Comparing the three, investigators were able to piece together that, by December 12, 1968 – about five weeks after his start – it had become clear to Crowhurst that his situation was hopeless. His boat was a mess. All *three* of his hulls were leaking so badly he was shipping about two hundred gallons of seawater per night – all of which had to be bailed out by hand each morning, because somebody had forgotten to load the suction hoses for his bailing pumps. One good storm, making bailing impossible, would have sunk his boat. In fact, most of his safety gear – including his new anti-capsizing system – had never been installed. His self-steering mechanism was disintegrating, and his starboard float had developed a serious crack.

Clearly, the *Teignmouth Electron* had been in no shape to risk the formidable Southern Ocean, which had already wreaked havoc among the race's far more experienced and better-equipped competitors.

That's when Crowhurst had hatched his devious scheme.

Such a scheme wouldn't have been possible a decade later, after satellite locator systems came into widespread use, but in the late 1960s, radio signals were still comparatively untraceable. Where there were exceptions, Crowhurst knew how to fake his way around them. Where even that was impossible – such as in the

Southern Ocean and the Tasman Sea – he had simply simulated generator trouble and sent no messages at all.

He had, however, received them, and during the four months when he was ostensibly sailing through those waters (while he was in fact merely sailing in circles off the coast of Brazil), he'd kept detailed records of shipping broadcasts and weather reports along that route, for eventual inclusion in his fake logbook. They made that "record" very convincing – so convincing that an instructor at London's School of Navigation found no navigational inconsistencies in it. In the absence of any other suspicions (the instructor noted admiringly), it would have readily passed muster.

And it probably *would* have passed muster, because what investigators also discovered was that Crowhurst hadn't intended to win the race. He'd intended, craftily, to come in second, a performance that would have saved his dignity, provided some measure of fame, and (most important of all) kept race officials from giving his logbook more than a superficial scrutiny.

Thus, Tetley's disaster off the Azores also became a disaster for Crowhurst. He knew his purported sailing speed had been sufficiently erratic – slowest at the start, fastest at the end – to have raised a few doubts. (He was right. Sir Francis Chichester, honorary chairman of the race, had already sent a letter to race secretary Robert Riddell urging that, should Crowhurst win, a particularly careful investigation be made of his navigational and radio records.)

So, with Tetley down, Crowhurst wasn't sailing toward triumph and riches at all. He was, in all likelihood, sailing straight into the devastating clutches of internationally reported exposure and disgrace.

But there was another danger that Crowhurst hadn't even

considered – the effect on the brain of seven months in solitary confinement on a limitless ocean. Sailors call it "sea-stoned"; landsmen call it "bushed." Either form can be lethal to unstable personalities, and Crowhurst was certainly that. But he'd made himself even more susceptible by becoming fascinated, during the latter part of his solitary ocean vigil, by a copy of Einstein's *Relativity, the Special and the General Theory*.

As his obsession with Einstein's theories grew, he began to have, and record, visions and revelations that enabled him to formulate his own theory of spiritual evolution. It was a theory at the culmination of which human intelligence abandons its physical constraints and becomes a disembodied god.

As his brain worked feverishly to fully understand and absorb these revelations, Crowhurst stopped bothering to sail, or even keep up his pretence of participating in a global single-handed non-stop yacht race. With the *Teignmouth Electron* virtually becalmed in the weeds of the Sargasso Sea, he lay naked on deck (as was reported by tanker sightings), filling page after page with urgent poems, partially completed essays, heavily underlined exclamations, and long, complex mathematical formulae.

"Will man accept," he wrote, "of his own free will, the stipulation that when he has learnt to manipulate the space-time continuum he will possess the attributes of God? The choice is simply this. Do we go on clinging to the idea that 'God made us,' or realise that it lies within our power to make GOD?"

On July 1, 1969, at 10:03 a.m., Crowhurst finally felt ready to answer that question. In a bizarre countdown to ultimate disembodiment, during which he kept an evolving time record on the left side of the page, with corresponding observations on the right, he documented seventeen realizations that led with mathematical relentlessness and inevitability to his final moments:

11 15 00   It is the end of my
my game the truth
has been revealed and it will
be done as my family require me
to do it

11 17 00   It is the time for your
move to begin
I have not need to prolong
the game

It has been a good game that
must be ended at the
I will play this game when
I choose I will resign the
game at 11 20 40 There is
no reason for harmful

Those were Donald Crowhurst's last words. At (presumably) precisely 11:20:40, he stepped off the deck of the *Teignmouth Electron* into the Sargasso Sea, and became a god.

The Mad Monarch of America

Emperor Joshua Abraham Norton I

On the morning of September 17, 1859, an impressively uniformed man – tall Kossuth hat with ostrich feather, cavalry sabre, huge gold-fringed epaulettes – marched into the office of the San Francisco *Bulletin*, saluted smartly, and handed editor George Fitch a rolled, ribbon-festooned document. The proclamation, heavily embroidered with ornate scrollwork and fancy penmanship, read:

At the peremptory request of a large majority of the citizens of these United States, I, Joshua Abraham Norton, formerly of Algoa Bay, Cape of Good Hope, and now for the past nine years and ten months of San Francisco, California, declare and proclaim myself Emperor of these U.S., and in virtue of the authority thereby in me vested, do hereby order and direct the representatives of the different States of the Union to assemble in the Musical Hall of this city on the 1st day of February next, then and there to make such alterations in the existing laws of the Union as may ameliorate the evils under which the country is laboring, and thereby cause confidence to exist, both at home and abroad, in our stability and integrity.

> Norton I,
> Emperor of the United States.

"I would appreciate having this published in your Saturday edition," the newly minted Emperor said politely but firmly.

And having thus formally launched his regime, Joshua Abraham Norton, formerly of the Cape of Good Hope, etc., tipped his hat, saluted once more, and left.

For several days, the fate of America's nascent monarchy hung in the balance. George Fitch was a busy man, and ordinarily had little time for foolishness. But over the weekend he found himself musing that, madness aside, there was an odd sort of sense to this. America's politicians were becoming increasingly reckless, a recklessness that might soon cause a full-scale civil war.

It raised the question as to who was sane and who was mad, the way they were going about it. In a way, this Norton fellow had a point. What they really needed, these childish political squabblers, was to have someone gather them together in the nation's sandbox and knock some sense into their heads.

The following Saturday, in a gesture of satirical whimsy, Fitch ran the piece on his front page under the sixty-point heading: HAVE WE AN EMPEROR AMONG US?

Bulletin readers' interest was obviously piqued. They replied in the language Fitch liked best: the purchase of an additional 136 copies of the day's paper.

America's congressmen, unfortunately, seemed less interested. Preoccupied with John Brown's attack on the United States arsenal at Harpers Ferry, they ignored Emperor Norton's edict and continued their eye-for-an-eye approach to solving the country's disagreements. This had been frustrating America's more rational citizens for a long time, and many were finding their patience fading fast. So there was a perceptible agreement among the readers of the *Bulletin* – expressed once more in significantly larger sales – when the Emperor, insulted at this congressional snub, appeared in the *Bulletin*'s office three weeks later to proclaim a subsequent edict (headline: CONGRESS ABOLISHED! TAKE NOTICE, THE WORLD!!):

It is represented to us that the universal suffrage, as now existing throughout the Union, is abused; that fraud and corruption prevent a fair and proper expression of the public voice; that open violation of the laws are constantly occurring, caused by mobs, parties, factions, and undue influence of political sects; that the citizen has not that protection of person and property which he is entitled to by paying his pro rata of the expense of Government – in consequence of which, WE do hereby abolish Congress, and it is therefore abolished; and WE order and desire the representatives of all parties interested to appear at the Musical Hall of this city on the first of February next, and then and there take the most effective steps to remedy the evil complained of.

Norton I,
Emperor of the United States
of America.

One might have thought that *this* was a gauntlet no red-blooded congressman could ignore – especially since it had been thrown down by none other than the Emperor of the United States of America himself. But Congress defiantly reconvened in January 1859 after its Christmas recess, evidently convinced that an Emperor's edict could be ignored with impunity. The readers of George Fitch's *Bulletin* – and, by now, most newspaper readers in San Francisco – waited breathlessly to see what would happen next.

They didn't have long to wait. With his regal authority clearly on the line, there was no room for pettifogging. The Emperor moved with decisive speed.

> WHEREAS a body of men calling themselves the National Congress are now in session in Washington City, in clear violation of our Imperial edict of the 12th of October last declaring the said Congress abolished;
>
> AND WHEREAS it is necessary for the repose of our Empire that the said decree should be strictly complied with;
>
> NOW, THEREFORE, we do hereby Order and Direct Major-General Scott, the Commander-in-Chief of our Armies, immediately upon receipt of this, Our Decree, to proceed with a suitable force and clear the Halls of Congress.
>
> Norton I,
> Emperor of the United States.

The mere contemplation of the bloodbath that might have resulted had General Winfield Scott been at liberty to obey the Emperor's orders was enough to drive sales of the *Bulletin* straight through the roof. Most San Franciscans had little doubt that the seventy-three-year-old hero of the Mexican War, "Old Fuss and Feathers" himself, could have cleared the congressional temple as effectively as he'd routed Santa Anna at Churubusco and Chapultepec. But Scott was occupied up in Washington Territory, settling an international boundary dispute with Britain over certain Gulf Islands located on the Canada–U.S. border. He appeared unable, or unwilling, to change those military priorities.

This was irritating, no doubt about it, but it wasn't the only disaster in a country stretched to the limit by civil strife. The election of Abraham Lincoln as president had already precipitated the first secessions – South Carolina, Virginia, North Carolina, Tennessee, and Arkansas – and more were expected at any moment. Senator Jefferson Davis had given up his Senate seat to become the breakaway confederacy's first president, and both sides had begun frantically stockpiling weapons and military supplies. All over the United States of America, men were swapping suits and overalls for uniforms.

Emperor Norton considered all these things. It was a complex dilemma, since virtually any move would benefit one side or the other to the ultimate detriment of both. That was the lethal contradiction of this disastrous debate – in a civil war, there are only losers. Then there was the fate of America's blacks to consider, a people who might well end up losers no matter which way the conflict ended. And who could be sure of the Spanish, once America had become sufficiently weakened from within to be successfully attacked from without?

All this was proof yet again that no country could hope to survive without a strong central authority and clear delineations of responsibility. Lack of clarity on this point, more than any other factor, was creating fertile ground for America's political opportunists and rogue generals. The American experiment in democracy was no longer working. It was producing only confusion and anarchy. One had only to compare it to the monarchies of Britain or France to see the difference.

This left Emperor Norton no other choice. When a country's political system was this hopelessly infected, there was really no option but to amputate. Radical surgery, but it couldn't be helped:

WHEREAS it is necessary for our Peace, Prosperity and Happiness, as also to the National Advancement of the people of the United States, that they should dissolve the Republican form of government and establish in its stead an Absolute Monarchy;

NOW, THEREFORE, WE, Norton I, by the Grace of God Emperor of the Thirty-Three States and the multitude of Territories of the United States of North America, do hereby DISSOLVE the Republic of the United States, and it is hereby dissolved;

And all laws made from and after this date, either by the National Congress or any State Legislature, shall be null and of no effect.

All Governors, and all other persons in authority, shall maintain order by enforcing the heretofore existing laws and regulations until the necessary alterations can be effected.

Given under Our hand and seal, at Headquarters, San Francisco, this 26th day of July, 1860.

Norton I.

This time, public reaction extended well beyond newspaper sales.

Norton's landlady, the redoubtable Mrs. Carswell of 255 Kearny Street, became so upset at this abrupt and peremptory dissolution of the United States of America that she abruptly and peremptorily evicted His Majesty from her boarding house. (She tried to camouflage her offended political sensibilities by claiming he hadn't paid his rent for the past several months.)

Editor George Fitch, on the other hand, was absolutely delighted. Norton's royal proclamations were becoming so popular that his paper's circulation had more than doubled over a five-month period. Interest in more particulars about America's new emperor was growing by leaps and bounds. It was time to let a few newshounds off the leash, to discover who he was and what he was all about.

✦

Joshua Abraham Norton had emigrated to San Francisco from South Africa in 1849, having just inherited a considerable fortune from the sale of his deceased father's ships' chandlery. He'd arrived in San Francisco at exactly the right time to take advantage of the boom brought on by the 1849 gold rush.

Norton wasted little time. He quickly established the "Joshua Norton Company – General Merchants" and plunged into the fray. He bought a clutch of oceanfront lots. He founded a cigar factory. He built a hotel and a large rice mill.

The following year – 1850 – San Francisco's population soared from about 500 to more than 30,000. The price of a $3,000* lot shot up to $62,000. The price of an egg rose from two cents to a dime. The value of both durables and comestibles seemed to double every few months.

---

* For consistency, all dollar amounts have been adjusted to 1999 values.

By 1851 Norton was a multimillionaire. He was now one of San Francisco's most successful industrialists and land barons. He was on a first-name basis with all its bankers and politicians. He was a member of its prestigious Masonic Lodge and its Four Hundred Club. He ate and drank at the city's most expensive restaurants and saloons.

And then, in September 1852, the city's rice supply dried up. China – America's primary source – had suffered a drought and banned all further rice exports. Within weeks, the American price of rice surged from 4 cents to 36 cents per pound. Norton's warehouses emptied and his rice mill ground to a halt.

It was at this point that a shipping agent for the brokerage Godeffroy and Sillem took Norton aside and offered him the deal of a lifetime.

The *Glyde*, a medium-sized British freighter, would be arriving within the day (December 22) with a full cargo of rice from Peru. The agent was prepared to sell the rice to Norton, before anyone else got wind of it, for 12.5 cents a pound – but there was a proviso. Norton had to commit to buying the entire 200,000-pound cargo sight unseen – and pay cash for it on the barrelhead.

It was a scary proposition, but the potential $3-million profit produced the required amount of adrenalin. Norton emptied his bank accounts, drew on his credit to the hilt, mortgaged his waterfront lots, and borrowed wherever and from whomever he could. Then he closed the deal. He hired a new crew for his rice mill and had them grease up the machinery. He cleaned out his warehouses and prepared them for imminent deliveries.

When the *Glyde* arrived in San Francisco harbour two days later, he had himself rowed out to her before she was even properly tied up at anchor. He waved his papers before the bemused captain's face, demanding to inspect her cargo on the spot, without delay, immediately.

What he found calmed his heart rate to a contented sixty-five beats per minute. It also pasted a serene smile on his face. The *Glyde* was indeed full of rice – and it was in good condition.

Norton spent the following day happily shuffling bills of lading. There was no hurry now – word of the shipment had flashed through the city and was driving its price higher by the hour. At this rate, the rice would be selling within the 50-cent range by the end of the day.

Norton hummed and whistled contentedly.

It was the last contented humming and whistling he would do for quite some time. The next day the Spanish freighter *Syren* sailed into port carrying another 100,000 pounds of Peruvian rice. A day later the *Merceditas* showed up with a further 200,000 pounds. Two days later the *Dragon* made port with 250,000 pounds, followed by the *Trident* with 175,000.

By the New Year, the city's harbour was dotted with eighteen additional ships full of Peruvian rice, and the market was totally glutted. The price of rice plunged to two cents a pound.

Norton never recovered from his fall. For a few years he drifted around the periphery of San Francisco's business world, trying to make a comeback as a coffee- and lima-bean peddler. When that failed, he tried the civil service. Nothing worked, and none of his former business colleagues were prepared to help him for long, because it soon became evident that Norton had lost more than his fortune when his business collapsed. He'd become bitter and morose, raging more and more incoherently about corruption and ignorance in American business and politics. He felt that the growing risk of civil war, as the rift between North and South widened, required nothing less than the strong hand of a monarch to hold the country together. "An empire should be ruled by an emperor, not a roomful of elected ignoramuses," he fumed. "Democracy is just a fancy word for pooling a country's ignorance and unleashing it wholesale on its citizens."

His address deteriorated as his fortunes sank. He moved from Battery Street to Sansome Street, from a ramshackle boarding house on Kearny Street to a rundown hotel at the bottom of Bush Street.

Then he seemed to disappear entirely.

✦

Though Joshua Norton's pedigree was soon discovered, the question as to whether he had truly lost his marbles along with his fortune remained in doubt.

On the face of it, he certainly seemed sane enough. The language of his proclamations, which he issued in increasing numbers over the next two decades, was flawlessly magisterial, refined, and coherent. His arguments, in public speeches, interviews, and letters to various newspaper editors, were cogent, well-reasoned, and in several instances (such as when he ordered the building of the Golden Gate Bridge and a cable-car system) downright visionary.

On the other hand, he seemed genuinely, obsessively convinced of his regal status – the only subject about which, if challenged, he became immediately irritable and peremptory. That's when his haughty, majestic side came out. In fact, it was probably this utter conviction on his part that made it easier for people to go along with his charade, and to treat him, in a kind of mock seriousness, as a real-life emperor. It wasn't long before the street-people, the fruit-vendors and delivery folk, and then the shop- and saloon-keepers, all began to address him as "Your Majesty."

For he certainly had the manner. Grave, dignified, but always unfailingly polite, he ambled each morning along Montgomery Street, the ostrich feather in his hat fluttering in the breeze, a silver-knobbed hickory stick pacing his stride, stopping here and there to answer a question, accept a petition, or reassure a subject. He held court every day on the public benches of Portsmouth Square, always surrounded by a large crowd, and attended synagogue every Saturday and church every Sunday. "I think it my duty to encourage religion and morality by showing myself in church," he explained to a bemused reporter. "And to avoid jealousy, I attend them all in turn."

He also attended city council and state congressional sittings, often rising to pronounce on issues of state or community in a way that initially amused, and then (as his newspaper popularity grew) intrigued and irritated the politicians. A city ordinance, for example, forbidding Sunday shopping (a bow to Christian churches) didn't take into account the Jewish Sabbath. His Majesty pronounced:

> Whereas it is our intention to endeavor to obtain some alteration in the doctrine of the Church, by which the Hebrew and Christian faiths will become united; as also by which the foreign churches will become Americanized;
>
> Therefore, We, Norton I, Emperor (etc.), do hereby prohibit the enforcement of the Sunday Law until our object is obtained and one Sunday is established for all.

These were often ideas that had been urged on him by ordinary people who stopped him on the street, or notions he drew from the newspapers, which he habitually read for several hours every day.

People liked his willingness to listen. They liked his earnest replies. They also got a big kick out of seeing some of their own ideas appear a day or two later, as proclamations, in George Fitch's *Bulletin*. It created the appealing illusion of direct access to political power, and the virtually instant conversion of one's ideas into direct action. If you couldn't get past the office door of your congressman or the secretary of your senator, you could always go talk to your Emperor and shortcut the entire process.

A flower-seller on Montgomery Street was apparently the first to recognize the business potential of the Emperor's growing popularity. Every morning he made His Majesty a formal bow and then pinned one of yesterday's unsold carnations to his lapel. In return, Norton graciously permitted the flower-seller to nail a sign to his barrow: BY APPOINTMENT TO HIS MAJESTY, EMPEROR NORTON I.

People got a big kick out of that, too. The flower-seller's sales soared.

It wasn't long before signs announcing HIS IMPERIAL MAJESTY, EMPEROR NORTON I EATS HERE or CULINARY PURVEYOR TO THE EMPEROR OF THE UNITED STATES, NORTON I popped up in the windows of restaurants and saloons all along Montgomery Street. They identified establishments where the Emperor was welcome to consume lunch or dinner "on the house." Walter and Tompkins, an upscale tailoring establishment, earned the right to become GENTLEMEN'S OUTFITTERS BY APPOINTMENT TO HIS HIGHNESS, NORTON I by furnishing His Majesty with a gratis pair of sailcloth trousers. Several San Francisco banks, having proved willing to cover His Highness's occasional modest overdrafts, became FINANCIAL ADVISORS TO EMPEROR NORTON I.

But Norton's biggest breakthrough occurred at a musical performance at Tucker's Hall in 1861, when the orchestra conductor, tipped off that Norton was coming into the hall, led the orchestra in a fanfare that brought the entire audience to its feet. The Emperor, startled but apparently pleased, merely responded with a majestic nod and wave of the hand – but a tradition had been established. From then on, all San Francisco's theatres sent the Emperor opening-night invitations, and his entrance was always accompanied by a musical flourish and ovation. His attendance, in time, became a necessary part of a show's success; if he failed to appear, people assumed the show was a bust and stayed away in droves.

By 1862, Norton's proclamations had become so popular that they'd even begun to spawn imitators. Editor Albert Evans of the *California Daily Alta* was known to be willing – for a suitable fee – to publish Norton proclamations that spoke approvingly of certain businesses or enterprises. Other newspapers published them simply to increase their own circulations, and political agitators faked them up to support their political causes.

Since San Francisco was split approximately down the middle on issues such as the Civil War, this began to make the Emperor seem inconsistent and confused. He complained bitterly to George Fitch about it, but even Fitch proved less than reliable – not above accepting the occasional bribe. Finally, in disgust, Norton abandoned the *Bulletin* entirely and made a deal with the weekly *Pacific Appeal*, designating it as his royal gazette. From then on, readers were more able to separate the wheat from the chaff.

With the advent of the telegraph, newspaper content became syndicated across the nation, and the Emperor's fame quickly spread beyond California's borders. Now, even the *New*

York Times ran the occasional Norton proclamation or Norton-related story. With no cable-cars or famous bridges yet available as tourist attractions, the Emperor became San Francisco's greatest tourist asset. Once the transcontinental railroad was completed eight years later, the first attraction most San Francisco- bound travellers demanded to see when they arrived was the city's famous emperor.

Soon every kiosk and souvenir shop in the city was selling Emperor Norton postcards, Norton dolls, Norton cigars, and Norton lithographs. He began being pestered for autographs, begged for photographs, solicited for advice.

"It is exhausting, but it is my mission and my responsibility," he informed a reporter who had urged him to take a breather. "A monarch's duty to his loyal subjects never ends."

He did, however, take the opportunity to replenish his Royal Treasury by gravely informing all train arrivals that Americans were now subject to an Imperial Treasury Tax of 50 cents per head – a levy that most citizens chuckled at and readily paid. In return they received a receipt bearing the official seal of the Imperial Government of Norton I, which the Emperor prepared on the spot by pressing an ink-smeared coin onto the paper. His Majesty also began selling twenty-year Imperial Treasury Bonds in denominations of $5, $25, and $100, all payable upon redemption at 7-per-cent interest. They proved enormously popular, and were always in great demand.

But probably the best gauge of just how popular the Emperor became was what transpired following his arrest, on January 21, 1867, on a charge of lunacy.

A newly hired police recruit from Oregon found His Majesty "loitering" in the lobby of the Palace Hotel. Unaware of the Emperor's history and stature in the city, the policeman gruffly ordered him to move along. The Emperor, properly incensed, informed the officer exactly whom he was talking to. In response, the officer changed the charge to lunacy and ran the old man in.

Half an hour later, after an apoplectic dressing-down by the chief of police, it was the young officer who was out on his ear, while the Emperor was being served hand and foot in the chief's office. The hastily summoned mayor was already there, apologizing over and over, while several councilmen fluttered about like frantic courtiers. Even the commissioner of health had hurried out of his board meeting at the news.

The Emperor seemed willing enough to overlook the incident, but it was already too late. Word had been leaked to the street, and every newsboy, reporter, and editor within a mile of Montgomery Street was hurrying down to the precinct office. Even Mark Twain, then a columnist for the San Francisco *Morning Call*, showed up to defend "The Emp" – which was only fair, since he'd often used His Majesty's name as a character reference when seeking newspaper employment.

The resulting wave of public outrage nearly swept the mayor and police chief out of office. "In what can only be described as the most dastardly of errors, our own Emperor Norton was arrested today in the Palace Hotel," George Fitch fumed in the *Bulletin*. "He is being held on the ludicrous charge of 'lunacy.' Known and loved by all true San Franciscans, the kindly Monarch of Montgomery Street is less a lunatic than those who have charged him – as they will soon learn when His Majesty's loyal subjects are fully apprised of this outrage!"

A flurry of telegrams and letters arrived from rival cities in California, Oregon, and Washington, all urging the Emperor to leave his thankless headquarters and relocate his throne to a more loyal metropolis. "We would love to be able to demonstrate our support and appreciation of Your Majesty," wrote the mayor of Oroville, California. "If Your Highness would but give the word, we would consider it an honor to whip the breeches off those proscriptive traitors in San Francisco!"

Being a peaceable sort, Emperor Norton wrote gracious acknowledgements to all his supporters and assured them that he would certainly visit their fair cities in the coming months (which he did, and was fêted royally in each city). He also publicly forgave the offending officer, and granted him a Royal Pardon.

But the police chief was taking no further chances. From that day on, all police officers in the San Francisco constabulary were required to salute His Majesty wherever and whenever they passed him on the street, and to offer any assistance he might require.

Just as anxious to make amends, the city council voted unanimously to buy the Emperor a splendid new uniform and hat, and to make its annual upkeep a regular item in the city's operating budget. The Mechanics Institute on Post Street extended to him one of its coveted memberships, dues-free. His listing in the city directory was changed from "Norton, Joshua Abraham, businessman" to "Norton I, emperor." (In the federal census three years later, the enumerator also listed Norton's official occupation as "emperor," but entered him in the category of "Male Citizen whose right to vote is denied." In the section labelled "Reason for Denial," he checked off the word "insane.")

The enumerator's judgement notwithstanding, Emperor Norton's acceptance continued unabated. By the early 1870s his daily schedule bulged with official functions both within and beyond San Francisco's city limits. He attended sessions of the

California legislature in Sacramento, accepted invitations to review the troops at military colleges in Oakland and San Diego, and gave speeches in public schools and colleges throughout the Pacific southwest. He inaugurated public buildings, led parades, and attended dozens of charity fundraising events.

No streetcar conductor ever requested a fare from him, and no ferryboat operator ever asked him for a ticket. The governor of California, Leland Stanford, personally issued His Majesty an unlimited free pass on his Central Pacific Railroad.

But while Norton was gentle and charming, he was also iconoclastic and fearless – which may well have been at the heart of his extraordinary popularity. He never argued for the sake of arguing, but, when he deemed it necessary, he had no compunction about biting the hands that fed him. When Stanford quadrupled his profits by selling off public lands that had been granted to his railroad for railbed purposes, while simultaneously gouging farmers with higher freight rates, Norton denounced him with a stinging proclamation. When the same city councillors who were paying for his uniform failed to see the future value of a cable-car system for the city, he issued three separate proclamations and one edict against them, ordering them, upon pain of dismissal, to commit municipal funds to the project.

Along with his popularity came increasing cultural fame. In 1873, the Metropolitan Theater on Montgomery Street featured a burlesque entitled *The Gold Demon*, which included a vignette of Norton in full regalia. The same theatre found it even more profitable, several years later, to depict Norton prominently in a revue entitled *Life in San Francisco*. In due course a comic opera entitled *Norton I* played to sellout crowds for several months at Tucker's Hall.

The novelists weren't far behind. Mark Twain put away the manuscript of *Captain Stormfield's Visit to Heaven* and focused on *Huckleberry Finn*, in which Norton occupies the role of the Hobo King (Twain's later *The Prince and the Pauper* also shows the Norton influence). Robert Louis Stevenson, also a San Francisco resident at that time, included a mad emperor directly modelled on Norton I in *The Wrecker*, a novel which he co-wrote with his stepson Lloyd Osbourne. Stevenson's stepdaughter, Isobel Field, featured Norton prominently in her memoir *This Life I've Loved*. Bret Harte, Ambrose Bierce, William Dean Howells, and Anthony Trollope all wrote about him.

And yet the question stubbornly remained: was Norton I a true or a fraudulent madman? Was he a man trapped in a genuine and obsessive delusion, or was he consciously and deviously making fools of an entire nation?

California Daily Alta editor Albert Evans, who saw the Emperor every day for more than a decade, remained convinced that he was a con-artist and a "calculating sham." The *Bulletin's* George Fitch, with identical credentials, resolutely defended "The Emp" as "more sane than those who claim to be." Mark Twain called him a "loveable old humbug," which, the more one reflects on it, could have supported either side.

Ambrose Bierce, the city's resident iconoclast, was least charitable. "In his own opinion he had a divine right to be maintained at the expense of others," he grumped. "To lead a useless, vagabond life, like other imperial mendicants; to get money and be supported like other kings out of a place. And who shall say that the Emperor was not right? Who shall presume to question the sanity of a mind that for years enabled its body to live in luxury and idleness, without physical or mental toil?"

In general, however, it seems safe to say that the majority of Americans rejected Bierce's view. There seemed a general consensus that, though he was probably making a tidy return on his bonds and imperial head tax, he wasn't being greedy about it. He lived, ate, and travelled modestly. He never misused his position for obvious material or political gain. That, too, contributed considerably to the public's affection for him. If he was indeed a con-artist, at least he was smart enough to accept that moderation kept the bubble aloft.

"The Emp" kept that bubble from bursting for more than two long decades – from 1859 until 1880. When he finally died, on January 8, 1880, it was of a heart attack on his way to an evening performance at the Academy of Natural Sciences on California Street.

The news flashed around the city in what seemed like minutes. Theatrical and musical productions all over the city were interrupted by the announcement. Within twenty minutes a huge crowd had gathered outside the city hospital.

The next morning, newspapers all over America, and then in a wider scattering across the Western world, announced the death of America's "bedlam emperor." LE ROI EST MORT, mourned the San Francisco *Chronicle*. The *New York Times* granted His Majesty an extraordinary, prominently displayed sixteen inches. California's new governor, George C. Perkins, searching for news of his public inauguration, which had occurred the previous day, found himself relegated to a thirty-eight-word mention on page three of the *California Daily Alta*, while the Emperor received thirty-four inches on its front page. The *Cincinnati Enquirer* ran what was probably the longest headline in the history of American journalism: EMPEROR NORTON GIVES UP THE GHOST AND SURRENDERS HIS SCEPTER TO THE

MAN ON THE PALE HORSE. THE CITY BY THE GOLDEN GATE
MOURNS HER ILLUSTRIOUS DEAD. AN EMPEROR WITHOUT
ENEMIES, A KING WITHOUT A KINGDOM, GONE TO KINGDOM
COME. SUPPORTED IN LIFE BY THE WILLING TRIBUTE OF A FREE
PEOPLE, HE DROPS DEAD AT A STREET CORNER AND NOW
KNOWS WHAT LIES BEYOND.

In his pockets they found a wad of imperial bonds (he died in
the year his first bonds came due), and a fistful of telegrams from
the likes of Alexander II of Russia, Queen Victoria of England,
and the president of France. No one could say for certain whether
he'd ever believed in the authenticity of such telegrams, but he
had always taken pains to answer them promptly.

More than fifty reporters crowded around the entrance to
the coroner's office several days later for the release of the post-
mortem.

"The cause of death was sanguineous apoplexy," Coroner
Douglass announced.

That wasn't what the assembled press had come to hear.
"Did you examine his brain, sir?"

"I did."

"And?"

"Nothing unusual."

"No sign of lunacy, then?"

"No pathological evidence of insanity was discovered."

The Emperor lay in state for three days, during which more than
six thousand people waited as long as four hours to view the
body. Some ten thousand mourners attended his funeral. The
cortège that followed the body to its official burial site was three
miles long. Some people drove in carriages, some walked in the
rain. They were, the *Chronicle* reported, from every walk of life,

"from the capitalist to the pauper, the clergyman to the pick-pocket, the well-dressed to the bowed with age, and prattling children."

They buried the Emperor as if he'd been the president himself, with full military honours and a twenty-five-gun salute.

Reminders of the Emperor can still be found around San Francisco to this day. There are Emperor Norton inns and hotels, Emperor Norton cigars and dolls. San Francisco's Sheraton-Palace Hotel still serves lunch in its Emperor Norton Room, and the *Harbor Emperor*, complete with Norton I figurehead, takes the city's tourists on cruises of San Francisco bay. At least half a dozen public and private museums are largely or entirely dedicated to the Emperor's memory, and a model of the Emperor, over ten feet tall, greets visitors at the entrance to Pier 39.

Since his death, more than a dozen biographies have been written about him, and a full-scale opera, *Emperor Norton*, was premiered by the San Francisco Opera Company in 1981.

Long live the Emperor.

Another Day, Another Picasso

The Astonishing Exploits of Prolific Master
Forger Elmyr de Hory

Elmyr de Hory never intended to become the greatest, most prolific, art forger of all time.

In fact, right until his death at the age of seventy-one, he remained embarrassed and in denial about the whole thing.

As a young Hungarian art student in the 1920s, studying under the famous post-impressionist painter Fernand Léger in Paris, he had high hopes of becoming a painter in his own right. When he was twenty, his work was included in a Salon d'Automne Exhibition alongside the likes of Chagall, Utrillo, Dufy, Monet, Derain, Vlaminck, de Chirico, and Courbet.

But de Hory had a very low tolerance for rejection and self-denial. He loved art, but wasn't terribly interested in suffering for it. As the spoiled child of rich aristocratic parents, his main crises tended to involve which outfits from his closetsful of shoes or jackets were most appropriate for which gallery openings. (More often than not the answer was none, requiring yet another new suit, coat, or pair of shoes.)

All through the 1920s and early 1930s de Hory hung out in the cafés and bistros of Montparnasse, playing groupie to painters like Picasso, Derain, Kees van Dongen, Matisse, and Vlaminck, and writers like Valéry, Stein, Hemingway, and Joyce. He was never a serious enough artist to keep their attention, but he studied their works with a sycophantic eagerness that made him one of their most knowledgeable fans. It was a knowledge that would pay big dividends decades later, when de Hory's own work was no longer "up and coming" but "down and out."

The crash came in 1938, when his family called him back to Budapest after Germany's annexation of Austria. Within the year, the Second World War was steamrolling over everyone's lives. Elmyr spent most of the war interned in various prisoner-of-war camps, avoiding the worst by painting portraits of the camp brass. By war's end his parents were dead, his family fortune in ruins, and his country under Communist rule.

Elmyr fled back to Paris.

But Paris in 1945 wasn't exactly an ideal place for a penniless playboy artist with a low threshold for rejection and suffering. The place was now crawling with impoverished aristocrats, each paying the rent by selling off what remained of their family treasures. You could pick up a van Gogh for a couple of thousand dollars, a Daumier for a thousand and change, and a Courbet for a couple of hundred.* Nobody seemed interested in the work of a clever but not particularly inspired forty-year-old Hungarian expressionist at any price.

---

* For consistency, all dollar amounts have been adjusted to 1999 values.

The only artists whose works were selling for premium prices were those at whose feet de Hory had sat before the war. Curiously, he'd always felt more in tune with their artistic sensibilities than with those of his own generation. He'd tried his hand at their style of drawings and watercolours once or twice, and the results hadn't been bad. A few of those efforts, unframed and unsigned, were hanging among his other paintings in his garret the day a friend, Lady Malcolm Campbell, dropped by for a visit.

She pointed casually at a line drawing of a young girl's head.

"I didn't know you owned a Greek-period Picasso, Elmyr. Would you be interested in selling it?"

Short of food and rent money as usual, de Hory agreed.

She paid him $750.

During the two months of Paris life that this money financed, de Hory struggled with a lot of guilt – guilt at defrauding a friend, and guilt at how much she'd paid him for a mere ten minutes' worth of work. But when he finally looked her up to confess, she confessed first.

"I sold your Picasso to a dealer in London," she admitted. "I got $1,400 for it. Can I make it up to you with lunch at the Ritz?"

She certainly could – though she found de Hory oddly distracted through the entire meal. Back at his studio he consulted a catalogue for a closer look at Picasso's Greek period. He spent the next hour practising its 1920s pen-and-ink style. He was amazed at how quickly he got the hang of it.

The next day he selected his three best results and took them to a Left Bank art gallery. He explained that he had received the drawings as gifts from Picasso before the war, but now was destitute and obliged to sell. The dealer glanced briefly at de Hory's old and worn (but obviously expensive) clothes and shrugged. It was a common enough story in postwar Paris. He busied himself examining the drawings.

For the next ten minutes, while he stumbled blindly around the gallery pretending to admire its artwork, de Hory almost disintegrated with anxiety. Every second he expected the Sûreté de Police to come bursting through the door to frog-march him off to prison. He was positive the dealer hadn't believed a word of his story. He was an idiot for risking his tenuous status as a stateless refugee in France for a few hundred dollars.

And anyway, deep down he still couldn't believe one could dash off three Picassos in an hour and get away with it.

"*Mais oui,*" the dealer said, coming back out of his office. "*C'est bon.* How much do you want for them?"

De Hory was so relieved, he let them go for a mere $2,400.

Though de Hory always insisted that such indiscretions were mere aberrations in his lifelong struggle to establish his own painting career ("even Michelangelo faked a sculpture now and then when he was short of funds"), this 1945 transaction marked the beginning of an increasingly deliberate, organized forging career. During the next two years, as his cost of living increased – classier studios, expensive wines, custom-tailored clothes, trips to fashionable resorts, and lavish gifts to young men – de Hory availed himself more and more regularly of this "temporary solution." By a rough estimate – he never kept records – his 1945–47 income from these "aberrations" exceeded $335,000.

Ironically, de Hory found producing fake Picassos far easier than selling them. Outwardly suave and charming, he was by nature timid and paranoid. While the production of pastiches (drawings or paintings in the style of a famous artist) wasn't illegal *per se*, signing them with a fake signature or selling them as the bona fide work of the imitated artist carried stiff jail terms all over the Western world. Before approaching a gallery owner or art dealer, de Hory invariably became so frightened that he would have to duck into a public washroom to throw up.

For a few months in 1946, de Hory teamed up with another young aristocrat, who did his selling for him. This worked well until he discovered his cohort pocketing more than his fair share of the proceeds. This was to be an ongoing problem for de Hory throughout his life.

Actually, *anything* involving money would prove to be an ongoing problem for de Hory. He was such an extravagant spendthrift, he simply couldn't save a nickel. He'd never had to plan ahead or think twice about where his next franc was coming from. Money slipped through his fingers like glycerine. He was always either rich or broke – the latter more often than the former.

On the other hand, because he stuck mostly to line drawings, and to a time in Picasso's career when Picasso hadn't kept careful records, never once, in these early years, was de Hory challenged or his forgeries rejected. Dealer after dealer held them up to the light, compared them with published reproductions, or even with originals hanging on their walls, and pronounced them genuine.

For a man convinced he wasn't really doing what he was doing, de Hory took an immense amount of pride in it.

In August 1947, after having produced more than fifty Greek-period Picassos and unloaded them on Europe's art dealers and galleries, Elmyr de Hory decided it was time to let the continental market cool down a little. He applied for a three-month tourist visa to the United States, climbed aboard a Vickers Viscount, and flew to New York City for a short, exploratory visit.

He overstayed that visa by some eleven years.

Postwar New York took to Elmyr de Hory like flies to sticky paper. Unlike Parisians, Americans in the 1940s and 1950s still found European aristocrats irresistibly exotic. Elmyr's classy smoking jackets, gold monocle, cultivated accent, and relentless charm proved highly marketable. Within three weeks he had a fancy East 78th Street address and was hobnobbing with the likes of Lana Turner, Anita Loos, Montgomery Clift, Averell Harriman, and fellow countrywomen Zsa Zsa and Magda Gabor. Zsa Zsa even commissioned de Hory to paint her portrait, nude, with a guitar leaning strategically against her thigh.

"She did complain," Elmyr confided to a friend, "that one of her tits – is this how you say it in America? – was too much in the centre. I was paid for it, but very poorly."

The rest of New York's art community seemed largely in agreement with Zsa Zsa. Despite a modestly well received one-man show at the Lilienfeld Gallery on 57th Street, nobody was terribly interested in de Hory's own work. The same, however, was clearly not true of his Picassos, two of which he had no trouble selling for a fast $5,000 to no less a gallery owner than the eminent Klaus Perls, president of the American Art Dealers' Association.

Klaus Perls thus achieved the dubious fame of becoming de Hory's first American victim.

Intent on widening his experience of America, de Hory continued on to California in 1948, and the American Midwest in 1949 ("I just had to get for myself a look at those cowboys!"). Once again, nobody was particularly interested in his own work, but his Greek-period Picassos – three or four of which, by now, he could knock off in the time it took to smoke a cigarette – sold for prices that raised even his own eyebrows.

Upper-class America, de Hory discovered, had made a lot of

money during the war. Now it was looking for the opportunity to buy itself a little of all that culture its troops had liberated.

And Elmyr de Hory was more than happy to sell it to them.

He took on the name Baron von Herzog, installed himself in a ritzy Hollywood apartment, invested in a large collection of post-impressionist artbooks, and began to expand his palette. He added drawings by Renoir, Matisse, and Modigliani. He threw in some gouaches and watercolours by Cézanne, Dufy, and Braque. He extended his range of Picassos into Picasso's early cubist period.

Then, for an even greater challenge – was it really so easy to fool the world's best-known art experts? – he began painting Modigliani and Picasso oils.

Faking oils was far more complicated than forging drawings or watercolours. Aside from additional factors like texture and complex colour mixes, there was always the problem of how to make them look their age. Oils dried infinitely more slowly than watercolours – often taking years to achieve merely a surface hardness. If you were going to fake oils, you had to be prepared to invest in a little long-range planning.

That was the down side. The up side was that even a modest Modigliani oil would put $100,000 in your pocket.

De Hory began to work on a cache of oils.

Meanwhile, Hollywood's art dealers were virtually tearing his fakes out of his hands, partly because they were getting better and better, partly because his stories were getting better, too. Having lived among the artists he was faking, de Hory could draw on a vast storehouse of Montparnasse gossip to embellish his pitch. He knew the names of Braque's mistresses, Matisse's friends, Picasso's business associates. He knew which Parisian art dealers had invested in the early works of these artists. He knew about the times the poverty-stricken Modigliani had dumped his studio's contents in the French equivalent of a garage sale.

This sort of knowledge made it easy to concoct believable explanations for how he'd acquired his drawings (from a mistress, friend, or early investor), and to give them the most important authentication any fake work of art needs: a believable provenance. You had to have a demonstrable, preferably traceable history of how the work had got from the artist to the seller.

Elmyr de Hory could give fabulous provenance.

During those early years in California, he only once encountered an art dealer who saw through him.

That man, by extraordinary coincidence, was the brother of de Hory's first American victim, Klaus Perls. Frank Perls owned a gallery on North Camden Drive in Beverly Hills, and de Hory had offered him several early Renoirs, two Greek-period Picassos, a few Matisses from around 1937, and a portrait by Modigliani, explaining that these were some of the last remnants of his family's once-vast art collection in Budapest.

As Perls described it many years later, he was impressed by what he saw. Enormously impressed. The Renoirs passed muster effortlessly. The Picassos did likewise. The Matisses were small masterpieces. But when he looked at the Modigliani – no less accomplished, really – his eye caught something about the composition that reminded him vaguely of the Renoirs he'd just examined.

He looked back at the Renoirs and then at the Modigliani. Back and forth, a second time.

Then he realized what he was seeing. The two works of art had been produced by the same hand. Different subjects, different styles, different techniques – but there was a faint, almost indefinable trace of similarity that couldn't be accounted for by any other explanation.

Perls gathered up the drawings, slid them back into their portfolio, tied up the strings, and flung the entire package at Elmyr de Hory's head.

"Get out!" he fumed. "You've got exactly two seconds to get out of my gallery and twenty-four hours to get out of town. If you're still around by tomorrow at this time, I'm calling the police. Every single one of those drawings is a fake!"

By this time de Hory had recovered his portfolio, his hat, and his composure. At the door he turned and gave Frank Perls a disarming grin.

"But they're very good, no?" he asked.

Perls snorted. "They came pretty close to fooling me," he acknowledged. "Now you've got one more second to get the hell out of here."

The experience rattled de Hory enough that he left Hollywood for New York, where he spent the next few weeks soothing his nerves at the Waldorf. He couldn't decide whether the Frank Perls incident had been a sign or a fluke. Was there a flaw in his talent? Had he in some way lost his touch? Was his affinity with the post-impressionists not as complete as he'd thought?

Eventually de Hory decided to submit his work to the most rigorous test he could conceive of. He took five of his newest Picassos and offered them for sale to the Galerie Paul Rosenberg, one of New York's most famous art galleries. Paul Rosenberg was America's most renowned Picasso expert, and Picasso's only authorized representative in the United States. He had been handling Picasso's work exclusively in the States for almost forty years.

Rosenberg took more than two weeks to examine de Hory's Picassos.

Then he bought them all.

De Hory paid his bill at the Waldorf, bought himself an only slightly used Lincoln Continental, and set out to sell America some more French culture.

Though his dealings with Rosenberg had proven gratifyingly restorative, de Hory had no interest in ever repeating the Frank Perls incident.

His solution was to go into the mail-order business.

For the next two years, working out of a posh apartment in Miami Beach under the name Louis Raynal, he wrote to art museums and galleries in several dozen large American cities, offering them "the remnants" of his family's art collection in Budapest – which had meanwhile grown to include works by Cézanne, Matisse, Picasso, Braque, Derain, Bonnard, Degas, Vlaminck, Laurencin, Modigliani, and Renoir. In each case he was prepared to send them any works in which they expressed an interest, for a free, no-risk, no-obligation examination.

No salesman would ever call.

Sears, Roebuck or Montgomery Ward might have taken a lesson. De Hory's success rate was nearly 100 per cent. Hardly anyone ever sent anything back. During two years in Florida he retailed more than a hundred post-impressionist drawings and watercolours, raking in almost $1.5 million. (Such sales figures, admittedly, were helped by his attractively priced Matisses, offered less than a year after Matisse's conveniently timed death.)

During this comparatively stable time in his life (1953–55), when he also entered into a domestic relationship with a young boxer, de Hory spent time further developing his talent for faking oils.

This was not easy, because French painting traditions differed from American painting traditions right down to the materials and frames. To fake pre–Second World War French oils, he had to import both canvases and frames from France, and, once the paintings were done, their frames had to be aged as convincingly as their paint. De Hory's studio became a veritable test lab of household chemicals and oils, and the substances he found most effective for ageing ranged from Lipton teabags to dirty linseed oil. Dozens of perfume atomizers filled with cleansers and varnishes and turps lined his shelves.

Then, one day, de Hory ran into trouble. He received a telephone call from a prominent Chicago art dealer, Joseph Faulkner, who'd been one of his better customers, having bought about $150,000 worth of drawings and watercolours and one small Matisse oil.

The usually cheerful dealer's voice had an unpleasant edge to it. He wanted to know if Raynal had a bill of sale, or any other papers, that would help in the further authentication of the Matisse painting.

De Hory winced. He'd known he should have waited a few more years before offering that Matisse oil for sale.

He assured Faulkner he'd have a look around and hung up. Half an hour later he was clearing out the apartment. By suppertime, when de Hory's boxer came home, the Lincoln Continental was heaped high with de Hory's possessions, and there was no room for anyone or anything else. The boxer, who'd found a good job he didn't want to give up, decided to stay behind.

Two days later the FBI showed up, asking to speak to a Louis Raynal. They searched the apartment, and asked when Raynal would be back.

The boxer said he didn't know.

The FBI said they'd be in touch.

On the run, not sure whether the FBI was following him, de Hory spent some time in Mexico and then flew to Montreal, where he set up shop to offer the remnants of his family's Budapest art collection to Canadians as well. His contented customers soon included "the head of an enormous Canadian corporation who did have a huge fortune and a house in Palm Beach," and "a man who did own a big Canadian whisky company." (The former reportedly paid $96,000 for a small selection of de Hory's Matisse and Dufy drawings, while the latter bought a de Hory Modigliani for an undisclosed price.) When de Hory left Canada to return to the United States some months later, it was via Windsor, Ontario, where he posed as a French-Canadian sightseer.

It would not be his last association with Canada, however.

In New York, Zsa Zsa Gabor mentioned to de Hory that the FBI had been to see her and several of her friends; they were looking for a Louis Raynal. So, apparently, were several art dealers and museum curators.

Obviously his trail hadn't cooled down as much as he'd hoped.

At the same time, de Hory was running into more and more evidence that his forgeries were penetrating deep into America's public art institutions. After crossing from Windsor into Detroit, he'd been startled to find several of his Matisse drawings prominently displayed in the Detroit Art Museum. His handiwork also hung in the Fogg Art Museum at Harvard University, the City Art Museum of St. Louis, the City Hall Art Gallery of New Orleans, and a dozen other large public art institutions. He was seeing eye-catching announcements and advertisements for "his" works in America's prestigious *Art News Annual*, and even scholarly and coffee-table post-impressionist histories and catalogues were beginning to include his forgeries in their indexed listings of the featured artists' works.

Every time he investigated, he found the prices these works were now fetching was five to ten times more than he'd been paid for them.

All things considered, it seemed high time to find himself an agent.

Naturally, since hiring an agent involved money and business, de Hory bungled it right from the start. Instead of teaming up with someone who already knew the art world, who could talk the talk and walk the walk, he allowed himself to be conned into an arrangement with a brash young Egyptian-born confidence man named Fernand Legros.

Legros didn't know a Picasso from a pistachio, but he had the larcenous instincts of a desert hyena. Short and lithe, with a long nose and dark, hypnotic eyes, Legros immediately sensed de Hory's essential spinelessness and moved in to take control. For good measure, he also took over de Hory's current boyfriend, a pretty nineteen-year-old Québécois drifter named Réal Lessard.

For the next ten years, de Hory patiently taught Legros everything a careful art forger should know about art and the art business. Legros listened impatiently, ignored everything de Hory told him, and yet, somehow, managed to sell everything de Hory produced. He had quickly intuited what de Hory had never been able to admit to himself: a large part of the art world *thrived* on forgeries, which probably made up as much as 60 per cent of its business, and as long as the work was convincing and the price was right, anyone – even an uneducated, uncultured thug like Fernand Legros – could walk into an art gallery and make a deal. The Frank Perlses of the art world were the exceptions.

Meanwhile, uncultured and uneducated didn't mean unintelligent. If de Hory's forging operation had been discreet and old-fashioned before Legros, after Legros it quickly became modern and high-tech.

It hadn't taken Legros long to discover that the most effective aid to selling forged art works was good authentication, and one of the most respected forms of authentication in the international art world was the French system of verification by licensed expert – a person who, due to years of study or association (for instance, having been the wife, mistress, agent, or secretary of the painter) was licensed by the French government as an *expert auprès du tribunal*. Such experts were permitted to charge a small fee for providing a work of art with an official certificate of authenticity, and for many it was their principal source of income. They were held in very high esteem in the art world, and any suggestion that they might be induced to betray the painter to whose memory they held such rare access was almost unthinkable.

Fernand Legros, of course, was always interested in the unthinkable. He had never gone far wrong operating on the assumption that, if there was any difference between himself and anyone else, it was merely a matter of degree. On his visits to these *experts*, he was never embarrassed to respond to a doubtful look by dropping a thousand-franc note onto the table. If that didn't make the doubt disappear, he followed it with a second.

That usually did the trick.

In the few instances when it didn't, Fernand simply forged the expert's signature – it hadn't taken him long to build up quite a collection of valuable letterheads – or applied a faked version of their official rubber stamps, *Expert auprès des Douanes Françaises*, to the back of the drawing or canvas.

Another convincing form of authentication was a bill of sale from a previous owner. It wasn't long before Fernand had also built up a list of "previous owners" who had fallen on hard times and weren't averse, in exchange for a few of Fernand's unembarrassed thousand-franc notes, to making up a "replacement" receipt for an earlier one that had been unaccountably lost. Naturally, Legros always made sure that the selling price on the reissued receipt was satisfyingly high, making a subsequent sale much more profitable.

One ingenious variation on this gambit was the rigged auction sale. Legros would put a de Hory Modigliani or Picasso up for auction at one of the more prestigious art auction houses, such as Parke-Bernet in New York or Hôtel Drouot in Paris. Then, he and Lessard would bid against each other in what appeared to be a pitched battle to acquire a much-desired painting or drawing. Since these auction houses kept the names of their consignors and sellers confidential, no one knew that Fernand and Réal were actually bidding against themselves. Once they had bid the work up to a truly astronomical price – well beyond anything any other bidder might have been prepared to pay – Fernand would cave in and Réal would buy the painting.

But what appeared to be a self-defeating exercise – especially since they now had to pay the auction house's 10-per-cent commission, too – was actually an exceedingly profitable way of establishing a previous owner, an entry and an illustration in a prestigious auction-house catalogue, *and* a handy astronomical price tag for a subsequent private sale.

Armed with selling ideas such as these, Fernand and Réal took de Hory in hand and on the road. "You just paint," they told him, "and we'll take care of everything else."

At first, this had sounded to de Hory like heaven, since he had always been in the habit of botching everything else. Now he wasn't so sure. For one thing, his two salesmen's ideas were so effective, and moved so much "merchandise," he could hardly keep up. Where he had previously drawn for an hour a day and played for the rest, he now found himself working like a wage-slave. And their ideas just became more and more ambitious. Now they wanted oils, big oils, masterpieces, works that would expose them all to massive risk. Yet his profits didn't seem to be keeping up with his output. Their "expenses," on the other hand, seemed to be getting larger and larger. He suspected he was being robbed blind but, whenever he complained, Fernand threw such violent fits that de Hory was left cowering in a corner.

One of their favourite sales gimmicks was to rent a luxurious mansion, load up its walls with de Hory's forgeries, photograph them with plenty of the mansion showing as backdrop, then announce that Baron von Herzog was being forced to liquidate his estate (that is, the mansion), along with all his priceless art treasures. This always flushed plenty of bargain hunters out of the woodwork, who were encouraged to bid on any work of art that caught their fancy. As the paintings slowly disappeared off the mansion's walls, the bidding frenzy invariably increased, and most ended up sold. Anything left over was offered to mail-order clients using the imposing photographs, and, if anyone ordered a gouache or watercolour that had already been sold, de Hory simply dashed off a copy.

In short, things had reached the point where de Hory was often forging de Hory forgeries.

Meanwhile, Legros was proving a veritable fountain of further scams. The most expensive large-format art books, he discovered, usually contained their art reproductions in detachable form, called tip-ins. This allowed the purchaser to remove and frame them. What Legros would do was remove one of these reproductions – usually held in place with just a dab of glue – and send it to de Hory. De Hory would then fake a watercolour or painting that was similar enough that the book's description and index entry still pertained – for example, "Modigliani, *Reclining Nude*, 1918, oil on canvas, 92 x 118, signed lower left corner, Private Collection, Paris." Once de Hory's fake was ready, Legros would have it photographed and reinsert this new reproduction (printed to the exact size of the original tip-in) back into the book.

The result: an instant, highly prestigious provenance for a de Hory forgery that Legros could then sell for hundreds of thousands of dollars. And since he was careful to choose only out-of-print art books for this scam, the likelihood of the purchaser encountering an identical copy for comparison purposes was almost nil.

One incident that occurred in 1962, and on which de Hory dined for years, involved the famous Fauve painter Kees van Dongen. Informed that van Dongen was still alive and living in the hills near Monte Carlo, Legros urged de Hory to fake up a variation of van Dongen's 1908 *Woman with Hat* – an oil portrait of a beautiful woman wearing a necklace of blue pearls – then sent Réal to visit van Dongen in hopes of getting it authenticated.

Van Dongen studied the portrait carefully. Then he smiled wistfully. Oh yes, he said, of course it was his. He remembered this model with particular fondness. He boasted to Réal about how many times he'd had to interrupt his painting to make love to her.

After he signed the portrait's authentication papers, he mused out loud: "You know, she must have posed for me at least a dozen times, but I haven't the faintest idea where half those paintings ever got to."

Réal couldn't get back to de Hory fast enough.

Over the next several years, de Hory painted more than a dozen additional van Dongen *Woman with Hat* portraits – and van Dongen happily authenticated every single one.

Then there were de Hory's dozens of Dufy watercolours, for which he'd petitioned the eminent Dufy expert André Pacitti for authentication. Pacitti was so convinced by de Hory's Dufys, and over the years authenticated so many of them, that, eventually, he began to reject *genuine* Dufys. He had become so used to de Hory's "hand," that the hand of the genuine Dufy now seemed fake!

For a man who still insisted that forging was just an incidental side-line, de Hory took an immense amount of pride in that, too.

By 1962, at age fifty-seven, Elmyr de Hory was so exhausted from thirty years of nomadic life, of rented apartments and endless hotel rooms, that he began to look for a place to settle down. It wasn't so much that he didn't want to travel any more, but he needed a more permanent place to park his easel. Fernand and Réal were now demanding so many fake oils that a permanent studio had become a necessity.

Of all the places de Hory had ever lived, the small Mediterranean island of Ibiza struck him as most suitable. It was warm, brightly sunlit, inexpensive yet cosmopolitan. You could fly there from Madrid in an hour, pick up the London *Evening Standard* at a local café, and dine out on superb Middle Eastern cuisine for a pittance. Best of all, it was neither French nor American.

Besides, it was time to put a bit more space between himself and his two frontmen. The deteriorating relations between Fernand and Réal had been making life miserable for de Hory. Though they were still an item, they fought like cats in heat. Fernand had taken to punctuating his diatribes against Réal by smashing glass coffee-tables or shattering bathroom mirrors. More than once he had broken into Réal's hotel room and flung every one of Réal's possessions down into the street.

Once, during a heated argument while the two were driving through Paris in Réal's brand-new Alfa Romeo, Fernand had begun to burn cigarette holes in the car's leather upholstery. Réal screeched to a halt beside a *gendarme* and charged Fernand with propositioning and sexually molesting him in his car.

The *gendarme* arrested them both.

When it came to business, though, the two never missed a beat. A man like de Hory was too valuable a golden goose to waste. By now they were selling de Hory's fakes throughout most of the Western world, and even into Japan and Egypt. Though de Hory's share never seemed to rise much above $5,000 per month, his two cohorts (unbeknownst to de Hory) had become multimillionaires. In 1963 Fernand (also unbeknownst to de Hory) bought a $3-million apartment on Paris's Avenue Henri-Martin that had once belonged to King Hassan of Morocco. Réal (unbeknownst to both Fernand *and* de Hory) owned a $2-million art-investment corporation registered in Liechtenstein, a million-dollar art gallery in Paris, and half a million dollars in Canadian government bonds.

To complicate things further, Fernand owed Réal about half a million dollars in IOUs, which Fernand showed no interest in repaying. So Réal (unbeknownst to Fernand) finally went to the French authorities to swear out a writ of seizure on Fernand's apartment.

Three nights later, as the two were dining by candlelight in Fernand's apartment, the doorbell rang. After a few moments the butler appeared, followed by a sheriff in a black raincoat.

"Monsieur Fernand Legros?" the sheriff demanded.

Legros stood up, looking puzzled.

"Monsieur Fernand Legros," the sheriff intoned, "in the name of Monsieur Réal Lessard, I am seizing your apartment, and the contents thereof, in settlement of your indebtedness."

Réal, who hadn't expected French justice to be served quite so quickly, dove behind the couch. The sheriff, who had expected behaviour more commensurate with the class of real estate involved, was caught completely off guard. Fernand, bellowing threats of murder and castration, hurled the salmon, the dishes, the cutlery, and the candelabra into smithereens on the floor. The resulting fire destroyed several square yards of carpet, the dining-room wallpaper, and a Matisse oil that unfortunately was genuine. The sheriff doused the fire with a soda dispenser.

"Gee, I really didn't think he'd take it that hard," Réal told de Hory the next day on the phone.

De Hory, who thought Réal was talking about some modest apartment in Montparnasse, couldn't understand it either.

No sooner had de Hory settled on Ibiza than Fernand was knocking at his door, urgent with plans. He was just back from another selling spree in the United States, where he'd met a multimillionaire oilman–art collector named Algur Hurtle Meadows. Meadows had struck Fernand as a sitting duck. The oilman had endowed his alma mater, Southern Methodist University in Dallas, with an art museum and a sculpture court, and now seemed hell-bent on filling it up with paintings before the world ran out of them. He had already put down a base of dubious Goyas and El Grecos from the "Infanta collection of

Isabel de Borbon" (Fernand laughed meaningfully), and was now eager to add a layer of post-impressionists.

Fernand wanted de Hory to get cracking. This guy was ready, willing, and loaded.

De Hory sighed and set to work.

Over the next two years he produced, for the "Meadows order," fifteen Dufys, seven Modiglianis, five Vlamincks, eight Derains, three Matisses, two Bonnards, one Chagall, one Degas, one Marquet, one Laurencin, one Gauguin, and one Picasso.

More than half of them were oils.

The bill (unbeknownst to de Hory) exceeded $44 million.

Fernand gave de Hory his share in the form of a red Mustang convertible.

Meanwhile, Réal and Fernand were still fighting. Fernand had never forgiven Réal for his attempt to seize the Avenue Henri-Martin apartment, and had been looking for an opportunity to reciprocate. It came one day, several years later, when Réal mentioned he'd be travelling to Rouen on the following Wednesday. Fernand was waiting across the street when Réal left his apartment that Wednesday morning; ten minutes later he had broken in and put all the necessary evidence in place. Before he left, he phoned the police as any responsible citizen would. When Réal returned from Rouen that evening, he ran right into the hands of a waiting *gendarme*.

They didn't find his protests – that the package containing a set of fake customs stamps, addressed to himself in his own handwriting, was a frame-up – very convincing. In fact, they took such a dim view of the affair that Réal didn't manage to make bail for an entire month.

He spent that month plotting revenge.

As it turned out, Fernand did the job for him. He had

decided to take advantage of Réal's stint in prison to sneak in a quick sale of some de Hory oils at a government auction in Pontoise and pocket all of the proceeds himself. He had already sent a listing of what he thought he had available to the auction catalogue, but on the day before the sale he found he was one painting short.

Once again Fernand operated on the assumption that he differed from most people only in degree. Since *he* had been quietly squirrelling away de Hory paintings whenever the opportunity presented itself (to sell them without sharing the proceeds), he assumed Réal had been doing the same. He checked a number of Paris storage warehouses and *voila!* a locker in Réal's name. One unembarrassed thousand-franc note enabled him to discover that the locker did indeed contain de Hory fakes. Fernand helped himself to a Vlaminck that looked particularly well aged, and headed for Pontoise.

And there, in an irony of fate, it was the kindness of strangers that knocked over the first domino that led to Fernand Legros's eventual downfall. An auction employee, noticing that Legros's Vlaminck looked excessively dirty, and thinking that a little cleaning would raise its price, gave it a few quick flicks with a turps-soaked rag.

What came away on the rag wasn't just dirt – it was a whole smear of Vlaminck's supposedly sixty-year-old sky.

The employee immediately called the police, who called Fernand. Fernand rushed down to withdraw the painting, but another officer, a stickler for the rules, had already confiscated it, as well as Fernand's forged certificate of authentication. Fernand was informed there'd have to be an investigation.

Fernand didn't wait around for the result. He drove back to Paris, burned all his business records, crammed nine suitcases full of clothes and jewellery into his Corvette, and shipped the whole works to Ibiza. There, he broke into de Hory's house, unpacked his bags, and made himself at home.

That had always been de Hory's worst nightmare. But it was only the beginning.

Algur Hurtle Meadows, it turned out, had just had a not-dissimilar experience. Introduced to a group of art experts at a Picasso exhibition in Dallas, he had boasted about his marvellous post-impressionist collection. Then he'd invited them all to his museum for a little look-see. Within minutes of entering the first room, Klaus Perls (who in the meantime had become something of an expert on de Hory fakes) turned to Meadows and said, "Before I go any farther, I would like you to tell me if you are prepared to hear the entire truth as we see it."

"By all means, tell me exactly what you think," Meadows nodded.

Forty-three fakes later, Meadows was in a state of shock and his visitors grim-faced. A day after that, on October 14, 1967, Meadows swore out a criminal charge against Fernand Legros, art dealer. An international warrant was issued for his arrest.

The up side for de Hory was that this forced Fernand to flee to Egypt, which had no extradition treaties with anyone. The down side was that it signalled the inevitable end for de Hory, too. There was no way he could remain untouched by his front-men's rapidly growing legal troubles.

And sure enough, it wasn't long before he was advised that the Spanish court in Madrid had initiated an investigation of the Ibiza resident whom more and more newspapers were calling the creative genius behind what seemed to be shaping up to become the art world's scandal of the century.

Pontoise and Meadows, it turned out, were only the tip of the iceberg. Beneath the glitzy surface of the international art world's business-as-usual façade, a growing army of increasingly alarmed art dealers and museum curators had been corresponding and investigating, trying to identify and track the vast and still-spreading post-impressionist virus in their collections, of which they were only just becoming aware.

What had fooled them during the previous decade was the plethora of different names behind the fakes: de Hory, Baron von Herzog, Baron Dory-Boutin, Louis Raynal, Baron von Houry, Viscount Cassou, and Baron von Hoffmann. Until only a few years before, no one had even suspected them of being one and the same man. As recently as February 1967, Klaus Perls had believed that the forger de Hory had died in prison in New Orleans. Stephen Hahn, another New York art dealer, had agreed that "de Hory had some talent, but the outstanding forger of our time was Raynal. He was a magnificent forger, a true genius. I heard he died in France around 1960."

Since then, dealers such as Joseph Faulkner and Klaus Perls had put two and two together, and had sounded the alarm. The grapevine had begun to hum. Now everyone was taking a hard second look at their collections – and what they were finding was causing widespread alarm.

During his twenty years of aberration, Elmyr de Hory had produced literally thousands of faked paintings, watercolours, and drawings – enough to insinuate half-a-dozen into every single public art gallery or art museum of any significance in the Western world. The amount of money these forgeries had generated – indeed were still generating, since not a single painting other than those fingered in the Meadows Collection had yet been officially denounced – exceeded $2 billion. De Hory, Lessard, and Legros alone had probably pocketed well over $200 million.

Throughout the summer of 1968, de Hory flew back and forth between Ibiza and Madrid, attending court hearings, conferring with lawyers, and cajoling influential people into acting as character witnesses on his behalf. A petition in his support made the rounds on Ibiza, and was signed by a majority of its residents. A committee of "citizens for the defence of de Hory" was struck and held meetings. Nobody seemed to want this courtly, generous, and charming gentleman to go to jail.

The Spanish court, when it rendered its judgment in August 1968, was sympathetic, but couldn't see its way clear to ignoring its international responsibilities altogether. It sentenced de Hory to two months in prison on Ibiza, to be followed by one year of exile from the island.

The second part of the sentence proved to be the harsher for de Hory. While in jail on Ibiza, his "cell" was more reminiscent of a community drop-in centre. He was permitted to bring in his deck chair, his stereo, his books, and even his art supplies. He ordered in lunch and dinner from nearby restaurants and hosted a party almost every night – parties that were attended by his guards as well as his friends. Since the prison had no refrigerator, he kept his drinks and ice next door in the town hall, in the mayor's personal ice-box. He hired a maid to clean his cell once a day.

When it came time for his exile, de Hory chose Portugal.

He was, by this time, an international celebrity. The French newspaper *L'Aurore* had already written a long, amused exposé of his misdeeds. *Look* magazine ran a feature article on him in December 1968. Clifford Irving (who would become similarly notorious for his faked autobiography of Howard Hughes) wrote a biography of him in 1969 entitled *Fake!* Eventually, Orson Welles made him the subject of a full-length documentary film.

The whole world, it seemed, was having a wonderful time talking about his antics and his genius, and the way he and his cohorts had fooled literally hundreds of the world's most notable art experts.

Unfortunately, neither the courts nor the banks saw it quite that way. In February 1968, Réal Lessard was picked up in Geneva for, of all things, passing bad cheques, suggesting that his house of cards had already collapsed. This brought Legros out of hiding in Egypt; two months later he was picked up in the same city, travelling under a false passport, intending somehow to spring Réal. Both men eventually jumped bail and fled to Brazil, which had, Legros believed, no extradition treaty with France.

He was wrong.

But it wasn't until 1976 that Brazil finally responded to France's extradition request and delivered Legros into the hands of the Sûreté de Police. He was sentenced to two years in French prison, which he served from 1977 to 1979.

(The French apparently didn't file an extradition request for Réal Lessard. The Québécois art dealer quickly disappeared from the international art scene, and was not heard from again.)

Also faced with an extradition request – from *both* France and the United States – Elmyr de Hory found the prospect of a genuine prison sentence too overwhelming. He committed suicide by taking an overdose of sleeping pills in December 1976.

Though his career as an artist in his own right had been a complete failure, de Hory's success as a forger was so remarkable that posterity eventually celebrated him as if the two had been one and the same. Even his victims appeared to have no objection. A Boston art collector who'd bought several de Hory Renoirs just shrugged. "I've had ten years of pleasure from my Renoirs – or Renoir-by-Elmyrs, if you like – and I'll have twenty more years if I'm lucky. Then I'll leave them to my two sons and tell them, 'These are things of beauty. Enjoy them for what they are, not for the signature they bear or what someone else tells you they are or aren't.'"

And a client of Joseph Faulkner, who had bought a de Hory Modigliani, was surprised when Faulkner offered him a refund on the purchase. "Are you serious?" he demanded. "Never! I wouldn't give it up for anything. All I want you to do is come up here to Minneapolis and write on the back of the drawing: 'I, Joseph Faulkner, certify that this is an original and genuine Modigliani fake by Elmyr de Hory'!"

Postscript: Item in a 1991 issue of the *Globe and Mail*: "Recently, paintings by Elmyr de Hory, one of the most successful forgers of our time, were sold at Bonhams, the auctioneers in London. De Hory's versions of famous paintings were so good that people started collecting them in their own right. Now, even the authenticity of some of his fakes is being questioned. According to former bookie Ken Talbot, who befriended de Hory in the last years of his life, some of the paintings at the auction were fake de Horys."

Calling All Drakes – Your Inheritance Is Waiting!

———◦—◦—◦———

Oscar Hartzell and the Drake Legacy Swindle

It was a summer evening in Des Moines, Iowa, and Oscar Hartzell was sitting with a group of people in a friend's living room, listening to a sucker-pitch.

The promoter was a fast-talking lady named Sudie B. Whiteaker, and her story sounded so far-fetched that Oscar was already feeling sorry for her. She claimed that there were millions of dollars* – *tens of millions* – just waiting to be pocketed by anyone savvy enough to invest in her still-secret campaign to probate the will of the famous British buccaneer Sir Francis Drake.

When Drake died in 1596, Whiteaker explained, he had left his considerable fortune to his only son – something the British

---

* For consistency, all dollar amounts have been adjusted to 1999 values.

government couldn't tolerate, because this son was not only illegitimate, but rumoured to be the issue of a scandalous affair between Drake and Queen Elizabeth I. The estate had been confiscated and the son imprisoned, forced to sign a promise never to claim his patrimony or his inheritance.

But now in 1913, 317 years later, a direct descendant of that son had been discovered, and he was prepared to challenge the British government in England's ecclesiastical court. His only problem was that he didn't have the money to hire the army of lawyers it would take to win the case.

To Hartzell's astonishment, Sudie Whiteaker wasn't laughed out of the room. In fact, a surprising number of listeners wanted to know more – much more. At least half a dozen eventually took out a "subscription." Others wrote down her address.

Hartzell found himself in a decided minority.

It was enough to make a man think.

Six months later, Sudie Whiteaker was arrested by United States Postal inspectors and charged with using the U.S. Postal Service to commit fraud. Many of her suckers had subscribed to her campaign by mail. The U.S. Postal inspectors in 1913 had powers of search and seizure that were positively breathtaking by modern standards. Their conviction record stood at an impressive 98 per cent.

It was enough to make a man think even harder.

Oscar Hartzell spent the following two years researching, pondering, and planning. By 1916 he had his story all worked out. By 1917 he'd managed to convince three confederates to join him as his agents. In 1918 he founded the Sir Francis Drake Association, whose stated purpose was "to wrest from the British Crown the illegally suppressed estate of Sir Francis Drake, Admiral."

Hartzell's agents now set to work hustling potential "donators" (as they were called) to raise the millions that would be needed to finance this extraordinary venture.

Hartzell's research had shown that there was just enough historical truth to Whiteaker's story to pass a cursory examination. Drake had indeed died officially childless, and his estate did seem to have become entangled for some reason at the ecclesiastical court. No Elizabethan historian would have dared to publish rumours of a liaison between Drake and the Queen, but the Spanish ambassador to the English Court, one Gonzalo De Mendosa, had apparently spiced his dispatches to Philip II with such suggestions. In fact, it seemed that Drake hadn't exactly cornered the market on royal hanky-panky; the Queen had apparently had a predilection for all sorts of buccaneers.

But it was Hartzell's organizational strategy that showed just how much he had benefited from Sudie Whiteaker's downfall.

First, he categorically banned the use of the mails for any part of his operation. All communications had to be sent by wire or private courier. All money had to be transferred via banks or Western Union.

Second, he conducted all his business behind a protective screen of agents. For years, no donator ever met Hartzell face to face.

Third – and this may have been his greatest inspiration – he limited his campaign to persons either named Drake, married to a Drake, or those who could prove they had Drake blood flowing in their veins. (The latter had to sign a document swearing to the truth of this claim.)

Finally, all donators had to sign a "silence, secrecy, and non-disturbance" pledge, promising to keep their involvement and the association's business strictly confidential, on pain of being "red-inked" off the association's register and forfeiting their investment.

Hartzell's pitch was not unlike Whiteaker's – he also claimed to have discovered Drake's sole heir, who had deputized him as his exclusive agent and representative – but Hartzell's numbers made Whiteaker's numbers look like spare change. He had actually done the math, and discovered that even a legacy of a mere £100 in 1596 would have ballooned, over three centuries, into an almost inconceivable *$250 billion* – enough to pay every donator at least $500 for every dollar invested.

In short, a return of at least 50,000 per cent.

Such profit fantasies proved so motivating that his investors couldn't give Hartzell their money fast enough. "Donations" arrived by the satchelful, the sackful, even in canning jars and lard pails. People rifled their life savings, their inheritances, the equity in their homes. One Farnhamville pastor sent in half of his church members' offerings every Monday morning, month after month, as regular as clockwork. In Webster City, twenty-six people pooled their pennies and invested them in the name of their recently deceased mayor, Leonard Drakester.

Far from limiting demand, Hartzell's restriction concerning the surname Drake merely increased his association's appearance of legitimacy and legality, whetting people's appetite even more. More than half of Hartzell's donators had surnames other than Drake, and many submitted long explanations, arguments, and pleas to justify their applications.

Hartzell, of course, couldn't have cared less about the explanations. He happily banked the cash.

In its first year alone, the Sir Francis Drake Association pulled in $3.7 million.

By 1920, Hartzell had fifteen agents operating full-time in nine Midwestern states. They, in turn, established dozens of local SFDA chapters, which hosted rousing promotional meetings – crosses between Bible-study sessions and pep rallies. Each meeting began with members saluting the flag and singing the national anthem. The study material consisted mostly of homespun history lessons about Sir Francis Drake, plus Hartzell's regular updates about the association's progress, cabled directly from Chicago.

These cables were always upbeat and encouraging. The association's lawyers had finally found a copy of Drake's original will! The ecclesiastical court had scheduled its first hearings on the Drake claim! The association had produced consternation among Britain's politicians by securing the legal services of one of Britain's most prominent King's Counsels!

Of course, such legal services were shockingly expensive, and everyone was urged to increase their donations, or better yet, to find more Drakes to assist in this formidable task. This was obviously accomplished, because various accounts reported groups in several Midwest cities with as many as two thousand members, their investments totalling several hundred thousand dollars each.

By 1921, Hartzell was able to report that the association's work had progressed to the point at which he was obliged to move to England to direct operations on site. His lavish digs in Basil Street, described to his donators as a modest but serviceable office, came complete with butler and maids, two security guards, and an automobile and mechanic. Hartzell splurged on Savile Row suits, bowler hats, and black umbrellas, and became a fixture at all the most fashionable restaurants and theatres.

The farm boy from Iowa had definitely arrived.

Meanwhile, his news just got better and better. He had managed to unearth the birth certificate of Drake's illegitimate son! The British government, faced with this evidence, had made an admittedly puny offer to settle, which Hartzell had scornfully rejected – but the politicians were now clearly on the run! The ecclesiastical court had conducted its first hearings, and the association's lawyers had performed splendidly!

Best of all, Drake's will had finally been translated from its almost unintelligible Elizabethan legalese, and the result proved that Drake's estate was actually worth many times more than the amount originally expected – in excess of *four trillion dollars*!

The response from North America (by now, Hartzell's agents had also expanded into Canada) could only be described as heartwarming. By 1924, Hartzell's take was rarely less than $150,000 a month, even after agents' expenses. He entertained lavishly, consumed extravagantly, and found particularly enthusiastic support among the actresses in London's theatre district.

He also spent a fortune on regular advice and reassurance from a haughty but perceptive London clairvoyant named Miss St. John Montague – whose insights were helped considerably by regular reports from a sexy assistant she secretly employed to fraternize with her more free-spending male customers.

One might have thought – indeed predicted – that more than a few years of this all-talk-no-action would have worn out the patience of Hartzell's donators. Some, after all, had sunk their entire life savings into his enterprise. But Hartzell had made it a point, right from the start, to warn his donators about the fierce political and legal opposition their cause would encounter – *especially as its success drew closer.*

On the heels of his report about the $4-trillion re-evaluation, for example, he reminded them that this re-evaluation might also make their cause harder to win, because a payout of such magnitude would virtually bankrupt the Bank of England.

Similarly, the delays that went on year after year were merely proof that the British government was boxed in and incapable of any other defence – triumphant evidence that a settlement was just around the corner.

As he composed his cables, reporting court squabbles won and lost, bureaucratic manoeuvrings proceeding crabwise through Britain's political undergrowth, and back-room dealings with the world's most powerful financial heavyweights, Hartzell became increasingly adept at making profitable use of everyday political events. A routine decline in the value of the pound against the dollar became proof positive that word of an imminent settlement of the Drake estate had leaked into the financial marketplace. Meetings between American and British politicians, as reported in the papers, were only *purportedly* about the aftermath of World War One; in reality, they were urgent discussions about the Drake inheritance. He sent quotes and clippings from financial and political magazines that had nothing whatsoever to do with the Drake inheritance – they didn't even mention the subject – but his agents read them to the faithful as further proof of ongoing progress and imminent success, and they were enthusiastically accepted as such.

And so, far from feeling that nothing was happening, Hartzell's donators woke up every morning to a crescendo of evidence that their cause was thundering inexorably ahead.

To up the ante even further, Hartzell periodically announced an actual date for the settlement: May 29, 1927, was set by the ecclesiastical court for a final showdown between the British government and its judiciary, with a payout to all donators no less than six months after that! (The SFDA promptly laid on workshops on how to manage sudden financial windfalls.) On May 30, Hartzell cabled Chicago that the principals were in intense negotiations, meetings going on around the clock, steady progress being made! A week later negotiations had become deadlocked; two weeks later there was a breakthrough, followed by the discovery that the accountants had made a $15-million error that couldn't be ignored. A month's recess.

No sooner had the negotiators returned than the Lord Chancellor fell ill, necessitating a substitute negotiator. He, naturally, had to familiarize himself with the entire gigantic portfolio. Another long delay. Then there was Christmas, Easter, the election of a new government – there was always something.

On October 24, 1929, three weeks after yet another definite settlement deadline, Hartzell's donators were given their most dramatic proof yet of the staggering effect their campaign could have on the West's financial markets. The 1929 stock-market crash, according to Hartzell, was actually the result of some very rough-and-tumble negotiations he'd been having with a consortium of Western bankers – a sign he'd finally got the inevitability of the Drake inheritance settlement through their thick skulls. Hartzell cabled his apologies; perhaps he'd pushed a little too hard. But he'd become impatient on behalf of his donators; it was an error (if it was an error) born of too much loyalty and dedication.

By now Hartzell's racket had been in operation for more than a decade, and though all his donators had pledged total secrecy, rumours of the deal had, inevitably, filtered through to the U.S. Postal Service. Its agents promptly investigated, but quickly found this operation an unusually hard nut to crack. Even after they'd pieced together Hartzell's basic *modus operandi*, they couldn't find anyone willing to lodge a formal complaint. Besides, Hartzell had been very careful not to use the mails for any of his business operations.

But in February 1931, after four years of fruitless effort, the Postal Service finally managed to find a tiny crack in Hartzell's armour. A few careless agents, impatient with Hartzell's postal embargo, had permitted some of their more far-flung donators to send in their payments by conventional mail after all.

These five agents were now served with subpoenas and threatened with a full-blown lawsuit if they didn't agree to immediately stop selling SFDA investments. Furthermore, the solicitor general of the Post Office called a press conference to denounce Hartzell's operation as an outrageous fraud, and many Midwestern newspapers picked up the story. Iowa attorney general John Fletcher also chimed in, calling the venture a worthless racket and Oscar Hartzell an unconscionable racketeer. The newspapers reported that, too.

If Hartzell had spent a fortune on the most effective advertising campaign in the country, he couldn't have done himself half as much good as these Postal Service attacks. Mindful of Hartzell's warning that public opposition would increase sharply as the settlement drew nearer, his donators were heartened and delighted by the attorney general's accusations. Their pep rallies grew more boisterous; thousands contributed additional donations. More than fifty thousand heeded Hartzell's request and sent vehement protests to the Post Office, the United States Congress, and even president Herbert Hoover. It was outrageous, they fumed, how American politicians and bureaucrats were brazenly protecting a foreign country (England) at the expense of their own citizens!

When his lobbying initiative actually seemed to be forcing the Postal Service to rein in its investigators a little, Hartzell decided to switch from defence to offence. Early in 1932, all SFDA chapters were informed of the exciting news that, given the vastly increased value of the Drake estate, Hartzell had succeeded in convincing the lone Drake heir to drop his surname restriction. From now on, absolutely anyone prepared to abide by the rules and regulations of the Sir Francis Drake Association, and to sign its "silence, secrecy, and non-disturbance" clause, was eligible to invest in this enormously profitable enterprise.

This was terrific news, enabling the SFDA's agents to cheerlead yet another massive wave of gullible donators into the fold.

By the summer of 1932, more than seventy thousand donators stood invested in the Sir Francis Drake Association, and more than a dozen new agents had been hired to replace the five that had been lost. Hartzell was now swaggering around England sporting an aristocratic title (the Duke of Buckland), which he'd either bought or appropriated. He was even talking Britons into investing in his scheme. One might judge his success by the fact that, when confronted by the pistol-wielding father of a young woman he'd seduced and impregnated, Hartzell managed to assuage the man's rage by relenting and permitting him to invest $30,000 in the Drake campaign. Only then did the outraged father put up his gun.

On November 14, 1932, however, Hartzell received a bit of a shock. A delegation of Scotland Yard detectives arrived at his London apartment for an "interview."

The detectives were civil, but only barely. They demanded information on the SFDA, Hartzell's political and legal contacts in Britain, a list of his "donators," and much more. When Hartzell refused to co-operate – in fact, threatened the detectives with all sorts of reprisals as soon as the Drake estate had been settled and he, Hartzell, had become a British citizen (the detectives' eyebrows rose) – his visitors seemed oddly satisfied.

Hartzell discovered why on January 7, 1933, when a U.S.

vice-consul, flanked by two policemen, banged on his door and informed him that he had two hours to pack for the trip back to the United States. The American State Department had applied to the British Home Office to have Hartzell deported back to Iowa to face charges of fraud, theft, and misrepresentation, and though Scotland Yard hadn't been able to determine whether Hartzell had broken any British laws with his scam, his behaviour during their interview had given them sufficient reason to have him declared an undesirable alien.

The postal inspectors who arrested Hartzell when his ship docked in New York two weeks later were convincing evidence that, occasional appearances notwithstanding, the U.S. Postal Service wasn't really in the habit of taking high-level lobbying by ingenious criminals sitting down. Hartzell was transported directly to Sioux City, Iowa, arraigned, and deposited behind the bars of the Sioux City Public Detention Building. The two SFDA agents who showed up to pay Hartzell's bail were told to come back the next week, when the judge assigned to the case *might* be ready to consider a bail hearing. Maybe.

If Hartzell thought he was safe from the law because he'd been rigorously careful never to use the mails, he had another thought coming. The postal boys simply handed Hartzell's case over to the FBI. The Bureau now sent one of its top detectives back to England to determine the facts about the Drake estate, bring back a copy of the will, and thus shed some objective light on the whole affair.

But Hartzell wasn't ready to throw in the towel just yet. When he finally made bail – after three weeks – he called in all his SFDA chapters for a huge, six-thousand-donator meeting in Sioux City's largest baseball park. There he harangued and charmed his suckers up one side and down the other. They were all the victims of government persecution; both Hoover and Roosevelt were in bed with the Brits; this outrageous deportation and court case was merely a last desperate attempt to keep them all from becoming hugely, enormously, unbelievably rich!

And did they know why? Because, unbeknownst to the public, but very well known to Western politicians and their moneybag friends, *the settlement had already been signed*! Yes, the deal was done, the papers had been initialled several months earlier, in strictest secrecy, in the Historical Document Room of Somerset House in London, where Drake's will was kept! The payouts were scheduled to begin in July 1933, only six months away, *and now their own politicians, in cahoots with their banker buddies, were making a last desperate effort to foil Hartzell's success*!

But it wasn't going to work. No sir, it wasn't; these crooks had been beaten before, and they would be beaten again. He, Oscar Merril Hartzell, hadn't sacrificed fifteen years of his life fighting for the world's Drakes only to give up now, when success and a life of leisure finally lay within the grasp of every single person sitting in this ballpark! Were they going to let a bunch of political crooks and their cronies tear this long-awaited and richly deserved payment right out of their hands?

The donators, for whom this was their first sight of the elegantly dressed and coiffed Hartzell, evidently liked what they saw and heard. No, they most certainly weren't going to let a bunch of corrupt politicians cheat them out of their rightful reward! In an impromptu gesture, they filled dozens of hats, which Hartzell's agents helpfully passed through their ranks, with $53,000 in cash, to help defray Hartzell's legal and living expenses while he prepared for his – for their – final triumphant trial. And before he adjourned the meeting, Hartzell reminded them all not to say a word to any detective who might be curious about the association's business or their donations. Pass it around to all the other donators too: mum's the word!

So mum was the word – a shoulder-to-shoulder stand against the forces of jealousy and evil – and it caused the FBI a lot more grief than they'd bargained for. Its agents had no difficulty discovering the real contents of Drake's will: a simple conveyance of all his worldly goods to his wife and his brother. They also found records in the ecclesiastical court, documenting a subsequent dispute between the wife and the brother over the disposition of some of the property – a dispute that had been duly settled. So the will had been quite properly probated and the property legally dispersed, not confiscated as Hartzell had claimed. There was also no reference anywhere to an illegitimate son, imprisoned or not, and the claim that he'd been forced to sign a promise not to pursue his patrimony appeared to have been a total invention. Besides, even if such a son had existed, a statute of limitations, first established by the British parliament during the reign of James I (1603–1625), limited the possibility of reopening matters of probate to a period of thirty years.

So that claim too was baseless.

But to convict an accused of fraud you need at least one victim and a witness, and despite eighteen months of probing, cajoling, and even bullying as many of Hartzell's seventy thousand donators as they could find, the FBI had no luck in producing either.

At the trial, the FBI's efforts to oblige self-confessed donators to admit that they had received nothing for their investments promptly backfired when these witnesses simply retook the stand for the defence and served as enthusiastic character witnesses for Hartzell. He was an honest man, they said, the salt of the earth, an utterly straight arrow. This trial was blatant proof of

the very conspiracy between the British and American governments that Hartzell had told them about. Every day, his supporters filled the public gallery to the rafters, loudly applauding
the defence and jeering the prosecution. The judge was forced
to clear the courtroom on more than a dozen occasions.

Hartzell's lawyers didn't even put him on the witness stand.
It clearly wasn't necessary. Day after day he sat in the prisoner's
box, his hair slicked back, a fresh carnation in the buttonhole of
his Savile Row suit, a slightly bored, exasperated expression on
his face. Despite their best efforts, the FBI couldn't lay a glove
on him.

In desperation, the prosecution called for a recess and sent
their investigators back to London. If they couldn't find or force
any SFDA donators to accuse Hartzell, their only other option
was to prove to a jury's satisfaction that Hartzell had accepted
their money *intending* to defraud them. It was a long shot, a blind
stab, and Hartzell laughed aloud when he heard about it. In
effect, the FBI was admitting it had been licked.

It probably had been – or would have been, had one of its
investigators not stumbled across a reference to a certain Miss
St. John Montague. She obligingly introduced him to her sexy
assistant. She supposed they'd have plenty to talk about, being in
the same business after all, tracking poseurs like that *dreary* little
American – what had he called himself, the Duke of Buckland?
Simply too preposterous for words. Could she interest them in a
spot of tea?

Several spots of tea later, the pot was empty and Hartzell's
goose was sizzling. Hartzell might have been extraordinarily
careful about his use of the mails, but his pillow talk had been
extraordinarily careless. He had been similarly careless with his
butler, laughing uproariously at the witless suckers back home
who were so enthusiastically financing his life on Easy Street.

That would be Basil Street, Your Lordship, the butler had always corrected punctiliously.

Their affidavits, presented at the continuation of Hartzell's trial six months later, didn't even make a dent in his supporters' faith – but they made an obvious impression on the jury. So did the fact that FBI investigators hadn't been able to find any evidence that Hartzell had ever spent so much as a nickel on the legal pursuit of the Drake estate. So did the story of the English girl Hartzell had seduced and then abandoned after their illegitimate son was born. (This was obviously news to Hartzell's American wife, who promptly sued for divorce.)

As for the money – an estimated $77 million – Hartzell seemed to have spent it like water. The Bureau's forensic accountants found less than $35,000 in Hartzell's bank accounts.

After deliberating for less than a day, the jury returned a verdict of guilty on all charges. The judge, in the same spirit, sentenced Hartzell to ten years in Leavenworth Penitentiary. It took police more than an hour to clear Hartzell's surprised and infuriated supporters from the courthouse.

His lawyers appealed, and Hartzell was released on bail within a day, but the FBI was no longer overly concerned. The trial had received widespread press and radio coverage, and Hartzell's fraud and methods were now well known all over North America. The public, in effect, had been inoculated against his blandishments. Besides, they had little doubt that the higher courts would sustain his conviction. They expected to see Hartzell behind bars very soon.

The higher courts denied Hartzell's various appeals, though it took a further two years and most of the SFDA's remaining funds to exhaust them all. Hartzell was finally hauled off to Leavenworth in 1935.

And that seemed to put paid to one of the most widespread and successful frauds ever committed in the history of American skulduggery. The newspaper stories ended, the radio commentaries stopped, and the U.S. postal inspectors found no further evidence of illegal use of the mails by the SFDA.

Then, about a year later, a Chicago man telephoned the Chicago police. He explained that his uncle had written him from Wisconsin, asking him to please check with the Sir Francis Drake Association in Chicago to ensure that the $3,500 he had sent by bank transfer had been received and properly credited to his account. This had reminded the Chicago man of Hartzell's conviction. Hadn't this guy been sent down to Leavenworth?

Then what was he doing still running a business that had been pronounced illegal?

The Chicago police sent a detective to the SFDA offices to pose as the Wisconsin donator's nephew. He found the place a beehive of activity, with dozens of people hard at work. He had no trouble at all confirming his "uncle's" bank transfer. In fact, the SFDA agent informed him that the Drake inheritance would be settled any day now, and urged the "nephew" to make an investment himself.

The incarceration of Hartzell had all been "in the plan," he explained. If the newspapers had reported the truth – that the Drake inheritance was legitimate – all the donators would have been hounded to death by agents and grafters, and some of the biggest donators might well have been kidnapped. Now that the public was off their backs, they could get their money in peace and quiet. And Hartzell, by the way, wasn't in Leavenworth, no matter what the papers said. Right after the trial the SFDA had negotiated his release, and he was now back at his desk and busier than ever, working to make his donators rich.

When the Chicago police raided the SFDA offices at 4:00 p.m. the following afternoon, they found and arrested thirty-five agents and five managers, who were in Chicago to attend a tactical meeting. They also confiscated a huge pile of cash, cheques, and negotiable securities. During the interrogations that followed, they discovered that Hartzell's new managers had introduced an even more sophisticated element into the scam: they were now using actors at promotional meetings to pose as government officials specifically seconded by Congress to supervise the imminent settlement of the Drake estate. (For variety, these "officials" were sometimes introduced as Scotland Yard or Secret Service agents, attending at the request of the SFDA to confirm the legitimacy of the Drake inheritance.)

With these and similar new methods, Hartzell's crew had managed, in the eight months following Hartzell's incarceration, to raise an astounding $12 million.

The resulting trial was essentially a rerun of the first, with donators refusing to register complaints and subpoenaed witnesses standing their ground. "I say, with all due respect to the courts, that I haven't changed my mind," said one donator under oath. "From all I've heard, the deal is still as strong as the Rock of Gibraltar."

Once again the prosecution had to fall back on its British affidavits, but this time the jury proved harder to convince. On January 30, 1936, only Hartzell (whom they deemed to have remained involved from inside Leavenworth), his brother (who had recently joined up), and five other managers were convicted. The thirty-five agents won dismissals.

The convicted all received a year and a day in Leavenworth. Hartzell's sentence was added to his original conviction.

This second trial, and the incarceration of the entire SFDA management team, finally did break the back of Hartzell's Drake inheritance swindle.

It did not, however, seem to convince many of the donators. During the following decade, incident after incident showed that many were still adamantly keeping the faith. A rumour that a Kansas City radio station had announced the Drake estate settlement on its evening news resulted in such a deluge of calls to the station that its announcers had to read a denial on every newscast for the next two days. A rumour that a ship loaded with the first instalment of the Drake inheritance gold had arrived in the dockyard at Galveston, Texas, proved so persistent that a well-meaning U.S. postal inspector in Houston actually took a group of Hartzell donators down to the docks to show them that the ship in question was loaded with nothing more exotic than oil pipes.

The donators merely shrugged. This proved nothing; the gold had probably been unloaded the day before, and might even be distributed within the next several days. And then the crooks who had jailed Oscar Hartzell would be forced to admit their conspiracy, Hartzell would be released, and everyone associated with him would be totally vindicated.

Everyone left the dockyard in good spirits – except for the postal inspector.

Oscar Hartzell, who had shown increasing signs of delusions of grandeur during his second trial, was sent to Leavenworth's psychiatric centre for further examination and was eventually declared mentally incompetent. He spent the following seven years at the Medical Center for Federal Prisoners in Springfield, Missouri, where he died on August 27, 1943.

Mau-Mauing the Military

Two Subversives in Uniform

1. Wilhelm Voigt, the Notorious Captain of Koepenick

At fifty-seven years of age, tired, haggard, and depressed, Wilhelm Voigt had almost reached the end of his rope.

Though he'd apprenticed as a cobbler in his native Prussia in the 1860s, the machines and factories of the Industrial Revolution had systematically squeezed him out of job after job, until he'd taken to stealing to make ends meet. But he hadn't been much of a thief either, and soon his prison record had made job-finding almost impossible. He had already spent twenty-seven years behind bars, and prospects were that he would die there. Even his present job – working in a Potsdam shoe factory under an assumed name – was likely to put him back there sooner than later. In Prussia it was a criminal offence to assume a false identity.

As he shuffled home after a long day's work, he was forced once again into the gutter by a passing column of goose-stepping soldiers. The Potsdam area, on Berlin's western outskirts, was one of Kaiser Wilhelm's main military centres, and it seethed with uniforms. All day long, over the whine of his shoe-sewing machine, he could hear the bursts of military bugles, the sharp bark of sergeants' commands, and the clatter of horse hooves on cobblestone. It was said that one out of three men on the streets of Potsdam was a soldier.

There wasn't much doubt about it: if you wanted respect and status, the military was the place to be. All the world bowed and deferred to a splendid uniform. Even ordinary civilians were legally required to show an officer respect in the Prussia of the early 1900s. Voigt had never served in the military, and recently he'd begun to consider this a big mistake. With a military commission, he'd have been in clover now, instead of in the gutter.

Voigt's most recent plan to rehabilitate himself had been the theft of a passport, to enable him to emigrate to greener pastures (felons weren't permitted passports in early 1900s Prussia). All police offices had blank passports, and, while under arrest for stealing a bag of apples, he had tried – unsuccessfully – to filch one from an officer's desk. That had merely lengthened his prison sentence, but hadn't put the idea entirely out of his head. Not every country was likely to be as unforgiving as King Wilhelm's Prussia.

As he passed a used-clothing shop near his tiny apartment, he stopped to admire a Captain of the Guard's uniform hanging in the window. Now there was an outfit that would have *everyone* stepping into the gutter! Even a policeman would snap to attention if you had one of those on your back.

The uniform was still hanging there the next day.

And the day after that.

It was still there when Voigt returned home with his month's wages in his pocket two weeks later.

On impulse, he went inside.

The clerk explained that the uniform was complete – jacket, trousers, cap, and even a sabre – but that it was in too poor a condition for further military use. Did the gentleman wish it for a costume? It looked a bit large for his size, but perhaps with a tuck here, a stitch or two there . . .

Now that he had it in his hands, Voigt could see that the clerk was right. It really was quite frayed and worn. It was also – when he tried it on – about two sizes too large. But perhaps with a tuck here, a stitch or two there . . .

It cost him half his month's wages. The clerk stuffed it into a cardboard box.

For the next few weeks, Voigt didn't have the nerve to make specific plans for his purchase. Any thoughts in that direction tended to engender panic. But he did find himself spending more and more time around the Kaiser's Berlin palace, watching the changing of the guard. He tried to decipher the officers' commands. He noted the different salutes and the body language. He also busied himself with needle and thread, taking in a tuck here, a stitch or two there . . .

A local brewery exhibition provided Voigt with his first dress rehearsal. He took half an hour trying to get the uniform to sit more convincingly on his scarecrow frame. He daubed his brown work boots with three separate applications of black shoe polish. He couldn't remember whether the Prussian insignia on the cap belonged above or below the Imperial German one, or exactly where to position the cap's cockades, but he did the best he could.

Then he stepped out into the street.

Almost immediately, it was as though he had entered a different world.

Suddenly everyone was bewilderingly, almost absurdly, helpful. People greeted him respectfully. Shopkeepers welcomed him with open arms. A flower-seller gave him a carnation. A policeman saluted.

The commissionaire guarding the exhibition door bowed low and threw open the door with a flourish.

It continued that way all evening. Booth salesmen were pleased to offer him samples. Company executives greeted him with deference. Women offered him their hands to kiss.

And everywhere, soldiers clicked their heels, saluted smartly, and stood rigidly at attention until he had passed.

Voigt waved at them all with an increasingly practised non-chalance. "At ease," he kept saying, not altogether sure what came after that. "At ease. At ease."

He returned home that night exhilarated and frightened.

For the next several weeks Voigt was unusually absent-minded and flustered. His landlord commented on it. Several of his co-workers grumbled about it. His boss deducted the cost of several pairs of ruined shoes from his wages.

Finally, one Saturday just before noon, Voigt put on his uniform again and went straight to the train station on Schlesenstrasse. Once again everyone raised their hats, nodded, and saluted. Once again, the whole world seemed eager to be of service. At the ticket window the agent stiffened and bowed.

"On military business, sir?" Confused, Voigt may have nodded. He asked for a ticket to Koepenick, a small town about twenty minutes east of Berlin. "Yes, sir. Immediately, sir." He was handed an expense chit. "If you would be so good as to sign this, sir." Voigt hesitated, alarmed, but made a few illegible scribbles. This produced, to his amazement, a free train ticket.

At the station restaurant, the same procedure produced a free lunch.

Captain Voigt grinned. This military life could become a habit.

At Koepenick station he signed a chit for a carriage ride to the centre of the town. In its Town Hall he made a quick reconnaissance of its corridors, noting the locations of the Mayor's office, the Treasurer's office, the office of the Chief of Police. For another chit, at a nearby *Gasthof*, he ate the best supper he'd ever eaten in his life. He pondered briefly whether to push his luck with a visit to a local vaudeville show, but finally decided against it. He took the next train home, and by 7:00 that evening was once again just plain old Wilhelm Voigt, factory wage-slave.

But not for long.

The next morning Voigt didn't go to work. Instead, he pulled on his magic uniform and headed in the opposite direction, to Ploetzensee, in Berlin's northwest suburbs. Ploetzensee was the site of one of Germany's most notorious hard-labour prisons – Voigt had done some time there several years earlier – but it was also the site of a large military swimming pool. As a prisoner, Voigt had watched a steady stream of soldiers from a nearby barracks enter and leave the pool in small units all day long.

At Ploetzensee, Voigt got out of the carriage, signed the chit, and took a deep breath. His hands were trembling. He was suffering from a severe case of the second thoughts. Perhaps escaping Prussia could be accomplished in a less risky way. Maybe the Hungarians or the Poles or the Russians weren't quite so harsh about their immigration rules. But then, three soldiers came marching around the corner, caught sight of Voigt, came to a screeching halt, slammed to attention, and stood there, straight as poles, awaiting his orders. They didn't even look at Voigt. They just looked straight ahead, unthinking. Voigt began to feel a little better.

"At ease!" he heard himself barking. "At ease." And then, "Carry on!"

The three soldiers obediently carried on.

By the time the next contingent of soldiers hove into view – five fusiliers and their corporal – Voigt was better prepared. "Halt!" he bellowed.

The soldiers stopped instantly and saluted. So did their corporal, though he registered enough surprise to momentarily rattle Voigt.

"Ah . . . where are you from?" Voigt demanded.

The corporal reported that they had just completed their swim and were returning to barracks.

"And where are you headed?"

The corporal blinked, then repeated that, having just completed their swim, they would be returning to barracks as soon as the Captain permitted.

"Fall in," Voigt ordered, recovering with an effort. "Fall in. Special orders." He began to walk briskly in the direction of the Putlitzstrasse railway station. Behind him, he could hear the instant clatter of soldiers' boots following obediently. Up ahead, four grenadiers stumbled out of an inn, slapping their thighs and laughing. At the sight of Voigt they transformed instantly into lantern stanchions. "Fall in!" Voigt bellowed again, pointing over his shoulder. "Fall in! Special orders. Forward, march!"

By the time they reached Putlitzstrasse station, Captain Voigt's little army had grown to fourteen. No one had hesitated to follow his orders, asked for an explanation, or even wanted to know their destination. The ticket agent proffered an expense chit without asking any questions. Voigt signed and took receipt of fifteen tickets for Koepenick. Then he signed another chit for a generous order of beer and sausages.

The mood of his army instantly improved from dutiful to visibly pleased.

At Koepenick station an hour later he arranged his soldiers into a column and marched them directly to the Town Hall. Though he tried to avoid making a spectacle – no loud orders, fixed bayonets, and so on – a column of soldiers marching through Koepenick was sufficiently unusual to attract a lot of gawkers. Voigt ignored them, ordered two men each to guard the Town Hall's three doors – no one was to enter or leave without his express permission – and marched the rest into the building and down the corridor to the Mayor's office.

The Mayor looked up from his desk, puzzled.

"You are Mayor Hugo Langerhans?" Voigt demanded, reading the name off the ornate wooden plaque on the Mayor's desk.

"I am," the Mayor affirmed. "To whom do I owe the honour?"

"You are under arrest," Voigt said brusquely.

"I beg your pardon?"

"Administrative irregularities," Voigt explained. "Nasty business, very regrettable, but my orders come from the highest authority. Please ready yourself for transport to military headquarters in Berlin."

The Mayor blanched and clutched at his desk. "I beg your pardon?" he stuttered again, and then stood up shakily. "What in the name of heaven are you talking about?"

"Please be ready in five minutes," Voigt said curtly. "I have other business to attend to."

One floor down, in the Treasurer's Office, he found everyone standing at the window, looking curiously at the increasing crowd gathering in the town square. "Who's the Treasurer here?" Voigt demanded.

A man with carefully slicked-back hair turned from the window. At the sight of Voigt and his soldiers he froze.

"Is it you?"

The man hesitated, then nodded.

"You are also under arrest. I will require all accounts fully balanced and the books ready to be transported, along with yourself, to Berlin. Please be ready in ten minutes."

The Treasurer looked alarmed. "We *never* balance the books before five o'clock," he said primly.

"You will today. You have nine minutes."

"But Herr Kapitän," the man protested, "I can under no circumstances do so without the authority of the Mayor."

"The Mayor is also under arrest. I am the authority in Koepenick now. You have eight minutes."

. In the basement, Voigt found the Chief of Police snoring contentedly in his big office armchair.

"So this is what we pay you for!" Voigt barked sharply, enjoying the way the police chief shot up out of his chair at the sight of a Captain of the Guard and eight fusiliers. "An enemy could have taken the entire town and you wouldn't have known until you'd read about it in the newspapers!"

The Police Chief stuttered incoherent apologies.

"Well, never mind; we'll overlook it this time. Now button up your uniform and get over to the town square. I want no public disturbance while I carry out my orders here."

The Police Chief rammed on his uniform cap and hastened out the door, desperate to repair first impressions.

Back on the third floor, Voigt found the Mayor rummaging frantically through his desk, totally at a loss as to what to take to Berlin. "Couldn't you *please* tell me what I'm being arrested for, Herr Kapitän?" he pleaded. "I have no idea what documents or records might be needed."

"Terribly sorry," Voigt commiserated, feeling a little sorry for the bewildered man. "I'm not at liberty to do so. I'm acting under orders."

The Mayor had a thought. "Could I take my wife?" he asked.

At that moment Frau Langerhans burst into the office, more indignant than frightened. "Herr Kapitän, Herr Kapitän, I beg of you! What is this madness I hear about my Hugo being arrested?"

Voigt bowed smartly and clicked his heels together. "I deeply regret having to carry out these unpleasant orders, Frau Langerhans. I am sure it will turn out to be a lamentable mistake. But in the meantime I have no authority to reverse my orders."

"But my Hugo has never hurt a fly!"

Looking at the Mayor cowering behind his wife, Voigt suspected she was right. He bowed again.

"Orders unfortunately are orders, my lady. But if it will help, you may accompany your husband to Berlin."

Frau Langerhans softened visibly and expressed her thanks. Then she threw her arms around her husband and patted him consolingly on the head. "Come come, Hugo, don't fret. Whatever you've done, I'll always stand by you. Now hurry and get ready, and don't forget your hat and muffler. You'll catch your death!"

Out in the town square the hubbub had been growing louder, and now Voigt saw a police officer on horseback forcing his way into the main Town Hall plaza. It turned out to be the Police Chief of the neighbouring town of Teltow, who had been out for an afternoon ride and had heard the uproar in the square. He appeared at the head of the stairs, demanding to know what was going on.

"I am here on orders from Berlin to arrest the town's Mayor and Treasurer," Voigt explained. "Administrative irregularities. Nasty business, very regrettable. Perhaps just an unfortunate misunderstanding. But orders are orders, as you'll appreciate."

"They are indeed," the Police Chief agreed. "I certainly do. Would there be anything I can do to assist you in your mission?"

"There is," Voigt nodded. "Your incompetent Koepenick colleague doesn't appear to be having much success keeping public order in the square. You might give him the benefit of your more professional advice and assistance."

"Immediately, Herr Kapitän!" The Police Chief clicked his heels together.

"In fact, why don't you just send him back up to me," Voigt suggested. "He'll probably just get in your way out there anyway."

The Teltow Police Chief suppressed a self-satisfied grin.

When the Koepenick Police Chief appeared in the Mayor's office, red-faced and chagrined, Voigt waved away his frustration. "At ease, at ease, Inspector. A man on a horse always has the advantage over a man on the ground. Besides, I need you for more important duties. You will get me two closed carriages, to transport my prisoners to Berlin. Have both prisoners and carriages brought into the inner courtyard, so they won't be seen by the crowd. It will be your duty to guard these prisoners

during their trip, and to deliver them safely to military headquarters. Is that clear?"

It was.

"Oh, and one thing more. Go down to your office and
bring me your entire inventory of blank passports. I wish to
verify their registration numbers."

The Police Chief looked relieved. This, at least, was one
thing that couldn't go wrong. "I can save you the trouble on that
score, sir," he said. "At the moment, we have no blank passports
at all. We issued our last one over a month ago."

"What? No passports?"

For some reason the Captain didn't seem at all pleased to
have been spared this extra work.

"No sir. We don't expect a new batch for several weeks."

The Police Chief hurried off to order the carriages.

In the Treasurer's office, Voigt found the town's books balanced
and ready for inspection. He flipped one open casually, as if
inspecting bewildering rows of letters and numbers were an
everyday part of his job. "Everything complete?"

"Yes, sir," the Treasurer assured him.

"So how much money do you have in your cashbox?"

"Our closing balance is \$42,385.32★ Herr Kapitän."

The Captain seemed to give this number a fair bit of thought.

"All right," he said finally. "Just put it in a bag and make out
a receipt."

"I beg your pardon, sir?"

"It's being impounded," Voigt said shortly. "It will be
double-checked at headquarters, so be sure you've accounted
for every penny."

★ For consistency, all dollar amounts have been adjusted to 1999 values.

The Treasurer looked offended, but hurried to the safe to bundle up the cash.

When Voigt had signed the receipt and stuck the money into his pockets, he issued his final commands. The Mayor and the Treasurer were to be driven by carriage to Berlin military headquarters, along with the Koepenick Police Chief and the Mayor's wife. His soldiers were to guard the Town Hall for another hour, then catch the next train for Putlitzstrasse station and return to barracks. He himself would return to Berlin immediately to make his report, and to prepare for his prisoners' arrival.

Was everything quite clear?

It was.

The Teltow Police Chief cleared a passage through the crowd in the square for the Captain. Later, the ticket agent at Koepenick station remembered this Captain of the Guard ("I thought his jacket needed brushing") boarding the 18:43 train for Berlin's Schlesenstrasse station. A cleaning woman at the Schlesenstrasse station believed she remembered a military man fitting the police description ("he looked very tired and grumpy") leaving the train and heading west down Flentzerstrasse.

After that, the trail grew cold.

Over the next two weeks the military police arrested and interrogated more than two thousand persons suspected of being the man who became known as the "Captain of Koepenick." Secret Service agents combed the suburbs of Berlin and banged on doors the length and breadth of its poorer inner-city districts. The owners of the city's uniform shops were questioned, and its innkeepers and carriage-drivers called in. Handwriting experts were consulted about the signatures on the military expense chits and Koepenick's treasury receipt. The pressure from military headquarters was enormous.

After two weeks of fruitless investigation, the press was informed. Though the generals weren't altogether blind to the possibility of public ridicule, they were convinced that Germany's prestige was in even greater danger if this impudent imposter was allowed to get away. A large reward was posted, and an appeal was sent out to all loyal citizens of the realm to aid in his capture.

The extent of their miscalculation caught even the generals' critics by surprise. First Germany, then Europe, and finally the entire Western world exploded with laughter. Everyone took the opportunity to poke fun at Germany's fetish with the uniform and its citizens' unquestioning obedience to uniformed authority. Even a few German newspapers, like the *Berliner Wochenschau*, echoed this criticism. "It is a disgraceful comment on all those high-sounding words like public spirit, civil courage before the mighty, rule of the law and so on. The fact is that the uniform is the supreme power in Prussia. They all lie on their bellies before a uniform."

The laughter grew even louder when, after a further two weeks, the Captain of Koepenick was finally caught, and it was revealed that he was nothing but a decrepit old jailbird, a lowly shoemaker, who had never even served in the army. As a further embarrassment, it was also discovered that, during all his imposterings, no one had noticed that the cockades on his uniform cap had been placed the wrong way around, and the Prussian insignia had been pinned above instead of below the Imperial German one!

"What an irresistible rogue!" wrote London's *Review of Reviews*. "How simple, almost infantile his craft; how ludicrous his adventures, and how cutting the satire of his exploits!" The French journal *Le Matin* was even more effusive. "If we were to be asked what human being last month deserved best to receive the Nobel Prize as a universal benefactor of humanity, the famous Captain of Koepenick would head the poll by a large majority. The worship of the military uniform, which has been carried to such preposterously extravagant lengths in Prussia, never received so effective an exposure. Now when it is seen how easy it is for ex-convicts to obtain a uniform, the cult has been hit in the vitals."

Wilhelm Voigt's trial, on December 8, 1906, drew standing-room-only audiences and a crush of Western journalists. Right from the start, it became evident that the military had once again badly misjudged public sentiment. Its bullheaded efforts to have Voigt pilloried for defaming the German military were booed by the onlookers and effectively disproven by a long line of witnesses – including the redoubtable Frau Langerhans – who testified that Voigt had been unfailingly polite, had behaved more like a gentleman than most military officers these witnesses had encountered, and had remained at all times a dignified and unruffled commanding officer.

Voigt's own testimony, in which he described his struggles to lead an honest life, and his repeated efforts to extricate himself from the vicious circle into which Prussian laws and the Prussian economy had thrown him, also made a visible impression on the presiding judge. He asked Voigt many questions, particularly about the problem of getting a passport once one had a criminal record. It soon became evident that, with the exception of the military, no one in the courtroom wanted this man to spend the rest of his life in jail.

"Had he been acquitted and set free," the *Berliner Illustrierte* commented, "the crowd waiting outside for the verdict would undoubtedly have carried him off in triumph, for he has created much goodwill by his ingenious coup, and his calm and modest manner in court."

He wasn't set free, of course. His theft of Koepenick's municipal funds alone would have made that impossible. But since he had returned virtually all of the money, and was adjudged not to have disgraced the German uniform, the judge sentenced him to four years of prison – with the condition that it not be hard labour. Then he shook Voigt's hand and said he hoped this would be his last stint in prison.

It was.

After twenty months as a model inmate at Berlin's Tegel Prison, Voigt had his sentence commuted by the Kaiser himself, who ordered Voigt released and his record expunged. Meanwhile, a group of concerned citizens had formed a committee to help Voigt break out of the vicious circle he had so movingly described at his trial; one of their first acts was to convince a rich Berlin industrialist to grant him a $12,000 annual pension for life.

When news of this pension hit the newspapers – anything about the Captain of Koepenick was now newsworthy – more than a hundred women wrote Voigt with offers of marriage, including two women from the United States and one from England. (There is no record as to whether he took up any of these offers.)

But there was much more to come. As soon as Voigt was released from prison, a German playwright wrote a widely acclaimed drama entitled *The Captain of Koepenick*, which played to sell-out houses all over Germany – with Wilhelm Voigt himself playing the lead. The play was so successful that it toured Europe and England and eventually even North America, where Voigt (his pardon having enabled him to get a passport) was cheered and mobbed and fêted like a superstar. When the tour ended more than a year later, Voigt teamed up with a ghost-writer to produce his memoirs under the title *How I Became the Captain of Koepenick*, and it became a bestseller.

Wilhelm Voigt eventually settled in Luxembourg around 1914; some sources suggest he even married at that point. Whatever the case, he had finally achieved his goal and by all accounts lived a quiet, contented life until his death, in 1922, at the age of seventy-two.

By a final twist of fate, a company of soldiers happened to be marching past the cemetery where his burial was in progress. In keeping with age-old military tradition, the commanding officer halted his company and ordered an honorary salute.

It wasn't until several days later that they discovered the man they'd saluted had been one of the most famous "captains" in European military history.

2. The Preposterous Escapades of Kanonier Schmidt

Nineteen-year-old locksmith apprentice Elfried Schmidt was in serious trouble. It was April 1938, the Germans had just overrun his Austrian village of Rampersdorf, and his family – outspoken Nazi opponents – had just received their first visit from the Gestapo.

It hadn't been a pleasant experience. The agents had expressed their opinion of anti-Nazi "agitators" in no uncertain terms. Schmidt still had an ugly bruise on his left cheek to remind him. There had been suggestions of worse to come.

Then there was the question of the impact all this would have on Schmidt's career.

Elfried Schmidt had a natural talent for heavy-transport engineering. For years he'd spent all his spare time hanging around the village's streetcar terminal, studying everything connected with rail transport. He knew all there was to know about locomotives, cars, tracks, and switches. He'd even designed and drawn a blueprint for a revolutionary new electric diesel locomotive, which hung in the hallway of his home. But his family simply hadn't been able to afford to send him to the Technical University in Vienna.

"What a pity you didn't become an engineer, Elfried," his girlfriend, Elsa, always said when she passed the blueprint in the hall.

Schmidt couldn't have agreed more. In class-conscious Austria, a locksmith's apprentice really didn't rate. He was worried that Elsa's parents might not allow her to marry a mere locksmith. Now the Gestapo's visit worried him for similar reasons. Nobody would care if a mere locksmith's apprentice was thrown into a concentration camp. But if he were an engineer, they might have to think twice.

And . . . if he were an engineer who'd been acknowledged by Adolf Hitler . . . they might have to think *three* times.

Three times was definitely preferable.

After musing about this for a week, Schmidt caught a train for Vienna. Several days later he returned with a satchelful of rubber stamps, the sort that were standard in any important bureaucratic office. INCOMING. OUTGOING. CONSIDERED. APPROVED. Some were more specific: TECHNICAL UNIVERSITY OF BERLIN. GERMAN STATE RAILROAD. GERMAN REICH TRANS-PORT MINISTRY. And some were of the sort that had only recently become *de rigueur* in the rapidly expanding Third Reich: a round stamp with a big swastika, and another with a proud, open-winged eagle.

Schmidt parked himself in front of a typewriter and pro-ceeded to become an engineer. His first construction was a letter from himself to the German State Railroad, generously offering them his fancy electric diesel locomotive. (He kept only the carbon of that letter.) His second letter, received from the GERMAN STATE RAILROAD several weeks later (OUTGOING. APPROVED), informed Herr Elfried Schmidt that his blueprint had been forwarded to the GERMAN REICH TRANSPORT MINISTRY for assessment and consideration. His third letter – this one from the GERMAN REICH TRANSPORT MINISTRY – was pleased to inform Herr Elfried Schmidt that his blueprint had been duly considered and accepted by the GRTM (CONSIDERED. APPROVED). Indeed, such gifted young persons as himself (the letter pointed out) could only expect to thrive under a National Socialist regime. He would be hearing from them shortly.

Naturally, all letters were liberally stamped with swastikas and eagles, and festooned with plenty of impressively illegible signatures.

Finally, a follow-up letter from the GERMAN REICH TRANSPORT MINISTRY bore the enormously gratifying news that authorization for production of Elfried Schmidt's diesel locomotive had been given by the Chancellery in Berlin itself, and that construction of a large factory for this purpose had begun. A position "commensurate with your exceptional talents" was being devised and would be offered to Schmidt shortly. (CONSIDERED, APPROVED, SWASTIKA, EAGLE; more illegible signatures.)

It didn't take long for word of Schmidt's extraordinary triumph to make the village rounds.

Even his mother was amazed.

But there was more good news to come. It wasn't long before a letter arrived from the Technical University in Berlin (SWASTIKA, EAGLE), informing Herr Elfried Schmidt that, on the basis of his extraordinarily visionary locomotive design, he had been awarded the engineering degree INGENIEUR HONORIS CAUSA by order of the Führer himself! It therefore requested him to present himself at the Reich Chancellery in Berlin on August 25, 1938, at 11:00 a.m., to be awarded this degree *by the Führer in person!*

This caused an uproar in Rampersdorf. The local newspaper ran a front-page story. The mayor called to congratulate Schmidt personally, and to ask him to pass on his most sincere best wishes to the Führer. Dozens of people shook Schmidt's hand, hundreds more waved and shouted congratulations from across the street, out of windows, and over tables. His boss gave him time off to have himself fitted for a new suit.

But best of all, the Gestapo suddenly seemed to lose all interest in Elfried and his family.

That was gratifying, but now Schmidt had an unavoidable date with Adolf Hitler. On August 24 he boarded the train to Berlin, waving resignedly to the crowd of townsfolk who had gathered to see him off. But the date went much better than Schmidt had expected. In a Berlin tourist shop he found a booklet about the Chancellery that contained, among many other useful facts, a complete description of Hitler's office suite. When he returned to Rampersdorf several days later, Schmidt was thus able to give the local newspaper a very detailed report of his Chancellery luncheon. At a municipal gala held in his honour the following evening, his endearingly candid depiction of the Führer ("he smiled at me benevolently, like a father") moved some of the ladies to tears. He also modestly displayed the diploma the Führer had given him: a large, framed placard imprinted with a maiden holding a laurel wreath, within whose circle of leaves the words HONORARY DIPLOMA and Schmidt's full name had been printed in an ornate font.

(Needless to say, the document was liberally stamped with swastikas and eagles and boasted a positively astonishing number of illegible signatures.)

There was only one bit of unpleasantness. A former schoolmate of Schmidt's, Peter Boehmen, demanded to know how he had addressed the Führer.

Schmidt hesitated. "I believe I said 'Heil, Herr Reichskanzler,'" he said finally.

Boehmen found that odd. "My dad was at a big reception in Berlin last month," he said. "And everybody was told to say 'Heil, mein Führer.'"

"Not in my case," Schmidt shrugged. His face had taken on a distinct pallor.

Boehmen couldn't understand that. He said he'd ask his father about it.

Schmidt didn't sleep very well that night. His brain was seething like a beehive under attack.

If Boehmen's father, who was rumoured to have high Nazi connections, became suspicious, Schmidt was sunk.

The next morning, Schmidt once again boarded a train for Vienna. In the city's downtown square, not far from the train station, he found several large uniform shops. In one, he bought himself a German major's uniform, complete with swastika armband and a silver lanyard that was worn only by high party dignitaries. In another, he bought a matching cap. For each transaction he proffered an authorizing letter, liberally stamped with swastikas and eagles. The purchases proceeded without a hitch.

Minutes later Elfried Schmidt began to experience what the Captain of Koepenick had discovered thirty-two years before: all the world defers to a splendid uniform. No sooner had he stepped out of the shop than everybody started saluting. Soldiers snapped to attention. Policemen bowed. Waiters scraped, hoteliers became obsequious, women glowed. Even military officers became remarkably co-operative and helpful.

Back in Rampersdorf, Schmidt explained that the uniform had been sent to him by the Führer to go with his new diploma. The silver lanyard, when worn on the left shoulder, as he was wearing it, constituted a Silver Honorary Cord of the Third Reich – one of the Reich's highest honours. The Silver Cord had been awarded only three times before.

The response in Rampersdorf was exactly as Schmidt had experienced in Vienna. Wall-to-wall kowtowing, fawning, heel-clicking, and deferential handshakes. Once again the local newspaper ran a front-page photo. People ogled through their windows as he passed by. Shopkeepers waved away his money. Even Peter Boehmen seemed convinced.

Only Schmidt's mother was unimpressed. "Just don't let that silly thing go to your head," she warned. "Keep in mind it was given to you by murderers."

Schmidt did, but he soon found the silly thing useful for a lot more than he'd originally intended. The first time it happened, his reaction was unthinking and reckless. Crossing Schwarzenberger Square in Vienna – where, as far as Rampersdorfers knew, he had moved to take up the illustrious engineer's position he'd been promised – he saw two Gestapo agents closing in on a Jewish family friend. By the time he'd sprinted to the friend's side the agents were about to handcuff him. "Just what is the meaning of this outrage?!" Schmidt demanded as imperiously as he could manage. "I am Engineer Schmidt, bearer of the Silver Honorary Cord of the Third Reich, awarded to me *personally* by the Führer! This man is Dr. David Silber, a loyal citizen of the Reich. I can vouch for him, and I won't have him maltreated!" And before the startled Gestapo agents could stop him, Schmidt grabbed Silber by the shoulder, pushed the agents aside, and walked the doctor quickly across the street.

That night he arranged for Silber and his wife to travel to Rampersdorf, and the next day his mother helped them escape across the border into Hungary.

That incident set the pattern for a flurry of similar nocturnal rescues, as word of Schmidt's influence and helpfulness spread. As the Gestapo became increasingly active in Vienna, more and more friends knocked desperately on Schmidt's door. Schmidt always did what he could. With the aid of his typewriter and satchelful of stamps he concocted impressively ornate letters of reference that obliged all Nazi Party officials and functionaries to extend to the bearer, Engineer Elfried Schmidt, Holder of the Silver Honorary Cord of the Third Reich, *on express orders of the Führer himself*, all possible aid and assistance.

It worked with startling effectiveness. No sooner had Schmidt slapped his letters down onto bureaucratic counters or desks than orders were rescinded, gates were opened, hands were uncuffed, priority transport was arranged. A steady stream of liberated Gestapo victims found their way to Rampersdorf, where Schmidt's mother helped them all escape across the nearby border. Schmidt still hadn't told his family the truth about his exalted position, but they must have suspected, because they never asked. They just hugged him anxiously.

Meanwhile, there seemed to be no limit to the power of Schmidt's letters. His greatest challenge came in October 1938, when he was informed that one of his mother's friends, a shopkeeper named Joachim Huber, had been carried off by the Gestapo the night before. A clerk at the Viennese Tenth District

Office explained to Schmidt that it was already too late; Huber had been sent to Dachau.

Schmidt demanded to see the district's top authority.

The clerk informed him that this was impossible.

Schmidt slapped down his letter.

Two minutes later Schmidt was sitting face to face with Kreisleiter Walter Kroener, District Chairman, demanding to know why Huber had been arrested. Kroener explained that Huber had been "detained for antisocial behaviour," as witnessed by a German citizen. Furious, Schmidt informed Kroener that the accusation against Huber amounted to nothing more than the denunciations of a greedy competitor. "The Führer told me only last week that he doesn't approve of this sort of thing," he snapped. "I'll be seeing him again next Thursday. If Huber isn't back in his store within forty-eight hours, I will personally report this appalling injustice directly to the Führer."

Kroener began frantically to apologize. Obviously, he hadn't been informed of all the facts. He could see that there had been a most regrettable error. He would personally see to its immediate correction.

"I hope so," Schmidt said grimly as he got up. "For your sake, I sincerely hope so. This is the sort of thing that really makes the Führer furious."

Huber was returned from Dachau within eighteen hours.

He was safely in Hungary twelve hours after that.

In all, Schmidt and his mother helped forty-one people escape from the Nazis' clutches in this way.

In November 1938, Schmidt was drafted into the armed forces. For the next two months he was hounded, yelled at, forced to remake his bunk until he was blue in the face, polish his boots to a positively eerie shine, and peel a million potatoes.

Ironically, he enjoyed the change. The responsibilities of being Engineer Schmidt, Holder of the Silver Honorary Cord of the Third Reich, had become enormously stressful. As Kanonier Schmidt of the German Luftwaffe, all that was expected of him was a lot of goose-stepping and mindless obedience. As he packed his kit for Christmas furlough back in Rampersdorf, he was actually sorry to have to reassume his former exalted position. Life as a grunt had its advantages.

But when Schmidt returned to barracks after an exhausting holiday – so many people with personal messages for the Führer – he was immediately ordered to report to the battery commander. He found the captain and all his staff officers gathered around the mess table, examining a newspaper clipping. One glance at the clipping sufficed.

"My *dear* Schmidt," the battery commander remonstrated benevolently. "We are overwhelmed. Why didn't you tell us this before?"

Schmidt was sweating profusely, but he remained standing at attention. Standing at attention always seemed a fairly safe bet in the Luftwaffe.

"There you are, gentlemen," the Captain said turning to his officers. "Just as I suspected. Modest to a fault."

"I didn't want any favours, sir," Schmidt quavered. "I just wanted to do my duty like any other soldier."

The Captain clearly liked what he was hearing. "As I said, gentlemen. The true spirit of a German soldier. Another proof of the fantastic foresight of our Führer, who singled out this simple Kanonier from among millions."

"Heil Hitler!" Schmidt shouted. Everyone promptly clicked their heels and saluted. Schmidt remained at attention.

"At ease," the Captain ordered. Schmidt relaxed slightly. "Now, Kanonier Schmidt, what are your duties at present?"

"Shovelling snow, sir!"

The Captain seemed embarrassed. There was an awkward pause. "Well, that's over now," he said apologetically. "Kanonier Schmidt, you are relieved of all military duties. You'll have an office set aside for your special work. You may come and go as you please. And you will wear your Silver Honorary Cord on your uniform at all times. Dismissed."

Schmidt saluted. Then he bowed and escaped.

From that day on, Schmidt lived the life of the military elite. He slept in his own Vienna apartment and didn't show up at barracks until after 8:00 a.m., just like the Captain. Whenever he showed up at the barracks gate, the sentry called out the honour guard, normally summoned only for a garrison commander. He spent his days touring engineering projects, studying incomprehensible air-force dispatches, and trying to look intelligent while inspecting anti-aircraft installations.

Several weeks later he was transferred to Luftgaukommando XVII, where his commanding officer, General Eduard von Loehr, promptly promoted him to the rank of colonel. He was assigned to a secret project involving aircraft engines, and given a sumptuous office, with a sergeant as an orderly. Since he knew nothing about aircraft engines, he asked the General's permission to study certain railway designs that would be "of vital interest to the Luftwaffe." Permission granted. During the following month, Schmidt spent every waking hour fulfilling a childhood dream that his family had never been able to afford.

He built himself a spectacular 1,200-square-foot model railroad, with 3 kilometres of track, 14 mountains, 17 railway stations, 18 bridges, and 33 trains, all chugging busily through hill and dale, hauling logs, freight, and industrial supplies. The layout was so detailed and expansive that it required the commandeering of two adjoining offices and the demolishing of three existing walls. His fellow officers, and even the General, were obviously enthralled, because they dropped by often to play with it.

On weekends, Schmidt accepted the General's offer of his Mercedes limousine, which he drove out to Rampersdorf to impress his friends. He enjoyed the way their jaws dropped at the sight of his General-Staff licence plates. When he swept down the town's central street, the policeman at the main intersection hastily stopped all traffic to let him pass. Once again, everyone bowed and scraped and saluted. Only his mother balked. In fact, she was so horrified at the sight of his entourage, with its flapping swastika flags and huge eagle hood ornament, that Schmidt finally broke down and told her the whole story.

It didn't make her feel any better.

"I just hope and pray that you know what you're doing," she said anxiously.

Schmidt's reassurances sounded a lot more confident than he felt.

Only a week later, on February 16, 1939, Schmidt's adjutant informed him that he was to present himself at the General's conference room. "General's orders, sir." Schmidt didn't like the sound of that. The General had always "requested" things before. He also didn't like the way the adjutant shadowed him as they walked over. In the conference room they found the General flanked by several prosecutors from the Luftwaffe court. The General's manner had suddenly become distant and frosty.

"Tell us exactly how you got your Honorary Diploma," he snapped.

Schmidt looked from face to face, but he couldn't tell how much they knew. He decided to bluff it out.

"Perhaps I should just call the Führer and let him talk to you," he said huffily. "He's given me his private telephone number, you know."

"You have the Führer's private telephone number?"

"Certainly," Schmidt said.

There was a long, uncertain pause. Then the General pushed a telephone in Schmidt's direction.

"Go ahead and call him," he ordered.

Schmidt was thrown into Floridsdorf Military Prison and charged with fraud and espionage. His jailers thought it was hilarious that he had hoaxed the brass like that. But Schmidt knew a charge of espionage was no joke. The penalty for espionage was death. And telling the truth wouldn't help. It would simply land his entire family in Dachau.

It took him several sleepless nights to come up with the solution.

He wrote a letter to his girlfriend, Elsa. In it, he explained his situation tearfully, despondently, remorsefully. He told her he had done it all for her. "Remember when you said what a pity it was that I wasn't an engineer?" he reminded her. "All I wanted to do was make a good impression on you and your parents. Oh, but how can I make them believe that here?" Then he gave the letter to his cellmate, who was being released the following day. The cellmate was to give it to the gate sentry, explaining that he'd been asked to smuggle it out to Elsa, but that he'd thought better of it, and had decided not become an accomplice to further crime.

The letter was duly surrendered to the guard. By noon the next day it was in the hands of the Chief Prosecutor.

Whether the Prosecutor genuinely believed the story, or whether it merely gave him an opportunity to sweep the whole embarrassing mess under the carpet, remains anyone's guess. There's little doubt that, if the press had got hold of it, the egg on the faces of at least a dozen high military officials would have been considerable. Whatever the explanation, Schmidt's trial proceeded with a degree of secrecy and haste that mere Teutonic efficiency couldn't possibly have explained. The charge of espionage was dropped completely, and the charge of fraud was narrowed to three counts: forging an official diploma, unjustified use of an academic title, and "insolently exploiting the name of the Führer."

Naturally, the last was the most serious charge, accounting for four months of Schmidt's six-month sentence.

Schmidt also had to sign a promise not to divulge his hoax to anyone – on pain of renewed visits from the Gestapo. His criminal record was then classified, and he was transferred to an army prison near the western front, where news of his hoax hadn't penetrated.

When he decided to get married (not, unfortunately, to Elsa) a year after his release from prison, alert Luftwaffe authorities obliged Schmidt to wear his phony uniform and Silver Honorary Cord of the Third Reich to his Rampersdorf wedding.

The good citizens of Rampersdorf didn't discover the true story until after the war.

Making Hay in Cathay

The Dubious Voyages of Il Milione,
a.k.a. Marco Polo

As medieval bestsellers go, *The Travels of Marco Polo* (sometimes entitled *The Book of Marco Polo, Citizen of Venice, Wherein Is Recounted the Wonders of the World*), has always been the book to beat.

From its initial appearance in 1299 until well into the nineteenth century, its enormous popularity never flagged – especially during the eighteenth and nineteenth centuries, when exploration, safaris, and "adventures" became all the rage with the West's aristocracies.

The book served as Europe's primary introduction to the Far East, and became the yardstick by which all subsequent reports about the mysteries of Mongolia, China, and India were measured. Originally written in French, it was eventually translated into 130 languages. Leonardo da Vinci never failed to keep his Italian version handy. Cervantes refused to allow his Latin version out of the house. Even Christopher Columbus, trying to reach China by sea in 1492, kept a copy of the book in his ship's library.

The Travels of Marco Polo actually describes two voyages. The first was a long trading venture by Marco's father and uncle, Niccolò and Matteo, who in 1260 undertook an extraordinary nine-year, 7,500-kilometre journey from Venice through Constantinople and Sudak to the Mongolian capital of Karakorum, headquarters of the great Mongol ruler Kublai Khan. There, they spent several years enjoying the khan's hospitality in his great white-marbled palace, where he lived surrounded by three thousand bodyguards and a retinue of some fifty thousand sycophants and courtiers (his four official wives alone maintained entourages of ten thousand servants each). The khan proved extremely curious about the West, and seemed quite knowledgeable about it, whereas his courtiers remained convinced that most Westerners hopped about on one foot and barked like dogs. (On the other hand, many Venetians back home still believed that Orientals were cannibals whose heads grew beneath their shoulders). The Polos also spent a good deal of time enlightening the khan about some of the more puzzling aspects of the Christian religion, and when they set off on their return journey in 1268, he gave them a letter for the Pope, asking His Holiness to send back missionaries and some sacred oil from the lamp that burned above the sepulchre of God in Jerusalem.

The brothers arrived back in Venice in 1269.

The book's second voyage was Niccolò and Matteo's return trip to the khan in 1271, this time accompanied by Niccolò's seventeen-year-old son Marco Polo. Marco quickly won the khan's favour, both for his storytelling abilities and the speed with which he learned various dialects of Mongolian and Chinese. Once again the Polos were honoured and fêted, and made an integral part of the khan's entourage. Over the following twenty-one years in his employ, they made themselves useful teaching his generals how to build great catapults during the siege of Xianyang, and travelling as his envoys to different parts of his realm. Marco himself was appointed governor of the city of Yangzhou for a period of three years, and undertook long voyages as the khan's envoy to Burma, China, and even India.

When the Polos became homesick and petitioned the khan for permission to leave in 1292, he consented but asked them to return to Venice by sea via Persia, so they could accompany and deliver a young Mongol princess to Tabriz, where she'd been promised in marriage to the Persian ruler, Arghun. The khan then provided the Polos with a flotilla of junks, a six-hundred-guard retinue, and several safe-conduct passports made of gold. The expedition left from the port of Zaitun, on China's eastern seaboard.

The trip proved difficult and perilous, with delays on the coast of Sumatra and south India and an outbreak of scurvy in the Indian Ocean. Of their retinue, only eighteen survived, but the remaining troop did manage, after making landfall in Hormuz and a 2,000-kilometre trek overland, to deliver their royal charge safely in 1294. It took the Polos another year to finally make it back to Venice, where they arrived gaunt and exhausted, though with a king's ransom in jewels sewn into the lining of their clothes. It was said that even their own relatives didn't recognize them.

In his next recorded appearance, in 1298, Marco Polo was imprisoned in Genoa, after the vessel he'd been commanding for the Venetian navy was captured in a sea-battle in the

Adriatic. But Polo's misfortune proved the world's gain, because it was during the following year's stint as a Genoese prisoner of war that Polo, "wishing to occupy his leisure as well as to afford entertainment to readers" (from his prologue), gathered his notes and journals and set to work on *The Travels of Marco Polo*. The project was completed in 1299.

The work proved an instant hit and was eagerly read throughout the Western world. At first it was circulated by the laborious method of readers making their own copies and passing on the original, but after the rise of the printing press in the fifteenth century, its readership and influence mushroomed.

Cartographers incorporated Polo's geographic and navigational reports into their maps. Adventurers and explorers studied the book in preparation for their own expeditions into the unknown. As both naval and land exploration gained greater popularity during the eighteenth and nineteenth centuries, world travellers used the book as a guide to try to replicate the Polo voyages themselves.

With the growth of Marco Polo's fame, an impressive array of discoveries and innovations were attributed to him. He was said to have given Italians their first recipes for pasta and ice cream. He was credited with introducing the West to everything from gunpowder and the mariner's compass to block printing. He was celebrated as a pioneer of scientific geography, and for filling in large empty spaces in the map of the world.

An army of scholars – both Western and Eastern – found purpose and careers busily analysing the more than 140 different versions of Marco Polo's manuscript that have been discovered to date. Thousands of studies and analyses have been made of every conceivable aspect and implication of the Great Work. Hundreds of books have been published on the basis of these studies, resulting in dozens of new and revised translations. Illustrated editions, children's editions, and newly annotated adult editions continue to appear year after year.

The book has spawned nothing less than a worldwide Marco Polo industry.

Despite all this attention, however, it wasn't until the 1960s – almost seven hundred years after its initial appearance – that a few courageous Marco Polo scholars finally began to discuss publicly some of the questions, suspicions, and outright doubts about this world-famous travelogue that had been bothering many of them privately for decades.

The fact is that *A Description of the World* is riddled with contradictions, dubious claims, and outright fabrications.

Marco Polo states, for example, that his uncles helped the great khan win the siege of Xianyang by introducing his generals to the use of catapults. In fact, catapults were already well known and in common use in both Persia and China at that time. More important, the siege of Xianyang was actually broken by Persian engineers in the khan's employ fully a year before the Polos even arrived in China. Chinese historical records also show that the Polos were not, as Marco Polo claimed, the first "Latins" ever seen by Kublai Khan, since the Mongul leader had always made a habit of surrounding himself with foreign advisers, including Italians and other Europeans.

In another puzzler, Marco Polo describes a conflict between Genghis Khan, Kublai's grandfather, and Prester John, thought by medieval Europeans to be a Christian ruler based somewhere on the eastern edge of the world – perhaps India. (Europe's Christian rulers were fascinated by the idea of an eastern Christian ruler, because this created the possibility of a two-pronged Christian crusade against the Muslims occupying the Holy Land.) Polo reports that Genghis wanted to marry Prester John's daughter, and, when John refused, the Khan declared war and killed him. But subsequent research has shown that Prester John never existed; he was a legendary figure about whom stories were invented in the tradition of St. Christopher and the Three Magi.

The work's itinerary doesn't add up either. European adventurers who mounted expeditions to follow "in the footsteps of Marco Polo" found it impossible to track his route-map much past Persia. Many of his stated distances and travel times turned out to make little sense. Nineteenth-century British historian Sir Henry Yule, trying to follow Polo's route from Yongzhang to the capital of Burma in seventeen and a half days, wrote in his typically understated manner: "I confess that the indications in this and the beginning of the following chapter are, to me, full of difficulty." Trying to follow Polo from Burma to Laos he encountered more than mere difficulties: "I do not believe . . . that Polo is now following a route which he had traced in person." Eventually he threw up his hands entirely: "We are obliged . . . to give up the attempt to keep a line of communicating rivers throughout the whole twenty-four days. Nor do I see how it is possible to adhere to that condition literally without taking material liberties with the text."

Studying the famous bridge just outside Peking, which has since been named the Marco Polo Bridge, and which Polo had described as having 24 arches, 24 piers, and 600 pillars with 1,200 stone lions, Yule was forced to conclude that Polo must have been looking at a different structure. This one had only 11 arches and a mere 120 pillars, with a much smaller number of stone tortoises, not lions. (In fact, scholars have never been able to find a bridge that corresponds to Polo's description.) In the city of Hangzhou, which Polo described as a Chinese Venice, Yule could find only 360 bridges; Polo had reported a whopping 12,000.

But it wasn't merely Polo's inventions or exaggerations that were troubling. It was also his astounding omissions.

How was it possible for a European like Polo to travel through China and fail to notice (or fail to report) such astonishing phenomena as the Great Wall of China (which Polo's claimed itinerary crosses on numerous occasions)?

Or the bound feet of Chinese women (a practice unknown anywhere else in the world)?

Or the fact that Chinese noblemen wore their fingernails so absurdly long that they had to protect them with foot-long nailguards?

Or the drinking of tea, the widespread culture of tea-houses, or the use of chopsticks?

Or Chinese calligraphy, the Chinese manufacture of paper, the Chinese use of paper money, or the Chinese book-printing industry (using wooden blocks), almost two hundred years before Gutenberg?

Was it perhaps because Marco Polo's book wasn't an eye-witness account at all?

Though billed as a travelogue, very little of *A Description of the World* actually follows a travel itinerary. It's also not written in the first person, as most travelogues are. The work is composed largely of a generalized chronicle of certain regions of Persia, Mongolia, and China, like a guidebook or a collection of fact-sheets. The Polos themselves make very few appearances – and when they do, they are almost always referred to in the third person.

This is a "travelogue," in other words, that could have been assembled by an armchair traveller, using pre-existing sources.

This notion, sidestepped, downplayed, and swept under the academic carpet for hundreds of years, has finally breached the discreet confines of scholarly magazines and reached the public arena – despite howls of outrage from the Marco Polo industry. Fifty years ago, books such as distinguished sinologist Frances Wood's *Did Marco Polo Go to China?* might well have constituted academic suicide. Today, they're a harbinger of research to come.

As the evidence continues to mount, Polo defenders find themselves forced into increasingly awkward contortions to explain away damning facts such as these:

1. Though Polo claims to have spent three years as the khan's appointed governor of the city of Yangzhou, there is no record of this appointment, nor any mention of Marco Polo in either the khan's – or the city's – carefully preserved and extremely detailed chronicles.

In fact, no scholar has been able to find a single verifying reference to Marco Polo or his uncles *anywhere* in thirteenth-century Mongolian or Chinese records or archives.

2. Though Polo claims to have learned to speak fluent Mongolian and Chinese, virtually every Mongolian or Chinese place name in *The Travels of Marco Polo* is identified only by its Persian name.

Why would an eyewitness, conversant in the local language, not use the appropriate local place names?

3. Marco Polo's account of his voyage from Zaitun to Tabriz to escort the Mongol princess to the Persian ruler Arghun appears in other historical-archival texts as well, notably the Persian Rashid al-Din's *World History* and the Imperial Chinese encyclopedia *Yung-lo ta tien*. However, neither account mentions the involvement of any Europeans or Italians, and no mention is

made of the Polos in any capacity. Was this story therefore borrowed from another source?

4. Though *The Travels of Marco Polo* has always been credited to Marco Polo – no other name appears on the book's title page – it turns out that Marco Polo didn't write the book himself. It was ghost-written for him by a popular romance writer named Rustichello, who was also in Genoa as a prisoner of war in 1298. According to a brief acknowledgement buried in the prologue, Polo "caused all these things to be recorded by Messer Rustichello of Pisa, who was in the same prison."

Very little is known about this Rustichello, except that he earned his living (according to the nineteenth-century critic Isaac D'Israeli) as a mercenary "celebrating the chivalry of the British court, when stimulated by largesses and fair châteaux." In other words, Rustichello was a freelancer who had successfully parlayed British royalty's penchant for Arthurian legends into a patronage position with King Edward I. In pre-Gutenberg Europe, this constituted the definition of a successful author.

A wondrous tale of two extraordinary voyages into the Mysterious East, filled with exotic peoples, bizarre customs, fabulous wealth, fairytale cities, and the exploits of heroic and powerful men, might well have struck Rustichello as an equally marketable idea.

It was certainly an idea appropriate to its time. There was a growing demand for scientific geographies in the late thirteenth and early fourteenth centuries, presaging the great age of discovery that was just around the corner. Writers such as Vincent of Beauvais (*Speculum Historiae*), Jacopo da Acqui (*Imago Mundi*), and even the notorious Sir John Mandeville (whose hugely popular *The Voiage and Travaile of Sir John Mandeville* was eventually proven a complete fake) had already gained, or were about to gain, much attention and success by producing such works.

It was a prospect that might well have appealed to Marco Polo too, because Polo was not, despite all claims to the contrary, a rich or well-positioned man. Venetian records give no indication that he was ever anything but a modestly successful merchant. The story about jewels in the lining of his clothing was apocryphal, the claim that he commanded a Venetian naval vessel unproven, and his family shield, long taken as proof of his nobility, has since been demonstrated to belong to a different family of Polos. He certainly could have used some patronage, and might have thought that Rustichello was just the man to arrange it for him.

So, did Marco Polo and Rustichello team up to fake the most famous and influential travelogue in the history of the world?

Yes, according to Frances Wood, now head of the Chinese department at the British Library – though she expresses some qualifications.

She feels the story of the first Polo journey, in which Niccolò and Matteo travelled only as far as Mongolia, may well be mostly true, and that Marco Polo may have used this voyage as a launching pad for his own fictitious one. If Marco travelled at all, she says, he may have travelled with his father and uncle to the family trading posts in Constantinople or Sudak, but the bulk of his purported journey – to Mongolia, China, Burma, and India – probably never happened.

But if it never happened, where did Marco Polo get his raw material?

This wouldn't have been as difficult as might be expected. Persian traders, who acted as middlemen between Europe and the East, had already established well-travelled trade routes to

Mongolia and China in Marco Polo's day. Their maps, reports, and travel accounts would undoubtedly have been available to the Polo family, since the Polos' own trading region extended as far east as the Crimean coast of the Black Sea. (This would also account for Marco Polo's exclusive use of Persian place names for Mongolian and Chinese locations.)

The reports of missionaries and travelling clerics were probably another source. Communication between Eastern and Western rulers was surprisingly extensive by the thirteenth century, and it was largely provided by travelling monks. Frances Wood comments that "it sometimes seems that medieval missionary travellers were practically nose to tail across Central Asia." The Franciscan friar John of Plano Carpini, also a "Latin," produced a widely circulated account of his visit in Mongolia with Kublai Khan's cousin, Guyug Khan, in 1246. William of Rubruck, another Franciscan friar, produced an even longer and more personal account of his life with the Mongols around 1254, including lively tales of their preposterous drinking binges, the khan's thousands of concubines, and his unbridled war games.

Conversations with visiting traders around the Polo supper table probably provided the young Marco with a good deal of the commercial and produce-related information contained in his book. Indeed, one of the features that makes *The Travels of Marco Polo* an uphill effort to read is its enormous amount of mercantile data, which all but overwhelms its tales of caliphs and concubines and combat. Visiting traders also probably passed on the latest rumours, hearsay, and political gossip, some of which Polo unwisely incorporated into his travelogue as observed facts. Whatever the case, there were obviously plenty of traders' reports to be had, because the Florentine merchant Francesco

Pegolotti was able, only a few decades later, to write a creditable guide to merchant travel in China (*Practica della Mercatura*, 1340) based entirely (and openly) on secondhand sources.

But there's an even more tantalizing possibility, and this is that Marco Polo used a major Persian or Arabic source that hasn't yet been unearthed. The tip-off came when scholars discovered that Rashid al-Din's history of China in his *World History* contained many stories and descriptions that closely parallelled Marco Polo's – and were marred by many of the same spelling, historical, or geographical errors. Like Marco Polo's, Rashid al-Din's work was largely impersonal, but unlike Polo's, it relied openly on a variety of (unfortunately unnamed) Persian and Mongolian sources.

The immediate suspicion, of course, was that this was Marco Polo's major source – until it was discovered that Rashid al-Din's work was produced in 1310. (The opposite possibility – that Rashid's work was based on Marco Polo's – has been discounted.)

The next development in this scholarly mystery came when noted sinologist Herbert Franke discovered the work of a Chinese Buddhist historian, Nianchang, whose accounts of Chinese history to the year 1333 contained parallels to Marco Polo's account that were even more striking and so numerous that some sort of relationship beyond mere subject and data simply had to be assumed. Since once again the dates didn't match up, Professor Franke concluded – and this appears to represent the thinking in Marco Polo research today – that all three writers made use of a common, possibly Chinese Buddhist, source that has yet to be found.

Finding that source has preoccupied a small army of Marco Polo scholars for the past three decades.

Whoever finds that source will undoubtedly become extremely famous.

Whether they will also become rich is another question. Marco Polo didn't, though he did achieve a small portion of his eventual fame during his lifetime. It wasn't, admittedly, sufficient to attract a patron, but it was enough to enable him to leave behind, upon his death in 1324, twenty-four beds, a great pile of silken linens, and a bag of medicinal rhubarb.

Supreme Naughtiness in the Forbidden City

———◆———

The Brazen Boondoggles of Sir Edmund Backhouse

For more than a century, both during his life and following his death in 1944, most people thought Sir Edmund Backhouse was a pretty swell guy.

He enjoyed a reputation as one of the most charming, charitable, cultured, and accomplished scholars and gentlemen you'd ever expect to meet.

His generous donation of a twenty-seven-thousand-volume collection of rare and extraordinarily valuable Chinese books and manuscripts to Oxford University's Bodleian Library had moved the university to engrave his name in marble on its permanent roll of honour.

His eyewitness accounts (co-written with J. P. Bland) of the last days of the Manchu Dynasty in Peking's Forbidden City, *China Under the Empress Dowager* (1910) and *Annals and*

Memoirs of the Court of Peking (1914) were regarded as timeless classics.

He'd been appointed to chairs at Cambridge and the University of Peking, and had served as negotiator and business representative for a veritable Who's Who of British and American corporations in Peking from 1895 to 1917.

It wasn't until 1973, almost four decades after his death, that the contents of a mysterious package, handed to British historian Hugh Trevor-Roper by a former Swiss consul for Peking at Basel's international airport, abruptly rolled up the Chinese screen of Sir Edmund's prestigious reputation to reveal what an amazing and duplicitous scoundrel he'd been all along.

The truth was, Edmund Backhouse had been a devious, secretive, and unpredictable spendthrift virtually from birth.

During three years as an undergraduate at Oxford, he ran up a gambling debt of more than half a million dollars* – but didn't finish his degree.

Two years later he was in the soup again, over dubious dealings in bogus art, antiques, and jewellery.

He wasn't at all the son his titled British banking family had hoped for.

But Edmund Backhouse had one overarching talent that tended to obscure all his faults: he could learn languages faster than any human being alive. He was fluent in Greek and Latin by the age of twelve. He picked up *both* Russian and Japanese in less than four months from foreign students at a boarding house. By age twenty-five he'd added French, Spanish, Arabic, Turkish, Mongolian, Tibetan, and three dialects of Chinese – including Manchu.

---

* For consistency, all dollar amounts have been adjusted to 1999 values.

It was on the strength of his fluency in Manchu that Backhouse's father, fed up with paying his wayward son's constant debts and fines, finally packed him off to China as a remittance man, on condition that he never darken his father's door again.

It was that same ability that convinced G. E. Morrison, head of *The Times*'s Peking bureau, to give Backhouse a job when he appeared on Morrison's doorstep in 1898.

Fluency in Manchu was worth gold in 1890s China. Despite the fact that Manchu was at this point the language of the imperial court, virtually nobody on the staffs of any European or American government legation or newspaper office in Peking spoke it. Translation and interpretation was a constant headache – made worse by the fact that the Chinese were considered, by popular stereotype, notoriously devious, secretive, and unpredictable. You could never tell exactly what they were saying or what they really meant, and their byzantine political system seemed almost impenetrable.

Within days, Backhouse was translating for virtually everybody in town.

Remarkably, he didn't seem to find the Chinese impenetrable at all. He seemed able to unpuzzle the complex relations between the court's hundreds of courtiers and concubines with astonishing ease. He was soon rumoured to be on a first-name basis with many of the palace's most powerful eunuchs and officials. It was even said that he'd been granted a secret interview with the Empress Dowager (known around the legations as the "Old Buddha") herself.

Maybe it was true, maybe not. You could never be quite sure with a fellow like Backhouse. Since his exposure to Chinese culture, he had learned to be the soul of politesse and discretion.

Gone a bit native, according to the chaps in the British legation. It was known to happen.

Not that anyone was complaining. It was a good thing that *somebody* was able to make sense of what went on behind the high walls of the Forbidden City.

British journalists in particular used Backhouse shamelessly, both to get the news and to translate it for their dispatches. They didn't credit him in their bylines, of course, but he didn't seem to mind – as long as he was paid. It wasn't long before Backhouse had become everyone's main source of information into and out of the imperial court. They all used him: the Americans, the British, the Germans, the French. Even the Japanese.

If anyone ever noticed that many of the world's most powerful governments – who all used the Western press to formulate their Chinese foreign policies – were in effect allowing themselves to be dependent on a nondescript little translator who had managed to position himself strategically at one of the main crossroads on their information highway, they didn't seem too worried about it. Yes, this was shaping Western perceptions of nineteenth-century China for decades to come, and, yes, this was frowned on by military strategists as putting too many of one's eggs in one basket – but given the extraordinary volatility of China's day-to-day political affairs, who had the leisure to worry much about those sorts of minor details?

Just take, for example, the Boxer Rebellion. Less than a year after Backhouse's arrival, Peking's diplomats, journalists, and foreign government officials found themselves pinned down in their own flimsily barricaded legations, fending off a ragtag army of Chinese patriots determined to overwhelm the city and kill every Westerner they could find. It was fifty-five days before they could be rescued by a hastily assembled allied naval force.

During the political sea change that followed, as Boxer leaders were executed and their supporters fled the city to avoid the same fate (leaving their homes and possessions unguarded), Backhouse was nowhere to be found – but his whereabouts weren't hard to deduce. Russian embassy records indicated he was collared by a squad of Russian soldiers "in the act of black-mailing, looting, and robbing."

Backhouse indignantly denied any such thing.

But when the Empress Dowager died in 1908 and a *Times* journalist, J. P. Bland, made Backhouse a proposal for a collabo-rative work on the Old Buddha – with Backhouse providing the translations – Backhouse surprised Bland by being able to provide a good deal more. In addition to a remarkable dossier of original material documenting the history of the Imperial Palace, he was also able to contribute the personal diary of one Ching-shan, a relative of the Empress Dowager and Assistant Secretary of her imperial household, who had been murdered during the Boxer Rebellion. This diary, which detailed the events leading up to the Boxer Rebellion from a perspective to which no Westerner could have hoped to have access – inside the Forbidden City itself – was an astounding find.

Questioned about the diary's origins, Backhouse insisted that he'd rescued it from Ching-shan's house, which he'd entered during the aftermath of the Boxer Rebellion, trying to stop a contingent of Sikh soldiers from torching the place. He'd found the book unbound and scattered all over the old man's study, with some of it already burned and trampled. He said he'd requested and received permission from the officer in charge to retrieve the document for safekeeping. (Since the officer had died by the time Backhouse gave this explanation, his story was given, at least for the moment, the benefit of the doubt.)

The diary had an enormous impact on the reputations of a number of prominent Chinese statesmen, notably Jung-lu, the Empress's Grand Secretary, whom Western diplomats and historians had tagged as virulently anti-Western, but who came across in the diary as a voice of moderation and restraint. Others, like Imperial Minister Li Ching-fang, lost some status, but the old Empress appeared far less devious, secretive, and unpredictable than she'd been believed to be.

Western historians took due notice.

China Under the Empress Dowager was a huge success. It established Backhouse as a noteworthy sinologist and paved the way, both critically and financially, for a second, equally successful, Backhouse–Bland collaboration, *Annals and Memoirs of the Court of Peking*, four years later. It also set the stage for Backhouse's amazing gift to Oxford University's Bodleian Library.

By this time Backhouse was forty years old and had come to rue some of his youthful indiscretions – most notably the part that had cost him his university degree. Of course, being the unacknowledged rudder that set the course for much of the Western world's Far Eastern foreign policy did have its benefits, but it would never provide the kind of life for which Backhouse had meanwhile developed a hankering: the leisurely pursuit of scholarly research in the august setting of a classy university. His recent books were an asset, of course, but hardly enough; there were plenty of published scholars of Chinese around, and most had the additional advantage of at least two sets of those Sacred Letters behind their names.

Thus, in the spring of 1913, Backhouse startled the Bodleian's librarians with a fantastic offer: if the library would pay the freight and guarantee him unlimited future access, he would donate to them his entire collection of rare Chinese books and manuscripts, "purchased cheaply from the Imperial Library," which he intended to use as a basis for future scholarly works, and which he also offered to properly catalogue "in the event that a Chinese lectureship may fall vacant one of these days."

To anyone without the prospect of a rare and extremely valuable gift dancing before their eyes, that might have sounded suspiciously like someone trying to bribe his way into an Oxford teaching sinecure. But the Bodleian librarians took one look at Backhouse's gift list and threw all caution to the wind. The money was found, and in due course twenty-nine crates weighing four and a half tons arrived at Oxford, bulging with books and straw.

What the librarians found when they unpacked those crates surpassed their wildest expectations. "It was like digging into King Tut's tomb," one remembered almost reverently years afterwards. "We were simply stunned."

The collection contained more than sixteen thousand volumes of literary rarities and treasures. It included six volumes of the famous *Yung-lo ta tien encyclopedia*, an immaculate copy of a Sung book, full of the autobiographies of the Ming emperors, samples of Sung printing from as far back as 1150 AD, and more than 150 rare scrolls, also dating back to the Ming and Sung dynasties. Its size (which at a stroke quadrupled Oxford's existing Chinese collection) and its value (more than $15 million) had the immediate effect of promoting Oxford University into the Western world's de facto primary centre for Chinese studies.

University officials expressed their gratitude in exactly the way Backhouse had hoped. They scrambled to assure him that his succession to Oxford's Professorship of Chinese – currently held by one T. L. Bullock, aged seventy-four – was a virtual *fait accompli*.

But a year later, following Bullock's death, the university's enthusiasm seemed to have cooled a little. Its Selection Committee fussed and fiddled until the outbreak of the First World War and then, inexplicably, decided to defer the decision until after the war was over – expected to be no more than a year or two.

Alarmed, Backhouse contacted the Bodleian and made a second gift. This one, packed in seventy-six cases and containing more than ten thousand additional volumes, included a splendid Chinese pall with printed inscriptions, fifteen manuscript rolls, 463 extremely old block-printed volumes ("chuan"), an extraordinary manuscript bound entirely in jade, and an autograph scroll by the great calligraphist Wang Hsi-chih.

Its value was estimated at a whopping $30 million.

Once again, the Bodleian's librarians yipped and cheered, and the university fell all over itself expressing its delight and gratitude.

But the university's Selection Committee, for reasons it seemed reluctant to divulge, stuck to its bureaucratic schedule. Perhaps the very extravagance of Backhouse's gifts was making its members wonder. Perhaps they had heard about some of his youthful indiscretions with bogus antiques and jewellery.

Or perhaps they had caught a whiff of the rumour going around London that the Ching-shan diary in *China Under the Empress Dowager* was a fake.

The rumour had apparently originated with G. E. Morrison of *The Times*, Backhouse's one-time benefactor, with whom Backhouse had had a subsequent falling-out. Morrison had goaded various London critics into expressing veiled doubts about the diary's authenticity, calling it, euphemistically, a "mistranslation" and worse.

Backhouse's publisher, William Heinemann, felt such a rumour could bring book sales to a screeching halt. He wrote to

Morrison and demanded he either prove his allegations publicly, or deny them categorically.

Morrison demurred. He insisted he had never said the diary was a fake, but had simply mentioned other people's doubts. For his part, he wasn't prepared to make a statement one way or the other.

This wasn't exactly the categorical denial Heinemann had hoped for, but he decided it would have to do. He issued a press release, quoting only the first half of Morrison's statement. Morrison didn't challenge the release, and book sales remained brisk.

By the spring of 1915 Backhouse was already back in Peking, having run out of money in London trying to convince Oxford to speed up its decision. He was so hard-up that he had just agreed to serve as the Peking agent for John Brown & Company, the British shipbuilding corporation, when an entirely new and different opportunity presented itself.

On June 15, 1915, Backhouse was contacted by the British Secret Service.

The war, at this stage, seemed to be favouring the Allies; the German offensive had been blunted, and its progress stopped. Everyone was digging in for a long trench war. Unfortunately, the Allies were short of weapons, and it would take at least a year to gear up sufficiently to produce them. While they did that, their agents were scouring the world for an interim supply.

China seemed to offer possibilities, since Japan's recent war with Russia, fought on Chinese soil in Manchuria, was rumoured to have left behind a huge stash of captured Russian arms. Could Backhouse use his Chinese contacts to secure some of them for the Allied cause?

The situation was admittedly delicate. Though China was now at peace and technically neutral in the European conflict, any sign that it was siding with the Allies might result in a German declaration of war. In addition, Chinese law expressly forbade the export of munitions.

More to the point, Sir John Jordan, Britain's minister in Peking, had already informed the Foreign Office that his diplomats had found no evidence of stockpiled arms remaining from the Russo-Japanese war.

But Backhouse surprised everyone by announcing, on July 17, that, after appropriately discreet inquiries among his many Forbidden City contacts, he had unearthed a gigantic stash of weapons in southeast China – to wit, 30,000 Mauser rifles in Hankou, 45,000 in Hangzhou, 26,000 in Tianjin, 30,500 in Mukden, and 20,000 in Nanjing. In Nanjing he had even managed to discover 100 Skoda machine guns. Did the Foreign Office want him to proceed with negotiations for their purchase?

Triumphant, the Foreign Office immediately wired instructions, ordering Sir John Jordan to make Backhouse an official agent of the Secret Service and to give him complete authority to negotiate the purchase of these weapons. Backhouse was to report his progress directly and only to Sir John and his Chinese Secretary. The memo reminded Sir John that Lord Kitchener at the War Office was also keeping a watching brief on this file, with direct reports to the prime minister, the cabinet, and even the King.

Suitably chastened, Sir John gave Backhouse his head.

It wasn't long before he had to give him a large line of credit, too. Complications arose and multiplied almost immediately. Mitsubishi of Japan, Backhouse reported, was also surreptitiously buying weapons, which was pushing up the price. The German legation was becoming suspicious, necessitating elaborate and expensive smokescreens. The Chinese generals who controlled the weapons were demanding much "gate-money" (bribes).

Sir John grimaced, but wrote more cheques.

To his relief, Backhouse eventually reported, on August 11, that the necessary contracts with the generals were ready to be signed – for 100,000 Mauser rifles at $100 apiece, plus 350 Krupp machine guns at $5,000 apiece, plus 30 million rounds of ammunition at $100 per thousand. Was this satisfactory to the War Office?

Delighted, Lord Kitchener accepted these terms personally, and wired Backhouse to put the weapons on British ships without informing the Chinese of their destination. He also informed Backhouse that a credit in the amount of $50 million was being transferred to the Hong Kong and Shanghai Bank for this purpose.

It wasn't long before Backhouse was able to reply, via Sir John, that all the complicated details for the transfer of the weapons had been worked out. They would be moved down-river in Chinese junks from their inland origins to the port of Shanghai, where they would be transferred to a "British bottom" for shipment to Hong Kong. Payment in cash would be expected in Shanghai. Backhouse also reiterated that the success of the entire enterprise depended on maintaining total secrecy, which could only be achieved if absolutely all negotiations were conducted by and through Backhouse alone.

This advisory was duly acknowledged and accepted by the War Office.

On September 8, Backhouse reported that the weapons were on their way. A total of six junks from the five cities in which the weapons had been warehoused were now making their way down the Yangtze River towards Shanghai, where they would turn south to rendezvous in Fuzhou. To maintain the appearance of a domestic operation, the flotilla's destination out of Fuzhou would be officially listed as Canton, but everything was arranged to have it change course at the last moment and slip into Hong Kong's harbour on September 18 under cover of night.

Everyone at the Foreign Office was jubilant. So was the War Office. The prime minister and the cabinet were informed. King George was said to be pleased.

Even Sir John was grudgingly placated.

Then, on September 15, Backhouse reported that the junks had been moving more slowly than expected, due to various unspecified difficulties. They were now expected to reach Shanghai on September 20.

On September 22, Sir John wired the Foreign Office that the Chinese officials managing the weapons transfer had informed Backhouse that the six junks had finally left Shanghai harbour that night, bound for Fuzhou. They were, however, not sailing as a flotilla, to avoid attracting attention. (This presumably explained why British naval vessels hadn't seen any sign of the convoy so far.)

On September 24, Backhouse reported that the shipment had hit a snag. The Germans and Austrians had got wind of it and had sent strong protests to the Imperial Palace. Whether Chinese president Yuan Shih-kai would continue to support the operation was now in doubt.

On September 25 Jordan wired the message that the Chinese officials in control of the operation had sent instructions to the junks, "accompanied by characteristic Chinese devices to get over the difficulty of the president's lack of support," to proceed to Hong Kong, but that, because of this unorthodox move, the chance of a miscarriage persisted.

On September 27 Jordan wired: "Backhouse reports that telegram from Governor of Fukien to Chinese authorities here [Peking] states that ships left Fu-chow [Fuzhou] Sunday night."

For the next four days there was silence. Then, Jordan's frustrated report that the governor of Canton, having heard of the flotilla's imminent (that is, official) arrival in his port, had apparently sent out a gunboat to bring it in – making the midnight dodge into Hong Kong harbour impossible.

The junks, Backhouse reported, were now corralled in Huichowon, where the governor was holding them hostage.

The next several days in the Foreign Office were taken up concocting and assessing a welter of possible scenarios, such as trying to bribe the Canton governor. (It was also spent trying to find the location of Huichowon, which no one recognized and no map seemed to show.)

Backhouse's response was a flurry of meetings, negotiations, and bribery (Sir John was kept busy writing more cheques), all laboriously described in a welter of telegrams and memos – but he didn't seem to be getting anywhere.

After two weeks of being driven crazy by Backhouse's confusing reports, contradictory explanations, and unanswered messages, Sir John decided to force the issue. He drove to Backhouse's home and banged peremptorily on his door. When Backhouse let him in, Sir John found his man deep in consultation with an American businessman, George Hall, Peking representative for the American Banknote Company. Backhouse introduced the two men, but Sir John was in no mood for lengthy civilities. He informed Backhouse that he was on his way to a meeting with Liang Shih-i (Controller of the Chinese Customs, and known around the legations as the "Machiavelli of China"), and that Backhouse must come along. "Your participation is mandatory," he said meaningfully.

Backhouse didn't argue, but the American businessman was clearly impressed.

The meeting with Liang Shih-i was, as Sir John had feared, unsatisfactory – at least by Western standards. Liang listened carefully, commiserated politely, but remained diplomatically noncommittal. He seemed to know something about the affair, but then again, perhaps he didn't. He said the junks were probably just offloading the weapons in Canton to convey them to Hong Kong by rail. Where exactly – just to refresh his memory – had Backhouse found these weapons?

By now the Foreign Office was seething with impatience. Lord Kitchener was breathing down their necks. Questions were being asked in cabinet. It looked as if the Secret Service might be called in.

Even King George was demanding an explanation for this frustrating hold-up.

Finally, Sir John decided to play his last card. Without informing Backhouse, he contacted the Chinese president himself.

To his pleasant surprise, the president willingly agreed to a meeting. To his enormous disappointment, however, Yuan Shih-kai professed complete ignorance of Backhouse's weapons transaction. He had no objection in principle, he assured Sir John, as he was sympathetic to the Allied cause, and he was quite willing to issue an export permit if such a large collection of weapons could be found, but he wasn't aware of such a stockpile anywhere in the country.

The experts at the Foreign Office hit the roof. This was, of course, another typical example of Chinese deviousness, secretiveness, and unpredictability. One minute the president was accepting protests from the Germans about the weapons, the next minute he was denying all knowledge of them to the

British – and all the while acting as if he weren't accepting thumping large bribes from their agent, Sir Edmund Backhouse.

Meanwhile, infuriated at Sir John's going behind his back, Backhouse stormed into the British legation to announce that this had short-circuited everything, that his carefully engineered house of cards was collapsing, that he could guarantee nothing further about the weapons, that they were now Sir John's problem, and that he would take no further responsibility for this utterly mishandled undertaking!

Having retaken control of the project, albeit under protest, Sir John spent the next four months trying to get to the bottom of it. He had little luck. No one within his range of official contacts in the Imperial Palace seemed prepared to admit to any knowledge of a flotilla of junks carrying one hundred thousand Mauser rifles and one hundred Skoda machine guns from Shanghai to Canton. No matter how diligently he poked and prodded, he encountered nothing more than the same Oriental deviousness, secretiveness, and unpredictability.

He finally had to conclude that, at the very least, Backhouse had been duped.

The Foreign Office was disappointed too, but, with a world war on its hands, its agents didn't have time to investigate the matter further. Besides, by now their worldwide search had produced other, more likely, prospects.

But for a man like Sir John, the matter simply couldn't be buried in paper. His professional pride and reputation was on the line.

During the following year, while the world war churned on around him, Sir John dug and burrowed more and more obsessively. And the more he examined the facts of Backhouse's voluminous and extraordinarily detailed reports, the more they didn't add up. Who, exactly, could Backhouse's contacts have been, since they didn't seem to be known to anyone else? How was it possible for an operation as large as this one to have reached the stage of involving dozens of Palace officials, generals, military bureaucrats, and port authorities, without ever producing a single piece of objective evidence?

By mid-1917 Sir Jordan had come to an inescapable conclusion.

Edmund Backhouse hadn't been duped at all.

Edmund Backhouse had simply retreated to his little house in west Peking, and there, shielded by the inscrutable world of Chinese politics, he had concocted an astonishingly complex tangle of detailed and convincing reports, describing dozens of completely invented meetings about the sale of entirely imaginary weapons from totally fictitious persons – all of whose hundreds of thousands of dollars of ostensible bribes and "expenses" had gone straight into Backhouse's very real pockets.

And, as a result of those machinations, dozens of cipher clerks had been kept frantically busy for more than half a year at both the Peking legation and Britain's Foreign Office, legation officials had been sent to Japan and Russia, hundreds of critical wartime hours had been wasted at Army Council, War Office, and cabinet meetings, a huge amount of money had been requisitioned and transferred to Shanghai, a lengthy, pointless diplomatic dance between the British Foreign Minister and the Chinese president in Peking had been occasioned – even involving the prime minister and the King of England himself.

The mountains of government files, reports, cables, minutes and letters this had generated didn't even bear thinking about.

But the worst of it was, the only man who realized the true

extent of this boondoggle couldn't afford to blow the whistle on Sir Edmund, because the bulk of the resulting public-relations mess would land directly on his own head.

Sir John requested and received a year's leave to recover his mental equilibrium.

It left the field entirely and unequivocally to Sir Edmund Backhouse.

Ironically, Backhouse's next victim was someone whom Sir John had unknowingly set up himself.

George Hall, a senior agent for the American Banknote Company of New York, had arrived in Peking with the hope of doing big business with the Chinese government. Getting nowhere, he'd decided to hire someone with "inside" connections to lobby for his firm. Someone had suggested Backhouse, and Hall had been meeting with Backhouse, not being terribly convinced by the man, when Sir John had stormed in and collared Backhouse to go see Liang Shih-i. Knowing who Liang Shih-i was, Hall was impressed, and changed his mind about Backhouse on the spot. When Backhouse returned from his meeting at the Imperial Palace, Hall promptly put him on the company payroll.

He didn't give him *carte blanche*, however. Hall was no fool, and he'd already had a bellyful of the vague, interminable, maddeningly polite way in which these Chinese jokers did business. His deal with Backhouse was reasonable expenses plus straight commissions, performance on the barrelhead, no maybes, possiblys, or likelihoods. It was going to be done the American way, with clear, demonstrable results. Hall was going to be impressed, or he wasn't doing business.

Backhouse, of course, was quite prepared to be as impressive as Hall required. After a mere three months, during which he overwhelmed his new boss with voluminous reports of extraordinarily productive meetings with Imperial Palace officials of the very top rank – meetings which admittedly cost the company many thousands of dollars in gate-monies – Backhouse was able to present Hall with a contract, signed by four top ministers plus the Chinese president himself (who also required a sizable "remittance"), committing the Chinese government to the purchase of an astonishing 650 million banknotes over a thirteen-year period.

This contract, worth more than $100 million in profits to the American Banknote Company, caused quite a celebration in New York. George Hall was promptly promoted to vice-president of its Far Eastern Department, with a hefty raise in pay. Backhouse's commission, with bonus and expenses, exceeded $150,000. It was paid to him on the spot, with fervent congratulations and thanks, even before the requisite follow-up order for that year's consignment of banknotes had been received from the Chinese government. While waiting for the order, the company spent more than a million dollars laying in the required stock of paper and inks, and designing the necessary plates and signature blanks.

When the order hadn't arrived several months later, anxious telegrams were sent to Backhouse and Hall. Hall contacted Backhouse; Backhouse checked with his Palace connections. The Japanese were intercepting China's mail, Backhouse reported, and Japanese–Chinese relations were souring. The president was very busy dealing with these difficulties.

Several months later, Backhouse reported that the president had informed him, during an interview which had cost Backhouse thousands of dollars to secure, that his "remittance" had been intercepted by someone – he implied it was the British government – and that the contract wouldn't be honoured until this money had been replaced.

Reluctantly, Hall handed over the required amount.

But the order still failed to materialize.

By September of 1917 Hall had begun to smell a rat, and that rat was an Englishman who had "gone native." Hall wired New York for a copy of the contract and then proceeded to petition the ministers whose signatures committed the Chinese government to its 650 million banknote purchase – one by one.

That's when he ran hard up against Backhouse's first line of defence. Getting an interview with any of the contract's exalted signatories proved utterly impossible for a mere agent of the American Banknote Company. Hall spent a small fortune and three months of effort before coming to that conclusion.

He turned for help to the American legation. Its minister, Dr. Paul Reinsch, judged the signatures on the contract to be genuine. So (at first) did Chinese Secretary of the British legation, Dr. Charles Tenney.

In the meantime the Palace had undergone yet another of its periodic upheavals, many of its major players had shuffled their portfolios, and Backhouse had a whole new set of excuses to choose from.

At this point, Backhouse's victims (who eventually grew to include railway companies, development corporations, and financiers who paid Backhouse millions for faked contracts that never earned them a penny) usually threw in the towel. Trying to follow Backhouse's elusive trail across China's constantly shifting political ground and into its bewildering political labyrinths just didn't seem worth it. And besides, in most cases a convenient war or yet another rebellion usually erased Backhouse's remaining incriminating tracks.

This time, however, Backhouse had met his match – at least in terms of determination and perseverance. Hall was able to convince Dr. Tenney to use a legation meeting with Chinese Grand Secretary Hsu Shih-ch'ang to have his contract's signatures examined more closely. The Grand Secretary pronounced them forgeries, though very good ones. This was eventually confirmed by the Chinese prime minister Tuan Ch'i-jui as well. Both men denied knowing, or ever having had dealings with, Sir Edmund Backhouse.

As soon as he realized Hall hadn't thrown in the towel, Backhouse went to ground at Canada's Empress Hotel in Victoria, British Columbia, where, it turned out, he'd often waited out the tempests his scams provoked. But this could never be more than a temporary solution, because, as soon as his ill-gotten gains had been spent – and Backhouse, we know, was a notorious spendthrift – he had no choice but to return to Peking. His father's instructions to his solicitors had always been ironclad: no remittance unless Edmund remained in China. But when Backhouse returned in the fall of 1918, hoping to slip back into China unnoticed, he found Hall right there waiting for him, more determined than ever.

And this time Hall wasn't interested in any more stories. He just wanted his company's money back. He'd sworn out affidavits against Backhouse in every country in which Backhouse had business dealings, including China, Japan, Canada, and England. The fact that Backhouse was totally broke didn't interest him either. Backhouse had a rich family in England, which was rather sensitive about its reputation – especially in banking circles.

It was a clever deduction, though not, he would discover, an original one. In fact, so many of Backhouse's victims had had the same idea over the years that the Backhouse family in England kept a lawyer on permanent retainer whose only job was to settle the suits and legal threats that resulted from Edmund's endless shenanigans.

This time, too, the matter was grudgingly settled to the victim's satisfaction. In the world of banking, reputation is everything.

But there were some scandals – as the Backhouse family was forced to discover – that money alone couldn't fix. By 1919, suspicions about the authenticity of the Ching-shan diary had grown to the point where they were once again being hinted at in both the American and European press. In 1920, Dutch sinologue Dr. J. Duyvendak expressed some of his doubts publicly, and, in 1926, an Italian biographer of the Empress Dowager, Daniele Vare, stated frankly that he considered the diary a fake.

The most damaging denunciations, however, came from British scholar and journalist William Lewisohn, who demonstrated that significant passages from the Ching-shan diary were actually verbatim quotes from a book by Ching-shan's contemporary, Grand Secretary Wang Wen-shao, and that some of the statements attributed to Jung-lu were actually quotes or paraphrases from – of all people – French statesman Charles Talleyrand.

Various Chinese scholars who examined the diary eventually came to the same conclusion. Chin-liang, editor of the official Chinese history of the Ch'ing Dynasty, found so many errors and discrepancies in the diary that he refused to include it in his historic references. Fan Chao-ying, writing in 1938, pointed out that many of the speeches ascribed to Jung-lu were in fact taken directly from various public memorials, and his colleague Ch'eng Ming-chou added an even more devastating kicker: not only the diary, but many of the other historical documents used in *China Under the Empress Dowager* were phony as well.

Backhouse's gift to the Bodleian Library, meanwhile, had also become tainted. While the collection did indeed contain many rare and priceless books – undoubtedly stolen by Backhouse from the homes of Chinese politicians who had fled Peking in 1900 – its six volumes from the famous *Yung-lo ta tien encyclopedia* of 1726 had proved not to be authentic originals but merely later lithographic reprints. More seriously, at least eighteen of its most rare and valuable manuscripts were now suspected of being outright forgeries.

By the end of the 1930s, both the diary of Ching-shan and the eighteen Bodleian manuscripts had been thoroughly discredited. The only remaining question was, had Edmund Backhouse been duped, or had he forged these documents himself?

Over the years, a growing consensus developed around the conclusion that Backhouse had not been duped.

But before he died, in 1944, Backhouse made one final, outrageous try at a comeback.

He wrote his memoirs.

Not actual memoirs, of course. Not an accounting of the dozens of companies he'd defrauded, or the hundreds of individuals he'd conned into investing in what invariably turned out to be phony antiquities, fake jewellery, or forged manuscripts or books.

They were, instead, yet another, even more triumphant, demonstration of his lifelong penchant for the devious, the secretive, and the unpredictable.

It should be said that Backhouse was not known to be homosexual during his lifetime, though he had raised money in his youth for Oscar Wilde's defence fund, and had always shown a particular predilection for the works of Aubrey Beardsley,

Arthur Rimbaud, Stéphane Mallarmé, Paul Verlaine, and Walter Pater. He had also managed to keep up, even from Peking, with the juicy gossip that swirled around some of the prominent politicians in England who were thought to be gay – such as Lord Alfred Douglas, Lord Drumlanrig, Lord Rosebery, and Sir Edward Grey.

His memoirs, however, suggest that Backhouse either lived his entire life as an extremely active closeted gay, or that he must have had access to some remarkably detailed sources of information about such a life. His account fairly seethes with libidinous frenzy. It is less a memoir than a non-stop two-volume homosexual bacchanal.

All this would be of merely passing interest if it weren't for the astounding list of sexual partners Backhouse claimed – and described in considerable and lurid detail. In addition to every one of the men already named, he included Pierre Loti, J. K. Huysmans, Lord Curzon, Pierre Louys, Villiers de l'Isle Adam, Maurice Barres, Charles Gore, Max Beerbohm, Harry Stanford, André Raffalovich, Henry James, Edmund Gosse, George Moore, and Herbert Spencer. Also included – though as intellectual rather than sexual partners – were Winston Churchill, Leo Tolstoy, William Gladstone, Joseph Conrad, Sarah Bernhardt, Sun Yat-sen, Empress Eugénie, Lord Kitchener, Cardinal Newman, Pope Pio Nono, and the Empress Dowager herself – the latter favouring Backhouse for *both* his intellectual and sexual prowess.

It was this two-volume manuscript, carefully wrapped and preserved, that British historian Hugh Trevor-Roper received from Dr. Reinhard Hoeppli in Switzerland in 1973. Hoeppli's stint as a Swiss consul in Peking in the 1940s had coincided with Backhouse's final years in that city. In fact, it was Hoeppli who had encouraged Backhouse to write his autobiography – though, when Backhouse had handed him the result in 1943, with the request that Hoeppli arrange for its publication, the manuscript had given the good consul quite a shock.

Hoeppli became the owner of the manuscript following Backhouse's death only a year later. Backhouse had spent his final years in the indigenous part of Peking as an increasingly eccentric recluse, wearing felt Chinese robes, keeping his hair in a long pigtail and his beard spaded like a traditional Chinese scholar. He'd become so paranoid about embittered suckers trying to serve him yet another legal summons that he always sent his houseboy ahead during walks or rickshaw rides, to warn of approaching Europeans.

Hoeppli had dithered for several decades, trying to decide what to do with the manuscript. His main worry had been legal; he'd been convinced the work was both obscene and libellous, and, though most of its characters were by then safely dead, there were their relatives and estates to consider.

There was also the question of the manuscript's accuracy. Though Hoeppli had known most of Backhouse's "partners" by name only, he had noticed – and pointed out to Backhouse – that Backhouse's tryst with Arthur Rimbaud, happening at a time when Rimbaud had already been dead for several years, seemed a trifle necrophiliac. (Backhouse had hastily changed the name to "Rambot," and explained that he'd simply confused the name with that of a certain local cobbler.) Hoeppli eventually decided that the determination of the work's overall accuracy – and its eventual fate – would best be left to an accredited historian.

Trevor-Roper's first impression was much the same as Hoeppli's; he judged the work pornographic and obscene. But unlike Hoeppli, he'd known a number of its characters personally, or was at least familiar with their histories. He immediately subjected the work to a more careful historical analysis.

He soon discovered that it was, as he'd suspected, very much a hoax – but one of the most brilliant and imaginative hoaxes he'd ever encountered.

What Backhouse had done was to carefully study the histories of each of his "partners," and pinpoint any periods of time left unaccounted for in the public record. Then he'd ingeniously melded his own life with theirs during exactly those times, claiming to have enjoyed wild flings, trysts, or affairs for the duration. Given the wide range of characters, times, and places he had available to work with, he'd usually found it possible to create these linkages without unduly distorting the known facts about his own life – or theirs.

Edmond Lepelletier's biography of Paul Verlaine, for example, leaves a blank in Verlaine's life from February 10, 1886, when he was known to have been in Paris, to July 19, 1886, when he was known to have entered Paris's Tenon Hospital. Since Verlaine was also known to have taught French in English private schools on several occasions, Backhouse filled in the blank by having him teach at his own private school – St. George's, Ascot – during that time, enabling the two of them to have a torrid fling. The poet's abrupt departure before term's end (to fit in with his known entry into Tenon Hospital) was explained by the sudden death of the school's headmaster on July 14, 1886. This death – a matter of record – neatly framed Backhouse's invention with known events and times, and may well have made his claim irrefutable, had subsequent biographies not filled in that blank by revealing Verlaine's true whereabouts. He'd never left Paris.

It was a deviously cunning and convincing tactic, made more so by Backhouse's remarkably fertile imagination, which garnished these experiences and adventures with such a rich embroidery of detail that Trevor-Roper sometimes found them very difficult to refute, even though he knew from a hundred circumstantial facts that Backhouse was undoubtedly lying.

Trevor-Roper eventually concluded that the work was simply too cleverly dangerous for him to imperil the reputations, even posthumously, of the people Backhouse had caught in his web. He decided not to have it published at all – which is why we have only his description of it in his 1977 biography of Sir Edmund Backhouse, *The Hermit of Peking*, to go on.

It was merely the final example of how Sir Edmund Backhouse, one of the most clever and imaginative con-men of the twentieth century, managed to protect his name and reputation for almost an entire century, despite the astounding facts.

Power to the People

A Dual-Fuel Utility

1. John W. Keely's Bargain-Basement Atomic Energy

In 1625 the famous German astronomer and scientist Johannes Kepler confidently prophesied that an "elemental force" would be discovered by mankind within his century – a force so powerful and pervasive, it would make all of mankind's previous energy-producing efforts look like child's play.

Kepler was a little optimistic.

It wasn't until 247 years later, in 1872 in New York, that the American inventor and electrical engineer John Worrell Keely announced that he had finally discovered – and harnessed – Kepler's mysterious energy.

He called it "Etheric Force," and explained that it was lighter than hydrogen, more powerful than steam or any explosives known to man, and that its vapour was so fine it could penetrate metal. But his most exciting news was that this force could be tapped using nothing more complicated or expensive than ordinary water.

Etheric Force, Keely assured the dubious-looking journalists attending his press conference in the Rochester Room at New York's Fifth Avenue Hotel, was so staggeringly powerful that, when harnessed to an engine he was currently developing, it could propel a thirty-car train from New York to San Francisco at a speed of 75 miles per hour in less than three days, using only a single quart of water for fuel.

Propelling a steamship from New York to Liverpool would require at most a gallon.

In fact, he had already run a 40-horsepower prototype engine at 800 r.p.m. for more than fifteen uninterrupted days on less than a thimbleful.

To demonstrate, Keely led them to a large platform on which he had mounted what he described as a "shifting resonator," a hollow brass sphere filled with a mass of wires, tubes, and plates. This resonator was coupled to a "vibratory liberator-transmitter," a large steel casing surrounded by a bristling array of variously sized hollow steel rods, ranging from needle- to pencil-size in diameter. The transmitter was connected to Keely's "hydra-pneumatic pulsating vacuum engine," which consisted of a heavy, flanged steel drum revolving inside a thick iron hoop. The whole contraption was bolted to a massive cone-shaped base that looked as if it weighed a ton and was made of either blackened cement or black iron.

"Observe," Keely instructed.

He poured a single shot-glass of water into an intake port in the drum of the hydra-pneumatic motor. Then he switched on the resonator and the transmitter. "This transmitter can accommodate seven different kinds of vibrations," he explained matter-of-factly, "though of course each individual vibration is capable of infinitesimal division. My earlier models used goose quills, which weren't nearly as versatile."

He picked up what looked like an ordinary tuning fork and struck it once, sharply. He held it close to the resonator.

Almost immediately, the steel rods of the transmitter emitted a fine haze of water vapour. Seconds later, the indicator needle of a pressure gauge on the motor leaped from 0 to 50,000 pounds per square inch. With a vicious hiss the drum began to spin, violently, its speed increasing to a fearful howl. "I will now apply the power of my motor to this length of industrial cable," Keely shouted, indicating a six-foot-long section of inch-thick steel cable that had been fastened between two enormous iron buckles on a second platform. He threw the lever on a huge hydraulic piston and quickly stepped back.

There was a loud twang as the cable stiffened to a vibrating rigidity. "Cover your heads!" Keely warned. There was a momentary drop in the howl of the motor and then individual wires in the cable began to snap with small sharp explosions. An instant later the entire cable ruptured with a stunning, teeth-rattling bang, showering everyone with sparks and tiny bits of hot cable. A mushroom of grey smoke enveloped the room.

Keely groped through the haze and shut off the resonator. The howl of the spinning drum dwindled to a low hum.

"And that," Keely told the shaken journalists with a satisfied grin, "is merely a very small demonstration of the extraordinary power of Etheric Force."

The headlines in the next morning's *New York Herald*, *New York Journal*, and *New York World* were everything Keely could have wished for. ETHERIC FORCE POWER OF TOMORROW.

ASTOUNDING DEMONSTRATION OF WATER POWER. SIMPLE TAP
WATER WILL POWER TRAINS, SHIPS. By noon, requests for additional demonstrations and talks were pouring in. Newspaper
editors who had ignored Keely's initial invitation changed their
minds. Scientists and engineers, both doubters and believers,
wanted a look. Businessmen smelled a hot new investment
opportunity.

Everybody wanted to see how a thimbleful of water could
power an entire freight train.

After several days of tearing apart more cables, Keely set up a
second demonstration, which effortlessly twisted enormous steel
bars into pretzels. Once again his spectators were immensely
impressed.

It wasn't long before John Keely was talking turkey with
some of America's most prominent businessmen and financiers:
John Jacob Astor II, son of the richest man in America; Charles
B. Franklin, head of Cunard Steamships; Henry S. Sergeant,
president of the Ingersoll Rock Drill Company; and John J.
Cisco, head of the Cisco National Bank. Patent lawyer Charles
Collier chaired the meeting.

Keely was quite content to let the financiers do most of
the talking. They were obviously in familiar territory. They
urged him to take out some patents on his astonishing discovery, and to protect himself by signing on with a couple of
prominent patent attorneys. They suggested he team up with
Thomas Edison, who was then at work developing America's
first electric-light power plant. They seemed to think it terribly important that Keely set himself up as a publicly traded
research-and-development company and get on the New York
Stock Exchange.

Keely went for the idea of the Keely Motor Company of
Philadelphia (where he'd already set up his laboratory), but he

nixed the idea of a patent. The potential of Etheric Force was too enormous, he said, to risk revealing even its smallest aspects. The information required for a patent application might well be enough to enable other scientists or inventors to fill in the blanks and render both his years of research and the huge profit potential of his prototypes worthless.

As for Thomas Edison, well, perhaps, perhaps. But for the moment, all he was willing to do was found the Keely Motor Company, register it on the New York Stock Exchange, and, if any of the gentlemen present wished to avail themselves of this opportunity, it was, of course, their eminent prerogative.

The moneybags liked Keely's independent style.

They committed to an initial purchase of $14-million[*] worth of Keely Motor Company stock, with an assurance of more to come. Keely, in return, asked each one of them to sit on his board of directors. Everyone consented. They all raised their glasses to a most profitable future.

The Keely Motor Company was duly registered on the New York Stock Exchange, the London Stock Exchange, and then the Frankfurt Stock Exchange. Naturally, news of the company's gilt-edged board helped give the stock some serious etheric lift.

Keely's motor soon became a popular topic of discussion in both mainstream and scientific journals. For the next twenty years, the theory of Etheric Force – as much as was known of it – was debated, defended, and debunked by an increasingly impassioned readership. Every prominent scientist or engineer interviewed by the press was invariably asked his opinion on Etheric Force.

---

[*] For consistency, all dollar amounts have been adjusted to 1999 values.

There was no shortage of scientists who thought the entire idea ridiculous. On the other hand, many were prepared to consider it, in theory at least, as possible. Even Thomas Edison was quoted as saying he was keeping an open mind on the subject, and was eager to see further developments. (Edison's remarks promptly provided KMC stock with even more etheric lift.)

Each year, at the KMC's stockholders' meeting, Keely reported steady progress towards the commercialization of his Etheric Force. In 1874, he used the occasion to demonstrate his latest "vibratory generator," which made a separate transmitter and resonator unnecessary. Several years later, he had refined this into an "advanced harmonic vibration liberator." The motor still ripped apart industrial cables and performed other astonishing feats of raw power, but Keely now foresaw its use in human flight (for power gliders) and in futuristic weapons of war. His "vibra-pneumatic Keely Gun," he assured stockholders, would soon become the deadliest weapon in America's arsenal.

But Keely's most intriguing discovery was that Etheric Force was most efficiently engendered by the sound of a violin. (A harmonica or a zither worked acceptably, but "less elegantly.") Over the next decade, from 1875 to 1885, Keely pursued this new physico-musical branch of Etheric Force with mounting enthusiasm. He developed an elaborate physico-musical chart, consisting of a series of overlapping circles, multiple cones of radiating lines, various other mysterious shapes and – most importantly – a series of musical notations, presumably denoting the most efficient and beneficial combination of tones with which to engender Etheric Force.

And indeed, his demonstrations became increasingly more explosive – smashing huge rocks and propelling projectiles through timbers two feet thick. This sometimes caused fires and considerable damage to his laboratory. Keely reported these triumphs as especially significant leaps of progress at his stock-holders' meetings, and all investors who held more than a million dollars' worth of KMC stock received enlarged, expensively framed reproductions of The Chart to hang in their living rooms or galleries.

Curiously, while Keely's pursuit of physico-musical Etheric Force lost him some of his less imaginative stockholders, it brought on board a large number of female investors, who, though perhaps less familiar with Keely's scientific theories, seemed irresistibly attracted to the idea of a motor energized by water and music.

One such investor, a wealthy widowed journalist who eventually bought more than $8 million worth of KMC stock, became so enthralled with this idea that she spent a great deal of time with Keely and began to write impassioned scientific defences of his theories for popular periodicals such as *Lippincott's*. In time, Clara Jessup Moore was moved to write an entire book on Etheric Force, *Keely and His Discoveries*, in which she explained how, in essence, quadruple negative harmonics caused just enough atomic disintegration of the fuel's water molecules to promote the triplification of the resulting air and water vapours into pure and intrinsically indivisible pulsating Etheric Force. (*Scientific American* called it all incomprehensible bunk, but John Keely was pleased to assure Moore's readers that, contrary to the "fulminations of vested interests defending established prejudices," the lady had got it exactly right.)

By 1890, the Keely Motor Company had taken in and spent in excess of $239 million, but still hadn't produced a commercially viable motor. Keely, however, remained unperturbed. He explained to his investors that all truly great scientific developments invariably took more time and money than first expected, and that a discovery as revolutionary as Etheric Force – which would inevitably necessitate a complete revision of physical theory – might quite reasonably take longer than most. It could expect to be attacked more virulently as well, and such attacks were bound to become more intense as his undertaking approached complete success.

Attacks on John Keely were indeed intensifying – and not only because his experiments weren't convincing the editors of *Scientific American*. His lifestyle as president of the Keely Motor Company was worrying some of his less patient investors. Over the years, its impact on the company's books had become down-right etheric all on its own.

The guest lists to his parties at his palatial Philadelphia mansion, for example, had risen from dozens to hundreds; his stable of custom-made automobiles (including a rare 1871 S. H. Roper steamer and an early single-cylinder Duryea) was rumoured to be priceless. Also, Keely seemed to be developing a marked preference for the company of the ladies over the requirements of the company. This might not have been as problematic if the work had continued under the direction of an assistant or partner, but Keely had always refused both; when it came to his invention, he mistrusted anyone and everyone.

So, when Keely wasn't in his laboratory, work on Etheric Force wasn't happening.

Even Clara Moore urged Keely to reconsider his decision not to team up with Thomas Edison. Surely, she reasoned, the most prominent inventor in America could be trusted to keep Keely's secret, and perhaps his assistance might speed up the work and produce the motor a little sooner. Even Keely couldn't deny that it was becoming harder and harder to keep investors convinced that the long wait was worth the candle.

But Keely remained unconvinced and unruffled.

He explained that his opulent lifestyle was necessary to attract additional research funds for the company. He lectured his investors on the sources of insight and inspiration. They didn't just happen in the laboratory, he said. One way or another he was *always* working on his invention – day or night, asleep or awake, in the laboratory or out of it. There was simply no way you could speed up such a natural process by unnatural means.

In fact, compared to other great pioneering scientific enterprises, work on Etheric Force was actually progressing at a positively meteoric rate.

Aside from the criticism of *Scientific American*, whose doubts over the years had escalated from cautious questions to open challenges, another dedicated Keely critic was Clarence Moore, son of Clara Jessup Moore. Clarence had been less than thrilled to see his inheritance slowly but inexorably falling into the hands of America's high priest of Etheric Force, and had tried for years to convince various engineers, physicists, and even psychologists at the University of Pennsylvania to take a closer look at Keely's claims. But Keely was so effectively buffered by his influential board of directors that no one at the university had shown much interest in committing professional hara-kiri.

All that changed on March 14, 1898, when John Keely died unexpectedly at the age of seventy-one – without ever having revealed the secret of Etheric Force to anyone.

For twenty-six years, he had successfully held his critics at bay. During all that time he had never given so much as an inch in his tug-of-war with his investors. Even his most intimate friends and supporters had never been able to coax a hint of the secret out of him.

So no one was surprised when, mere hours after the news of

his death, Keely's laboratory became the scene of an unseemly free-for-all. Directors, investors, friends, and enemies yelled and flailed at each other, everyone trying to find and pilfer whatever of Keely's documentation and equipment they could get their hands on. In the year that followed, threats, legal action, counter-offers, and surreptitious meetings became the order of the day, as the more successful of the grave-robbers tried to piece together a system for which they'd only managed to purloin unconnected parts.

It proved impossible – not only because of too much greed and technical ignorance, but because there were strong indications that Keely had foreseen the debacle. He had, apparently, already removed various vital parts of both his motor and its "liberator," so that no one would be able to unpuzzle the secret of his Etheric Force posthumously.

But Keely had failed to anticipate the strength of an equivalent power: the anger and determination of a son who believed he'd been robbed of his mother's affections.

Frustrated at his lack of success in trying to negotiate with Keely's former investors and friends, and at an impasse with his still-infatuated mother, Clarence Moore finally managed to rent Keely's former laboratory and then went to work on it, exploring it inch by inch, looking for anything Keely's grave-robbers might have overlooked in their indecorous haste that March 14 night.

It wasn't long before he discovered an anomaly.

The laboratory's floor had been raised.

It had to be, because there was a short, two-step riser at the entrance, and – he then realized – the laboratory door had been shortened by about a foot.

Moore hurried home for a crowbar.

By midnight the laboratory floor was a splintered mess, and Moore was well on his way to unpuzzling Keely's secret.

Between the false and the original floor lay a network of steel pipes, all nine inches in diameter but with only a three-inch bore. That meant they were designed to withstand enormous pressures. Concealed under a thin veneer in several places immediately under the floor, and also in the walls, Moore found spring valves that could be operated unobtrusively by foot or elbow, releasing or stopping whatever flowed through the pipes.

The pipes led into the walls and down several floors into the basement, where Moore found an immense steel globe half buried in dirt. Hauled out, it weighed more than 6,600 pounds, and was fitted with connections for an industrial-sized compressor, which appeared to have been removed.

And that, it turned out, was the secret of Keely's Etheric Force: ordinary air, compressed to spectacularly high pressures. The air had been produced by the compressor in the basement, stored in the buried steel globe (a pressure tank) at 50,000 pounds per square inch, then drawn up as needed whenever Keely pressed a hidden spring valve with his foot or elbow to "run" his motor.

Playing a violin wouldn't have had any effect on his apparatus at all. It had simply been a device to distract his audience while he pressed the valve.

As for the motor's enormous power, highly compressed air does indeed have extraordinary power, enough to run trains and ships and large industrial engines, just like steam — but like steam, it takes a great deal more than mere water to generate.

Moore's investigation of Keely's past turned up even more fraud. Keely's "credentials" as an inventor and electrical engineer were totally bogus; Keely had spent most of his youth working as a circus carny and an occasional carpenter. Ironically, he had stumbled across Kepler's famous prophecy in the very magazine that eventually became his loudest critic: *Scientific American*.

During his twenty-six years as president of the Keely Motor Company he had managed to relieve some of America's most sophisticated money-men (not to mention some of America's richest ladies) of close to $1.5 billion. Unfortunately for them all, he had spent most of it by the time he died.

His bank accounts, at any rate, contained little more than uncompressed air.

2. Louis Enricht's Gas from a Garden Hose

The timing couldn't have been better for Louis Enricht.

It was 1916 and the First World War was raging in Europe. Gasoline everywhere was scarce and getting scarcer. Even in the United States – which hadn't yet entered the war – it was already selling for an unprecedented $3.75 per gallon, and the price was going nowhere but up. The U.S. government was urging all Americans to conserve fuel wherever possible.

Enricht had spent much of the previous decade working on a solution to the rising price of gas, and now the seventy-year-old inventor and tinkerer had finally found it. At a press conference that brought dozens of newspapermen out to his home in Farmingdale, Long Island, he announced that he had discovered an additive that turned ordinary water into automotive fuel.

Even better than that, the additive was so common and widely available that America's gasoline shortages were effectively over.

Best of all, it reduced the price of gasoline to a mere ten cents a gallon.

Naturally, Enricht was prepared to demonstrate his product. He invited the newspapermen to examine the automobile that was parked in his driveway. He urged them to check that there was no false bottom in its gas tank, and no hidden auxiliary tanks anywhere within the car's body. He pointed out that there were no extra fuel lines connected to its carburetor.

When the newsmen were satisfied, Enricht opened his gas tank's drain and demonstrated that the tank was empty. He tapped a stick against its side and it rang hollow. He shoved the stick down its filler tube and showed that it was dry.

Then he filled a white china pitcher with water from his garden hose. He offered it to several reporters to taste.

Everyone agreed that it was ordinary tap water.

Now Enricht produced a small vial filled with a green liquid. He poured the liquid into the china pitcher, stirred it, and dumped the mixture into the gas tank.

"Okay, crank her up!" he instructed.

Several newsmen leaped to the task. The engine roared into life, then raced furiously.

"Go ahead," Enricht grinned. "Take her around town for a spin."

Half a dozen reporters jumped into the car and drove off. Fifteen minutes later they were back to let four more of their colleagues run the test. Everyone had to admit the car had run smoothly and strongly, with no problems and plenty of power.

"Will that stuff run in my car, too?" one reporter challenged.

"Of course," Enricht said. "Bring it over."

The gas tank in the newsman's car was drained and refilled with Enricht's mixture. His car too ran on the fuel without problems.

Now everybody wanted to fill their gas tanks with Enricht's mixture.

"I don't have enough for everybody," Enricht apologized. "Just enough for two or three. You guys decide who gets it. Then go and tell the world."

"He's pulling the wool over your eyes," shouted William Haskell, publisher of the Chicago *Herald*, over a bad connection to his reporter in New York. "Yeah, I know he put the stuff in your tank, I read your dispatch, but there's gotta be a hitch there somewhere! Hire some mechanics!"

Three days later, when his man reported back that the mechanics hadn't been able to find anything wrong, Haskell decided to investigate for himself. Giving Enricht no warning, he arrived at his door unannounced, identified himself, and asked the inventor to give him an on-the-spot demonstration.

To his surprise, Enricht agreed. But before he gave Haskell the demonstration, he made some phone calls to check the publisher's credentials. He explained that the oil companies had begun sending out investigators disguised as newspapermen, and he was being followed in the streets. "I've got to be careful to know who I'm dealing with," he said.

Haskell spent the entire afternoon with Enricht. He came to like the old man's stern mien and careful manner. It gave an impression of reliability and straightforwardness. There didn't seem to be anything of the snake-oil salesman or carpetbagger about him. He could be a bit nervous, and inclined to name-drop ("Henry Ford is interested in my formula too, you know"), but overall his grain seemed pretty straight. He was even willing to let Haskell examine his green tincture more closely, and to daub a little of it on his tongue.

"What's the bitter-almond taste?" Haskell asked.

"Prussic acid," Enricht shrugged. "But it's not an active ingredient. I just add it to disguise another odour that would let you recognize my main ingredient far too easily."

The two men grinned at each other.

Haskell drove around town on Enricht's fuel for more than an hour. He used his own car rather than Enricht's. Enricht came along, but merely to ensure that no one got the idea of draining off a little sample. By the time the publisher dropped the inventor off in front of his house, he'd become a convert.

"I have just sat in on the beginning of an industrial revolution," he enthused in the *Herald* the next day. "A couple of turns of the crank and the engine started, racing fiercely with an open throttle. It ran even and true. I got in the car and drove it all around Farmingdale, and never had a bit of trouble. It was a most remarkable demonstration indeed.

"If anyone had tried to convince me of what I witnessed myself, I would not have believed him."

After the appearance of Haskell's unequivocal endorsement, Enricht's telephone rang non-stop for a week. His mailman complained about the deluge of mail that arrived every day. Newspapers from all over the country wanted interviews, backgrounders, demonstrations.

One organization that was especially curious was the Automobile Club of America. Its chief laboratory engineer, Dr. Ferdinand Jehle, wrote asking whether Enricht might be willing to submit a sample for testing by the club's laboratory. "Merely to see whether it's of value," he explained. He promised not to attempt to discover the tincture's ingredients. "We just want to find out if it's worth all the excitement," he told a reporter. "Or, to be plain, if it's a fake."

Enricht turned down the club's request, but he did divulge to Jehle that the formula's principal ingredient wasn't combustible in itself, but that it had an affinity for oxygen in water. This affinity, he said, caused the water's oxygen molecules to separate from its hydrogen molecules, which then recombined in an engine's combustion chamber with explosive force. That, in a nutshell, was how the formula worked.

Enricht's explanation provoked his first serious challenge from America's scientific community. "No chemical can be added to water that will make it combustible," huffed Columbia University chemistry professor Thomas Freas. "Water may be broken up by electrolysis, but the energy required will be exactly equal to that produced on combustion. That is, nothing would be gained."

Dr. C. F. Chandler, an internationally acclaimed metallurgist, was similarly unimpressed. "The proposition is absolutely impossible," he insisted. "It's trying to get something out of nothing. True, several substances – metallic sodium, for example – will release hydrogen from water, but to get enough hydrogen to equal the energy in one gallon of gasoline would take 57.5 pounds of sodium. At 25 cents a pound, such energy would cost $14.37 a gallon!"

Louis Enricht simply shrugged. "Then it's a damned good thing I'm not using metallic sodium, isn't it?" he grinned.

One of Enricht's most prominent supporters was his next-door neighbour, Benjamin Franklin Yoakum. Yoakum was a former president of the St. Louis and San Francisco Railroad, a member on the board of directors of several other railroads, and a well-connected financier.

"I've known Louis Enricht a long time," Yoakum was quoted as saying in the *New York Times*. "I have confidence in his invention. I have used it in my own motor car."

The public debate grew so heated that even Henry Ford became tantalized. He telegraphed his Washington press agent (who had indeed made an exploratory call to Enricht in response to the inventor's initial press conference): "PUT ENRICHT ABOARD WOLVERINE EXPRESS RAIN OR SHINE; DELIVER F.O.B. TO MY OFFICE IN DETROIT."

Enricht took his time replying, and when he did he explained that, with all this uproar, he was afraid to leave his house unattended. Besides that, he was disinclined to travel. But if Mr. Ford wished to see him, he was available in Farmingdale at his convenience, any time.

The extent of Ford's interest became evident three days later when the *New York Times* reported: "Ford Visits Enricht about Motor Fuel. Tycoon and Inventor Talk for an Hour. Ford Will Come Again and See Ten-Cent-a-Gallon Mixture Work."

Interviewed after the meeting, Henry Ford's New York sales manager, Gaston Plantiff, acknowledged, "Mr. Ford is something of a chemist himself, you know, and he asked Mr. Enricht a number of specific questions. The answers must not have been unsatisfactory, or the matter would have been dropped."

They weren't, and it wasn't.

The next day the *New York Times* quoted Henry Ford as saying that he would buy Enricht's formula outright if it passed certain stringent tests. "I wrote Mr. Enricht today," Ford said. "We will have a test in a week or so, and I'll be there. I don't know what to think of it, but we've had men working along that line for some time."

Several days later, three Ford employees delivered a brand-new

Ford sedan to Enricht's home, for use in the upcoming tests. They also dropped off an envelope containing $15,000 in "earnest-money."

Enricht cheerfully banked the cash and enjoyed the car — but if Ford had expected that a mere $15,000 would be enough to instil a sense of obligation in the wily inventor, he was seriously mistaken.

Less than a week later, Maxim Munitions of New Jersey, one of America's largest weapons manufacturers, announced that it had not only negotiated exclusive rights to manufacture Enricht's gasoline formula, it had also made a deal with the town of Farmingdale to buy enough of its industrial land to accommodate a laboratory and factory to manufacture Enricht's key ingredient. The company reported that it had applied for a patent on Enricht's behalf, and pointed out that the beneficiaries would include not only America's motorists but also America's farmers, who would now get inexpensive power for their harvesting and wood-cutting. "Experiments prove that Enricht's invention, perfected in some minor details, will be revolutionary in character," a company spokesman said.

The company refused to reveal financial details of the deal, but the U.S. *Patent News* felt no such constraints. "It is said that Dr. Enricht received $15 million in cash and 100,000 shares of Maxim stock ($157.50 a share)," it reported.

Over in Detroit, Henry Ford practically choked on his caviar. But, after a day of burning up the phone lines and several strategy sessions, he seemed to have regained the driver's seat. "We are going ahead as before," he replied to a *New York Times* reporter. "I was talking with Mr. Enricht today, and he said there was absolutely no truth in the statement that Maxim Munitions had acquired the rights to his mixture."

"Not so," denied Maxim Munitions treasurer William Benson. "I do not think Mr. Enricht was correctly understood. We certainly have the contract."

The *New York Times*, which was obviously being used as the facilitator in this game of chicken, permitted itself this wry editorial at the expense of Enricht's doubters: "It looks at least a little as if the wise ones had been somewhat hasty in saying offhand what can and can't be done, and it may be that – not for the first time – they are to be proven wrong by an inventor whose pretensions they had loftily ridiculed."

The first outward sign that Henry Ford had been finessed was a suit against Enricht by the Ford Motor Company to recover its car.

That didn't surprise too many people. Ford had a reputation for overselling his hand.

But the next development surprised almost everyone. After seeing its stock gain 50 per cent at the news of an Enricht deal, and then surge yet again at the news of Ford's capitulation, Maxim Munitions admitted that it, too, had failed to hold on to the elusive formula.

Then who was holding the winning hand? It was obvious that *somebody* was pumping a lot of dollars into Enricht's bank account. Signs of his new wealth were everywhere. A huge new home was being built on a hill above his existing house. Foundations for a large laboratory and factory were going in at the back of his property. The Ford sedan had been swapped for a fancy imported number, and Enricht was strutting about in clothes that were clearly a match for those of any of the industrialists he'd been taking on.

And then things became *really* mysterious.

In a legal suit against Enricht that incidentally revealed the holder of the winning hand to have been none other than Enricht's next-door neighbour, Benjamin Yoakum, the railroad financier charged in U.S. Supreme Court that, contrary to an agreement he had signed with Louis Enricht on April 12, 1917 – six days after the United States had entered the First World War – Enricht had still not handed over his formula. And the reason for this, according to Yoakum's charge, involved not merely fraud, but treason.

Yoakum's company – the National Motor Power Company – which he had founded specifically to market Enricht's formula, had quickly found a potential customer in the British government. Several high-ranking British infantry officers had promptly arrived to investigate Enricht's claims. Enricht had demonstrated his mixture for them, exactly as he'd previously done for New York's newspaper reporters, and the officers had hurried home with a favourable report. It was when they'd returned to New York with the authorization to buy a production licence for the formula that problems had started.

At first, Enricht had merely dragged his feet. Then he'd obstructed the negotiations with a lot of irrational objections and demands. Finally, he had informed Yoakum that he was not in a position to licence the production of his formula until "after the war."

This bizarre condition had struck Yoakum as suspicious enough that he had hired a private detective to investigate. And indeed, the detective had soon discovered that Enricht had met secretly on several occasions with a Captain Franz von Papen, a military attaché with the German embassy in Washington, who had recently been expelled by the U.S. State Department for "behaviour incompatible with diplomatic protocol" (that is, spying). These meetings had taken place on board the German submarine *Deutschland* while it was tied up in Baltimore harbour from July 1 to August 3 of the previous year.

At the conclusion of these meetings, the detective claimed, the German government had paid Enricht the sum of $24 million.

This was the nub of Yoakum's accusation. "We have grave fears," he said, "that Enricht has already disclosed his secret to the German government, and that the seeming plentifulness of gasoline in that country is due to the fact that they are already manufacturing Enricht's liquid on a large scale." He demanded that the U.S. attorney general, Thomas W. Gregory, seize Enricht's papers and close down his factory until the matter could be fully investigated.

Acting under wartime powers, Gregory did just that – but to little avail. Trying to find a formula that no one had ever seen was like searching for a message in a dictionary. There were boxes of scribbled papers, but no one could make sense out of any of them.

Enricht, meanwhile, readily admitted to his meetings with von Papen, but claimed the Germans had offered him $150,000 for an older invention that had nothing to do with gasoline. They'd been interested in his method of producing artificial stone, which had no military use and was therefore quite legal to sell. Despite this, however, he had turned them down. "I'm a patriot," he insisted. "If the American government wishes to have my most recent discovery – a new process for extracting nitrogen from air – I'd be happy to give it to them."

Refusing to be sidetracked, Yoakum got a court order to search Enricht's safety-deposit box at the First National Bank in Farmingdale. It turned out to contain nothing but a few Liberty bonds.

The formula, Enricht now informed the court, didn't exist on paper any more anyway. He had burned all his notes for fear of theft by the oil companies. The only place where the clues to the formula for his gasoline substitute remained was in his head.

A court order to search someone's head being something that even wartime powers couldn't provide, Yoakum threw in the towel. There wasn't any point in trying to get his money – rumoured to be in the order of $10 million – back from Enricht, because the war would probably be over by the time the courts got around to dealing with such a suit. Besides, Enricht had already agreed to hand over the formula at war's end anyway.

Assuming his word would be any more reliable then.

Which Yoakum had growing reason to doubt.

Louis Enricht, meanwhile, was living the life of Riley. Though no one in Farmingdale (or anywhere else) could figure out what his game was, the upshot was that he was suddenly a very rich man and seemed to have played at least three very large, rich, and resourceful corporations to a draw. He had somehow managed to convince each of them to fill his pockets with a great deal of money, and had then managed to put himself safely beyond their legal reach while he enjoyed the benefits of their largesse. In addition, it seemed distinctly possible that he had convinced not one but two foreign governments to line his pockets as well.

For anyone keeping score, his take so far ranged anywhere from $12 million to $35 million – and no telling what was yet to come.

All this for an elusive formula that no one had yet seen, for a mixture that no one had yet produced.

Or if they had, they'd lived to rue the day.

Shortly after Louis Enricht died, in 1924 at the age of seventy-eight, having managed never to divulge the secret of his mysterious formula to anyone, a Dr. Miller Reese Hutchinson, then chief engineer for the Thomas Edison Corporation, set himself the task of discovering Enricht's formula. It struck him that this shouldn't be as impossible as it sounded, what with various clues that Enricht had mentioned, his demonstrations that various New York reporters had described in their newspapers, plus Hutchinson's own prodigious knowledge of chemistry and internal-combustion fuels.

It wasn't long before he believed he had the answer.

To prove it, he poured a little vial of colourless liquid (Enricht had probably added colour as a disguise) into a gallon of water and took it to the Brooklyn Navy Yard for a test. He poured the mixture into the gas tank of a Navy dockside loading machine and cranked it.

The engine roared into life, then raced furiously.

Hutchinson mixed up a larger batch and ran the engine at various speeds for several days.

The test ended when the engine seized. When Navy mechanics took it apart, they found its cylinders so badly corroded, they pronounced it beyond repair.

"Enricht's secret ingredient was undoubtedly acetone," Hutchinson explained. "It's a volatile, inflammable liquid, commonly used to make smokeless gunpowder. It's very cheap, you can mix it with water, and it will indeed run an internal-combustion motor."

He grinned.

"But it will eventually destroy it in the process."

Gangs That Couldn't Loot Straight

A Bungling Trio

"Success," according to British author Stephen Pile, "is highly overrated. Man's real genius lies in quite the opposite direction."

To promote this fact, Pile founded the Not Terribly Good Club of Great Britain, a gathering of like-minded failure enthusiasts "from all walks of ineptitude," who exhibited their art in their own *Salon des Incompetents* and parallelled Britain's famous Henley Royal Regatta with a regatta of their own – featuring only a single air-mattress, to avoid contamination by the "baser competitive urges." (The regatta, unfortunately, was so well attended that it had to be cancelled for fear of suffering a demonstrable success.)

But the club's most disastrous project was the publication of *The Book of Heroic Failures*, which celebrated some of England's most abject flops in politics, sports, business, and crime. When the book made the bestseller list, Pile was summarily ejected as the club's president for bringing the shame of success upon its membership. When the book's continued success resulted in more than twenty thousand inquiries from readers interested in joining the Not Terribly Good Club of Great Britain, its members saw no alternative but to disband the organization entirely, since its roaring success had become incompatible with its stated objectives.

Pile, however, went on to assemble a second volume, *Cannibals in the Cafeteria*, which celebrated the substandard in human endeavours throughout the Western world – notably in the area of crime. Some examples:

1. The Safecracker Suite

British safecracker David Balfour had it all figured out. On the night of the second-last day of the month – the night before payday, when the Cheltenham Credit Union's vault would be bursting with money to cash all those paycheques – he would break in, drill his way into the vault, load up the cash, and live happily ever after.

To improve his chances, he invested in a fancy new pneumatic chiselling drill, a tool that can drill and hammer at the same time. This, apparently, was considered by the safecracking fraternity the *sine qua non* of safecracking equipment.

Breaking into the credit union proved a piece of cake. Access to the vault proved no problem either. But once he'd begun to drill, Balfour realized he had himself a serious challenge. The vault's walls, made of alternating layers of steel and reinforced concrete, were pushing his drill's capabilities to the limit.

He forced his entire weight against the handle. He drilled and hammered until the vibrations shuddered through his body like a fibrillator. The bit ground and pounded valiantly, but progress was slow.

By midnight, he was less than halfway through. He was soaked in sweat and coated with concrete dust. The drill against his stomach was so hot that he had to fit a glove between his shirt and the handle to avoid scorching himself.

By 3:00 he was three-quarters of the way through. By dawn he was chiselling out the last barrier, absolutely exhausted. But all that money, that glorious payola, was now just minutes away.

That's when the vault's door suddenly swung open – by itself.

It had been unlocked, Balfour discovered, all along.

It had been unlocked because the vault was empty. No cash. No securities. Just some credit forms and a stack of deposit slips.

The answer was staring him in the face from the calendar on the vault wall. It was Thursday, May 1, 1980. It wasn't April 30, 1980. All the paycheques had been cashed the previous day.

What Balfour said to himself at that point was undoubtedly unprintable. What he did was throw his expensive, now useless, drill into his duffel bag and hightail it out of the credit union. He hid the bag in the bushes on a nearby empty lot for future recovery and swung clear. He would return for the bag when the heat had cooled off a little.

When he returned a few days later, he walked straight into the arms of the law.

His overheated drill had scorched the fabric of the duffel bag. Some passing schoolboys had smelled it, investigated, and taken the bag to the police. The police had returned the bag to the vacant lot and staked it out.

Balfour received eight years behind bars to mull over his tactical errors.

2. Getting with the Concept

Another British safecracker, from Chichester, had designs on the safe of Chichester's posh Southern Leisure Centre. He broke in on a Saturday night (the centre didn't open until noon on Sunday) and laboriously hauled in a brace of acetylene tanks, gas hoses, torch tips, and other metal-cutting equipment he'd recently bought in an effort to improve his safecracking performance.

But, when he lit the torch and applied it to the safe's door hinges, it didn't improve his performance one bit. There was a satisfying shower of sparks and an impressive splattering of metal, but the results were puzzlingly additive rather than subtractive. The more he applied the torch, the more the metal puddled and clogged, building up on the hinges, the frame, even the doorlock. There was clearly something wrong with this equipment, but several hours of continued fireworks didn't bring success any closer. Our safecracker finally had to abandon his efforts at self-improvement, gather his equipment, and beat a strategic retreat.

Investigators the next morning stared uncomprehendingly at the mangled mess.

The safecracker, it turned out, had used a *welding* torch instead of a cutting torch. Instead of being cut open, the safe's door had been welded shut so thoroughly that it took a professional welder more than two hours to undo his nocturnal colleague's efforts.

3. Timing *Is* Everything

A gang of four Italian bank-robbers spent weeks casing a regional branch of the Credito Italiano in the peaceful little town of Artema, about a two hours' drive from Rome.

Since the credito was the town's only bank, there was good reason to believe that its vault would make for excellent pickings. The gang had drawings of the building's floor plan, its entrances and exits, even its electrical circuits and outlets. Everything was planned to proceed with split-second timing and military precision.

They would arrive at the bank in their stolen getaway car at exactly two minutes before closing time (3:00 p.m.), get out, form up, then follow their leader into the bank at a dead run. Inside, both bank personnel and customers would be made to lie face-down on the floor by the leader, while the other three scooped the tills. At the end of precisely three minutes, the operation would be terminated, no matter how much money had to be left behind. (They were always very textbook about this, it seems.) The getaway car would be abandoned within a mile of the village, with a second vehicle – also stolen – substituted for the return run to Rome.

On Friday, February 3, 1980, the robbers made their move. At precisely 2:58 p.m. a blue Renault screeched to a stop in front of the Credito Italiano. Four masked men spilled out of the car. They formed up, pulled out their pistols, and headed for the bank's entrance at a dead run. At the door the leader reached for the handle, gave a powerful tug, and slammed straight into unyielding plate glass. He fell to the sidewalk, out cold.

For a moment the robbers milled about in confusion. The door to the bank was locked. Two startled clerks stared back from their perches behind the bank's main counter. Strollers along Artema's main street stopped short to better witness this surreal spectacle.

Left with no other option, the robbers grabbed their unconscious leader, dragged him hastily into their car, and zoomed off down the street. Their three minutes, after all, were up.

It had all occurred with split-second timing and military precision. Every eventuality known to bank-robbing had been considered and taken into account. A contingency plan for every variation to the formula had been memorized.

The only element they had not foreseen was that Friday, February 3, 1980, had been a slow day.

And on slow days, the bank's employees often closed the bank a few minutes early.

Extortion by Remote Control

The Amazing Ingenuities of Dagobert Duck

At first, it seemed a routine case of ordinary extortion.

On June 14, 1992, just after midnight, an exploding pipe bomb made an impressive mess of the china/housewares section of the Karstadt department store on Hamburg's Moenckeberg Street. Besides reducing a roomful of Rosenthal, Seltmann, Villeroy, and von Hutschenreuther chinaware to rubble, the bomb also triggered the sprinkler system, which flooded the entire second floor.

Only hours after the store opened for business that morning, a courier-delivered letter from the extortionist demanded the payment of $1 million* to avoid further bomb blasts. "This one

---

* For consistency, all dollar amounts have been adjusted to 1999 values.

was just a Christmas cracker," it stated. "The next one will be a catastrophe."

The letter was signed DAGOBERT DUCK.

The signature caused a few anxious grins around the administration office. Dagobert was the German name for a Walt Disney creation, Donald Duck's Uncle Scrooge, the notorious miser who loved taking baths in whole tubfuls of his heartlessly acquired money.

This sounded like an extortionist with ambitions.

But the German state police in Hamburg weren't overly concerned. Extortion had one of the lowest success rates of all federal crimes in Germany. Almost anyone could set a bomb or kidnap a victim as an opening gambit; the real challenge was getting away with the ransom money. That's where more than 95 per cent of extortionists got caught. And the German police were well experienced in this department. Decades of postwar terrorist attacks – by the likes of the Baader-Meinhof gang, Hamas, Black September – had given them plenty of opportunity to develop effective counter-measures. This Dagobert was as good as in handcuffs already.

Dagobert's second letter, bearing a Berlin postmark, arrived on July 14. It contained a small key.

"Be ready for action tomorrow," it read. "Pack the money in thousand-mark bills into a sealed plastic bag. You'll need a car with a full tank of gas. I'll be in touch sometime after 4:00 p.m.

"P.S. Don't lose the key."

Deducing that a full gas tank meant the handover wouldn't be attempted in Hamburg, the police ordered several helicopters and mobile units to stand by. The instructions about the plastic bag resulted in an alert order for all marine policing units within range of Hamburg. A standard protocol with the German Federal Railroad – trains had occasionally been used in hand-over attempts – already existed. This gave the police permission to board any train targeted by an extortionist, and to require its engineer to stop the train anywhere along its route.

Dagobert was back in touch by 3:55 p.m. the next day. In another letter he ordered the money couriers to drive to Bad Doberan and to use the previously delivered key on a box fastened to an electrical pole at kilometre 79. "You'll have to hurry," he added cryptically.

Bad Doberan was about two hundred kilometres northeast of Hamburg. Three police officers dressed as civilians roared off in an unmarked car.

They found the power pole just before 6:00 p.m. There was a large wooden box attached to it, about eighteen inches square by ten inches deep.

Inside, they found their first indication that Dagobert Duck was a lot smarter than your average extortionist.

It was a black metal box with an antenna on top. Its back was fitted with four electromagnetic disks. There was a zippered plastic pouch attached to its front.

"Continue on to Rostock," a note in the pouch instructed. "Put the money into the pouch and attach this entire device to the rear bumper of the last car of the Rostock–Berlin Express, departing Rostock at 8:58 p.m. To activate the magnets, move the lever on the left-hand side."

As they drove on to Rostock, another twenty kilometres farther east, the officers conferred by cellphone with a police electronics engineer in Berlin.

"It's probably got batteries inside, to power the electromagnets," the expert suggested. "Once you activate them with that lever, they'll keep the contraption magnetically stuck to the train while en route. Then, from some hiding spot along the tracks, he'll presumably deactivate that circuit with a remote-control device. That, in turn, will deactivate the magnets. The contraption will drop off the train, money and all."

"Ingenious bastard," one of the officers grinned.

"When does the Berlin Express leave Rostock?" the engineer wanted to know.

"At 8:58 p.m."

"It'll be dark by the time he hits the button. You guys won't be able to see a thing."

The same thought had obviously occurred to the brass back in Hamburg. "Okay, we're outnumbered on this one," the officer in charge telephoned a few minutes later. "There's not enough time to get inventive. So let's just get to know him a little better. You guys attach that thing to the train with the magnets like he said, but tie it with some loose rope too, so it won't fall off completely. Make it look like a mechanical failure. We'll have mobile units deployed along the tracks and two helicopters in the air, just in case. When the contraption lets go, you yell."

It was pitch-dark when the Rostock–Berlin Express pulled out of Rostock station. One of the police officers on board kept watch on the east side of the tracks, another on the west. A third trained a flashlight beam on Dagobert's black box.

Nothing moved for well over an hour.

Suddenly, as the train neared the shore of Kaebelick Lake, the box shuddered. Then it separated from the rear bumper.

"He's hit it!" the flashlight-man yelled. "It's just dangling by the rope! Can you guys see anything?"

The other two officers strained frantically, trying to make out anything suspicious in the dark.

From outside, they could now hear the rhythmic banging of Dagobert's deactivated black box against the train's rear bumper.

That was all.

No sign of anyone along the tracks. No lights. No vehicles. There wasn't any point in stopping the train.

At a debriefing session the next day, the police pooled their findings.

Their man appeared to be extremely cautious, an electronics expert, and no fool.

The parts for his money-drop device appeared to have been bought from an outlet of Conrad Electronics, a country-wide chain of electronic hobby shops, which had a particularly well-stocked outlet in Berlin. The device itself had been remote-controlled on a radio frequency set aside for model-airplane pilots.

Fortunately, Dagobert also seemed willing to accept that the reason for the failed money exchange had been an electronic malfunction. During the following three weeks, no further bombs exploded at any Karstadt store.

Instead, on August 13, his next letter (bearing a Berlin post-mark and, once again, a key) simply stated: "We'll give it another try tomorrow. This time it'll work."

That pretty well summed up the police's attitude, too. This time, they mobilized both the entire crew from the previous handover attempt (two helicopters, several hundred line officers, marine units), plus three dog teams, half a dozen crack motorcyclists, and some fifty cars and all-terrain vehicles to patrol the railway wherever parallel roads made this possible. When Dagobert's next instructions ordered the money couriers to the Altona train station in west Hamburg (where they found an identical remote-controlled device in a baggage locker, with instructions to fasten it to the rear bumper of the last car of the 4:08 p.m. Hamburg–Berlin Express), it took these units less than two hours to fully deploy along the train's route.

This time the police had filled the money pouch with a carefully assembled arrangement of real bills (about $4,000) covering a fat roll of shredded paper. The roll also contained a battery-operated directional locator, enabling the two helicopters to home in on the pouch with pinpoint accuracy.

They didn't have to wait long.

Barely outside Hamburg, as the train passed the small forest of Kraehenwald near Reinbek, Dagobert's contraption jerked, slipped a few inches, then plunged onto the railbed. At virtually the same moment a man, crouched low, burst out of the bushes along the forest's outer edge. He sprinted frantically towards the still-skidding box.

Almost instantly, all hell broke loose.

The train, its wheels shrieking protest amid a shower of sparks, began grinding to an emergency stop. One of the helicopters dove straight towards the extortionist, its rotors thundering like high-speed cannon shots. Several motorcycles raced towards the man from a nearby road, engines screaming. Uniformed men spilled out of the still-moving train.

But the extortionist had already grabbed the box and was bounding back into the bushes. For a few seconds he disappeared completely; when he became briefly visible in a small clearing, he was pedalling madly away on a bicycle.

The nearest of the two helicopters swooped low over the forest, flattening its bushes and grasses. Two of the motorcyclists drove their mounts recklessly through the undergrowth. Within minutes, several dozen men were crashing through the low-hanging branches, their flashlights stabbing frantically into the dark.

But the extortionist had evaporated.

Not only that, the helicopters promptly lost the signal from the directional locator. This suggested either that the equipment failed or that the extortionist had expected something of the sort and had immediately disabled the device.

"This guy sure seems to know his alphabet," the director of operations had to acknowledge at the next day's debriefing. "But at least we're scoring on evidence." On a table before them lay the remains of Dagobert's second money-drop device (pouch emptied), his remote-control circuit deactivator, a wig, a pair of sunglasses, and a collapsible mountain bike. The bike was a Phoenix, a brand sold exclusively by the very store Dagobert was extorting.

"They oughta use that in their advertising," an officer smirked. "*Even our extortionists remain loyal to our brands.*"

The humour seemed to elude the director.

"Tell the store to put its personnel on full alert," he ordered. "I have a hunch we've pissed him off a little bit."

On September 9, just before midnight, a pipe bomb loaded with screws and washers blew up in the automotive accessories section of a Karstadt department store in the city of Bremen, about 100 kilometres southwest of Hamburg. The bomb had been hidden behind a rack of automotive oil. Though it didn't start an oil fire, it did puncture a large number of the oil containers and also set off the sprinkler system. The damage, in the words of a store employee, was "indescribable," exceeding $4 million.

Six days later a much weaker bomb exploded in the house-wares section of a Karstadt store in Hanover, 125 kilometres to the south. The damage was comparatively minor, destroying only some shelving and part of a dropped ceiling, but the explosion occurred during store hours and gave two customers a case of ringing ears. (A doctor later established that neither had suffered permanent harm.)

This time Dagobert sent his letter to the newspapers. "The police are playing games with the lives of thousands of innocent customers," he warned. "As you can see from my bomb in Hanover, I'm quite prepared to set one off during store hours, too. Sincerely, Dagobert."

In a letter to the Karstadt administration a day later, he kept up the pressure. "You ought to cut loose from the police," he advised. "Those jokers should have known I wouldn't let them catch me. Next time, I want them to back off. If I see another helicopter, or they stop the train again, you'll get another bomb. Oh, and by the way, do you think I don't know all about directional locators? So quit faking up the money packages. Sincerely, Dagobert.

"P.S. The logistics of using letters to give you my final instructions is too complicated. Give me a dedicated phone number where I can reach you directly."

The two bomb blasts did a good deal more than just thicken the plot. Now that the press was more directly involved, the police and the department store found themselves embattled on two fronts. Though the police tried to keep some degree of control over the story, it wasn't long before newspaper reporters had ferreted out the fact that an extortionist named Dagobert had already committed three bombings, had escaped the police's clutches twice, and had effected a money handover with one of the most ingenious devices known to extortion. So who was this Dagobert? What was the significance of the name? Where was he from, and what was his background? Was he committing extortion for political, economic, or sociopathic reasons?

Or was he just a kidder?

Despite their dozens of experts, the police still knew little more than the obvious. Dagobert was a technically proficient, extra-cautious perfectionist who seemed to know a lot about police procedures – especially in the area of electronics. Police psychologists would only venture that his motives seemed economic rather than political, and that he seemed, generally speaking, disinclined to hurt anyone.

"And that's the best that Germany's billion-dollar police force can do?" scoffed commentator Berndt Klosser. "Any ten-year-old could have produced the same insight for the cost of a pack of cigarettes!"

Dagobert's next letter arrived on October 12. This time he instructed the money couriers to buy a mobile CB radio suitable for use on a train. Further instructions would be delivered by telephone at the dedicated number the store had made available. (A "Dagobert Line" had been installed with connections to both Hamburg police headquarters and the German Post Office, which operates Germany's telephone system. Any calls on the line would be immediately traceable.)

The call, on October 13, came in just after 3:00 p.m. The voice was computer-distorted and hard to understand – the police had to replay the tape several times – but the gist of it was that the money couriers were to board the last car of the 4:21 p.m. Hamburg–Berlin–Dresden inter-city train at Hamburg's Central Station. They were to have the million dollars stuffed into a securely tied canvas bag and their portable CB radio tuned to channel 4. At a predetermined command over the CB radio, they were to toss the money through the back door, out onto the tracks.

(Shortly after the phone call the Post Office rang up to apologize. The extortionist had cleverly placed the call from somewhere in the former East Germany, where a telephone's location wasn't yet traceable.)

When the 4:21 p.m. train for Dresden left Hamburg's Central Station, the three money couriers were aboard, complete with money and CB radio. So were several dozen plainclothes cops. So, too, to the officers' surprise, were at least a dozen journalists. Within the next half-hour, the motorcyclists and all-terrain drivers deployed along the tracks also reported groups of roving journalists.

There were journalists hanging around every station between Hamburg and Berlin.

Somewhere, there'd obviously been a leak.

It was completely dark by the time the Dresden inter-city train pulled into Berlin's Spandau Station. Only a few passengers got off, and hardly anyone got on. Next stop was Berlin's Heerstrasse Station.

The radio came alive just as the train was slowing down for the station. One long beep, then two shorts.

"That's it!" the officer with the earphones yelled. "That's the signal! Throw the damn thing out the door!"

The officer with the bag yanked open the rear door and flung the bag in a high arc into the air. It landed with an audible thud on the side of the railbed.

The train didn't even have to stop. The policemen spilled out of every door and platform. Sirens began to wail from nearby streets. Rockets hissed into the air, flooding the area with a brilliant, purplish light. Cars and motorcycles sped towards the train. The entire motorized capacity of Berlin's city police seemed to be converging on the Heerstrasse Station's parking lot.

The only thing missing was the helicopters.

And Dagobert.

This time, he didn't even try to pick up the bag. But he'd been within fifty feet of it. In bushes only a stone's throw from where the bag had landed, searchers found his CB radio transmitter with a Dictaphone taped against its microphone. They also found his set of highly effective Russian army night-vision binoculars.

"Aw, jeez," one of the policemen groaned. "The son-of-a-bitch must have seen every move we made all night."

DISNEY DUCK STILL LEADING POLICE GOSLINGS AROUND BY THE NOSE was one headline typical of the press reaction to this latest handover attempt. PUPPET-MASTER DAGOBERT HOLDS ALL THE STRINGS was another. The thrust of the articles was humorous, cheeky, and irreverent.

Some also seemed fairly inventive. One journalist claimed that Dagobert had left the canvas bag untouched because it had contained a tear-gas bomb. Another suggested that all the fireworks had simply been camouflage to hide the fact that the tear-gas bomb had exploded prematurely.

Police strategists were sufficiently alarmed to call an internal press-strategy meeting. Its first few hours were filled with tactical debates on how to better muzzle the press. The discussions droned on until the utter futility of such a plan became clear to even the most dedicated control freak. In the absence of any other idea that had ever worked, it was finally decided to go to the opposite extreme – virtually total co-operation. Feed the press as much as they could handle. Give them the extortion letters. Give them transcripts of the phone calls. Inform them about upcoming handover attempts. Provide bus service to the sites! Hope that such co-operation would make the press more helpful, or, failing that, that the resulting profusion of fact and speculation would give Dagobert at least as many red herrings as leads.

It was a daring tactic that would eventually produce some rather unexpected results.

In the meantime, the technical details of Dagobert's latest handover attempt rattled the memories of certain police old-timers, who now recalled a remarkably similar extortion attempt four years earlier in Berlin. On May 25, 1988, a bomb had exploded in the sports section of the Kaufhaus-des-Westens (KaDeWe) department store, and an extortionist had sent the store a ransom demand for $500,000. The handover had been arranged in almost identical fashion, via a CB radio signal on an S-train in Berlin; the only difference was that, in that instance, the operation was successful – for the extortionist. None of the marked bills had ever been recovered by the police.

Though the 1988 extortionist's letters had remained unsigned, the identical form of bomb manufacture, the same electronics, and the similar *modus operandi* were too much to ignore. Also, the police still had a tape recording of the 1988 extortionist's voice over the CB radio, ordering the money to be thrown off the train. Police experts immediately began studying electronic comparisons of the two extortionists' voices.

Dagobert announced his next attempt for October 29. Once again it would be a CB-radio-based delivery, and once again from an inter-city train, #545, Hanover to Berlin. This time, however, he added a curious alternative plan. If the handover failed on the Hanover–Berlin route, he instructed the money couriers to transfer to intercity train #174, Berlin to Hamburg, departing from the Zoological Gardens Station at 5:47 p.m. (Due to this longer message, the Post Office managed to trace the call to a public cardphone in Berlin's Charlottenburg district.

Officers were immediately dispatched, but, by the time they got there, Dagobert was gone.)

When train #545 pulled into Hanover's Central Station, three dozen policemen pushed their way in, closely followed by more than twenty journalists. Additional agents squeezed in with the engineer on the head end. On the ground, a special task force had prepared a large-scale map of every railway line in northeastern Germany, identifying each point at which bushes or forests lay within a hundred metres of the railbed. By the time the #545 departed Hanover at 11:00 a.m., a veritable army of officers and special agents had taken up positions at every point on its route that fit that description.

Nevertheless, it was hard to be upbeat. A handover attempt in broad daylight seemed out of character for the overcautious Dagobert. This suggested a high likelihood they were all wasting their time, that Dagobert was simply countering the police refusal to hand over the money with a calculated plan to provoke frustrations to the point where the police became tired of the game.

If that was his plan, a police spokesman assured the accompanying journalists grimly, Dagobert had another think coming. As the train passed each patrol point en route to Berlin uneventfully, the freed-up patrolling officers promptly departed for similar points on Dagobert's plan B, the Berlin–Hamburg route. By the time #545 pulled into the Zoological Gardens at 5:30 p.m. to disgorge its load of tired and bored police and journalists, the entire Berlin–Hamburg route was fully manned and under observation.

At 5:47 p.m. the inter-city #174 pulled out of Berlin's Zoological Gardens Station with another full complement of journalists and police.

At 5:58 it passed through Berlin's Savignyplatz Station.

At 6:06 it slowed to cross Kaiser-Friedrich Street over a bush-covered embankment, on approach to Berlin's Charlottenburg station.

Without warning, the CB radio in the last car bleeped the agreed-upon signal.

"There's our song, boys! Let's dance!"

Somebody yanked open the back door. The cotton money-bag flew out into the dark. It landed in a bush beside the tracks, its white cloth still faintly visible through the branches.

A smallish man dressed in dark clothes appeared out of the bushes less than ten metres away.

For at least a full minute Dagobert remained crouched, scanning the tracks and adjacent bushes, watching the train disappear into Charlottenburg station.

Then he crept toward the bag.

Suddenly a twig snapped in the bushes to his right.

Dagobert froze. His head snapped in the direction of the sound. Then – even though the bag was only another step or two away – he spun around and disappeared into the bushes.

Seconds later he reappeared at the bottom of the embankment, heading quickly towards a bicycle half-hidden in a filbert bush.

As he swung his right leg over the saddle, a hand reached out of the bush and grabbed the left arm of his jacket. "All right duck-face, we've got you now!" a low voice growled.

Dagobert jammed his right foot onto the pedal and pushed down with all his might. The bike's wheel tilted and spun, jerking forward, pulling the police officer half out of the bush. The officer grabbed at his quarry with his other hand but missed.

By now Dagobert had managed to fully mount his bike. Gripping the handlebars, he rose on the pedals and aimed a desperate kick at his assailant. An strangled yelp indicated success. Then he flung his weight forward and hit the pedals. The bike dragged the officer completely out of the bush, his grip on Dagobert's arm still clenched, but slipping. One more lunge on the pedals broke it free.

As Dagobert disappeared around the next corner, the officer regained his feet and sounded the alarm. Within minutes, the entire area was surrounded.

But Dagobert had once again evaporated.

This latest failure opened yet another front in the war between the German police and Dagobert.

No sooner had the press had its day than the politicians came to have theirs – and they weren't remotely as amused.

"This is getting out of hand, gentlemen," an internal-affairs representative pointed out to a hastily called meeting of federal police officials. "This man absolutely must be caught. If he's allowed to keep this up, he'll make a laughingstock of us all. We're already receiving a lot of mail from the electorate."

The police pointed out, diplomatically, that they had almost caught the man several times already.

"From the public's perspective, half-full is the same as half-empty," the official replied. "We believe this case requires a more dramatic initiative. So we want you to set up a special commission of the country's top forensic and investigative experts. Its sole purpose will be to bring this Dagobert fellow to justice. Hire whatever manpower you'll need to get the job done. Whatever money you need will be found – somewhere."

By the time Dagobert got back in touch, on November 15, a fifteen-member Dagobert commission had been set up in Berlin, with a top-priority draw on all police resources. Since the KaDeWe and Karstadt extortionists had meanwhile been determined to be the same man, the commission's first act was to make a sample recording of Dagobert's voice available to the public. Citizens anywhere in the country were urged to dial 01166, toll-free, and listen to a three-second clip of Dagobert giving instructions to a KaDeWe money courier. It ended with his CB-radio-transmitted command: "*Achtung!* This is the extortionist. Throw the money out the door! I repeat: throw the money out the door!"

Anyone recognizing this voice was urged to call their nearest police station. A reward of $100,000 was offered for information leading to Dagobert's arrest. Tens of thousands of curious citizens called the number in its first week alone.

Although the widely announced phone number and reward resulted in disappointingly few leads, they clearly pumped Dagobert's sense of self-worth. In his November 15 letter, he not only warned Karstadt officials that any more handover failures would result in a whole string of daytime explosions at the height of the Christmas shopping season, he also announced that he was increasing his ransom demand by $500,000, to $1.5 million.

Remote-control electronic parts, he explained, had been getting more expensive.

For the next handover he instructed a money courier to come to Central Station in Hanover on the afternoon of December 3 to await further directions.

On December 3 he telephoned from a cardphone in Brandenburg (according to the Post Office), ordering the money couriers onto a train bound for Düsseldorf.

When they arrived in Düsseldorf after an uneventful trip, he called from a cardphone in Dortmund to order them onto a train bound for Bielefeld.

This kept a contingent of almost five hundred police agents, in an armada of cars, trucks, motorcycles, and all-terrain vehicles, racing futilely across the country for almost sixteen hours.

When the train finally pulled into Bielefeld, releasing its contingent of worn-out police officers, electronics experts, and journalists, nothing had happened.

"We believe the extortionist has embarked on a systematic program to exacerbate frustration levels," a noticeably irritated police spokesman suggested at the next day's press conference.

Dagobert's letter a few days later begged to differ. "If you guys keep practically running me over with your unmarked radio patrol vehicles, we'll never get anywhere," he wrote. "I'm not blind, you know. Frankly, I think you've given me plenty of reason to plant more bombs; take it as a Christmas present that I haven't. The next date for the handover will be December 29. Sincerely, Dagobert.

"P.S. I wish you a peaceful Christmas."

On December 28, after more than six hundred police agents had already been marshalled and prepped, Dagobert cancelled the next day's handover and rescheduled it for January 5, 1993.

While Germany's citizens celebrated the 1993 New Year with champagne and noisemakers, its policemen had little to cheer about. In seven months of matching wits with their increasingly famous extortionist (even *People* magazine had begun to take note), the score stood 9–0 for Dagobert. And though the wily extortionist hadn't managed to accumulate much money, he'd accumulated ink and broadcast time like a film star.

The German public was clearly taking a liking to this ingenious rascal.

Some liked him for his resourcefulness and his attention to detail. Some liked him for his politeness, and his obvious efforts not to hurt anyone. Almost everyone could relate to his dream of bathing in a tubful of money – after all, Germany's reunification was costing everyone either money or jobs. And his choice of victims, Germany's most profitable department stores, wasn't causing ordinary Germans a lot of sleepless nights either.

But perhaps his most significant appeal was his extraordinary success at tweaking the noses of Germany's much-vaunted police. That made it a sporting event of the highest order.

In fact, in a Germany-wide opinion poll, an astonishing 62 per cent of respondents admitted to rooting for the extortionist, or at least sympathizing with him.

All this was causing the new Dagobert commission in Berlin to consider some eyebrow-raising measures.

Several journalists reported that the police were testing miniature personnel bombs that could be hidden in a ransom-money pouch. They claimed that sides of pork were being used to test the bombs' effectiveness.

A less drastic measure involved telephone booths. The Post Office had noted that almost all Dagobert's traceable phone calls had been made from public cardphone booths located in Berlin's inner city. Since Dagobert's handover instructions invariably began with a letter announcing both the date and the time he would call the Dagobert line, police strategists began to toy with the idea of putting all cardphone booths in Berlin under surveillance during the time of his call. The call itself could be traced in a few seconds, giving the police about half a minute (the usual length of his calls) to close in.

The personnel required for such an operation would be nothing short of extravagant. There were about 2,300 cardphone booths in the target area. About 2,500 undercover operatives would be needed to do the job properly. To come up with that number, police officers from all over Germany would have to be bused into the city over a two-day period. The logistics and costs would be staggering.

Still, when you were losing 9 – 0 . . .

It was decided to go along with one more Dagobert hand-over play. If that failed, Operation Cardphone was on.

At 4:52 p.m. on January 5, Dagobert called from a cardphone booth in downtown Berlin's Wittenbergerplatz (he was gone by the time the police got there) to instruct the money couriers to open locker #21A in Berlin's Central Station. He said they would find it unlocked.

They did. Inside, they found another of his familiar remote-controlled electromagnetic black boxes. Its pouch contained instructions to affix the device to the right side of the second-last car of the Berlin–Stralsund Express, leaving Berlin's Central Station at 6:17 p.m.

With by now practised efficiency, the mobile police units fanned out along the 335-kilometre train route between Berlin and Stralsund. Once again, every stretch where bushes or forest lay within a hundred metres of the track was put under observation. Police vehicles were hidden in or behind hundreds of thickets or windbreaks.

And, as usual, dozens of journalists also took up positions in train stations along the route, joined the police mobile units, or bought seats on the Berlin–Stralsund Express. Many now carried cameras equipped with night-vision lenses, or had switched to infrared film.

Barely ten minutes after the train had left the station, the black box slipped slightly and began to buzz. The buzzing was caused by a police device inside the train that had been set up to briefly interfere with Dagobert's deactivating switch. The idea was to delay the time at which the box fell off by some two to three seconds, just long enough to draw Dagobert a little farther out of his hiding place.

But when the box fell down onto the tracks and skidded onto an embankment, Dagobert didn't bite. The box lay there for about an hour, with half a dozen police and journalists' field glasses trained on it.

Finally the police retrieved it and called off the exercise.

Operation Cardphone was on.

In his next letter, dated January 16, Dagobert was clearly annoyed. "Did you honestly expect me to *chase* after that thing?" he demanded. "You messed around with it. Now you fix it. Make sure it's working properly again by January 21. I'll contact you by phone at 2:30 p.m. on that day."

That deadline gave the Dagobert commission just over four days to prepare Operation Cardphone. Thousands of police operatives, drawn from at least a dozen different police organizations throughout Germany, had to be contacted, hired, and bused into Berlin. They had to be housed, fed, instructed, and deployed throughout a carefully defined operations area within the city – an area bound by the Spandau district to the west, the Wedding district to the north, the Kreutzberg district to the east, and the Steglitz district to the south. (To minimize the possibility of a leak, it was decided not to alert the press this time around.)

It was a formidable job, but by 2:00 p.m. on January 21 everyone was ready and in place. From that moment on, every Berliner who stepped into a cardphone booth within the operations area was being surreptitiously observed and photographed.

But that was just a warm-up exercise.

At 2:32 p.m., the very instant Dagobert called Karstadt's Dagobert line, a predetermined radio signal sent all 2,500 operatives rushing out of their hiding places to secure the phone booths. They did this by simply slamming the doors. Anyone caught inside was an automatic suspect.

That's when their superbly organized operation began to fall apart.

At this point, their instructions called for the police to identify themselves to their captives. But the booths were fairly soundproof, and many of the captured telephoners couldn't understand what their plainclothes captors were trying to tell them. They assumed they were being mugged, and reacted accordingly. Some actually fell to their knees, begging for mercy and fervently offering up their wallets and jewellery. Some feigned heart attacks or fainting spells – and since the police couldn't be sure, dozens of ambulances had to be summoned. One particularly enraged voter simply tore the phone booth's door off its hinges and then knocked the protesting police officer out cold. One called orders to his dog – tied to the booth's outside door handle – which promptly attacked the officer and bit him in the leg.

Fortunately, once police officers succeeded in explaining the purpose of Operation Cardphone, most of its involuntary participants became a bit more co-operative. Some were even thrilled to be involved in an attempt to capture Germany's most famous extortionist.

Unfortunately, an attempt was all it turned out to be.

For some reason, Dagobert had chosen not to call from central Berlin this time. He'd called from a cardphone booth in Neukoelln, a suburb far to the south of the operations area.

When the press found out about Operation Cardphone – despite strenuous police efforts to keep the cork in the bottle – their reaction wasn't overly sympathetic. OVER 2,300 POLICEMEN CHASE "THE DUCK," one headline read. STILL NO LUCK. "Twenty-five hundred police took it into their heads to catch Dagobert by putting virtually every cardphone booth in Berlin under observation," another paper scoffed. "The only one they missed was the one he used."

Naturally, this suspicious coincidence promptly renewed speculation about Dagobert's identity. Could an ordinary crook have been this lucky ten times out of ten? Wouldn't you have to be a former policeman, or a man with police connections, or perhaps a former German Secret Service agent? Or how about an out-of-work Stasi or KGB operative? God knows there'd been plenty of those kicking around since the fall of the wall. It was a line of thought that even the Dagobert commission was beginning to take seriously.

In the meantime they still had absolutely nothing of substance to work with. Nothing useful from the more than seven hundred tips they'd received from their toll-free number to date (which had already cost several hundreds of thousands of man-hours of investigation time). Nothing from their interrogation of all known extortionists in the police data bank. Not even – despite ten "contact occurrences" – a workable composite mugshot of the extortionist. The one that had been prepared on the basis of a description by the police officer who had almost caught Dagobert on October 29, 1992, had been strongly challenged by another officer, who had also seen the extortionist pedal away from the handover scene. The two men's descriptions had been so contradictory that the commission had decided to withdraw the artist's rendering. Besides, the darn thing had turned out to look disconcertingly like the head of the Dagobert commission himself, and the commission knew full well what a field day the press would have had with that.

To no one's surprise, at this point Dagobert promptly stopped using public cardphones to call the Dagobert line.

In fact, to the police's unease – and after scheduling several further handovers that he cancelled one after another – Dagobert fell strangely silent. This put everybody on tenterhooks.

"We don't know what he's cooking up, but we're not diminishing our efforts," a police spokesman said. "He's not the type who gives up easily."

An enterprising Berlin wholesaler began producing white T-shirts imprinted with the question DAGOBERT, WHERE ARE YOU?? A competitor promptly countered with T-shirts announcing I AM DAGOBERT. Both sold by the thousands.

Spurred by the success of the T-shirts, a novelties manufacturer produced a line of pre-printed postcards addressed to the Hamburg police, demanding: "Please put the money where I can find it! Sincerely, Dagobert." Another sold Dagobert masks, and buttons reading: "If You Wanna Be Rich, You Gotta Know How To Wait!" A clothier offered Dagobert ties and scarfs for "alternative evening-wear."

Various newspapers and radio stations began offering sizable fees for an exclusive "confidential" interview with the extortionist. Their offers ran daily in their classified and advertising sections. Though some hinted at clandestine negotiations, there was never any evidence that Dagobert responded to any such offers.

In the meantime the Dagobert commission was trying another tack. Assuming the extortionist might be working on another ingenious gadget, it assigned undercover agents to stake out every significant electronics hobby store in the country. The stores were given a list of the parts Dagobert might try to buy, and their clerks were asked to signal the agents whenever a customer tried to buy or order any of them.

After a two-month hiatus, Dagobert finally resurfaced with a letter to the Karstadt department store, naming April 19 as the next handover date. He also apologized for the delay, explaining he'd been ill. The couriers were to take the money to Berlin's Central Station and wait there for further instructions.

At 8:04 p.m. that evening, he phoned from an ordinary pay-phone in Neukoelln (gone when police arrived), directing them to take an S-train to Berlin's Zoological Gardens Station, and to open luggage locker #613 (unlocked) for further instructions.

The locker contained a key.

"This key fits a municipal sandbox (the sort containing the sand used on sidewalks during icy winter conditions) located on a parking lot at Gutschmidt Street and Gruener Way," an accom-panying note explained. "More instructions in box."

By the time the couriers had found the parking lot and trained their headlights on a grey, weather-beaten box on its northeast corner, they had been joined by two unmarked radio vans and a dozen unmarked police cars full of plainclothes officers. Once again, the money pack had been filled with shredded newspaper, but this time, in addition to a directional locator, the police had included a motion detector. Even in the dark, they would know immediately if the money pack was being touched – let alone moved.

The cars and one of the vans faded unobtrusively into nearby streets and alleys. Minutes later their occupants were taking up equally unobtrusive positions within sight of the parking lot. The second van had parked so that the box remained clearly visible to both its occupants and in range of its bristling array of electronic surveillance gear.

The courier with the key, the money pack, a flashlight, and a radio throat-mike and earphone, approached the box.

He unlocked and pulled up the lid.

The box was about one-third full of a grit made of sand and salt. The note lying on the grit read, PUT IN THE MONEY, CLOSE THE LID, DISAPPEAR.

"So what should I do?" the courier murmured into the mike.

"Search the box," came the reply through his earphone.

The courier ploughed his hand through the gritty mix.

"Nothing," he reported.

"Dig right to the bottom," his earphone instructed. "Dig all around."

"Still nothing."

"Okay, drop in the pack, and back off."

The courier lowered the lid and withdrew into the dark. A moment later he was climbing into the radio van.

"Anything yet?"

"Not a peep," said the radio technician. He was wearing earphones and watching the sandbox on a small computer screen.

Total silence. The minutes dragged by.

Suddenly, the technician snapped upright and gazed suspiciously at the screen.

"What the hell?" he grumbled.

"What?"

"The motion detector's signalling."

The courier trained a pair of infrared binoculars on the box. "Can't be. There's nobody there."

"Then why's the damn thing signalling?"

The technician began fiddling furiously with dials and knobs. Suddenly there was a sharp series of beeps, and a red light began to blink.

"Now the direction locator's firing! I tell you, the damn thing is moving!"

"*But there's nobody there!*"

The technician tore off his earphones, grabbed a flashlight, and yanked open the door. He set off at a dead run for the box. The courier grabbed his own flashlight and followed.

The technician yanked up the lid.

The box was almost empty. All that remained of its former contents was a rim of grit around a yawning black hole about thirty centimetres square in the bottom.

Both men trained their flashlights into the hole. From their angle, the light disappeared into the dark without hitting anything. A foul, rotten odour wafted up.

"It's a goddamn sewer shaft!"

"Gimme a hand with this thing!"

The box without its load of grit tilted up easily.

Down at the bottom of the shaft they could see the dim outlines of the burst money pack, its paper shreds still bobbing gently on the black sludge.

Dagobert, of course, was nowhere to be seen.

"The extortionist pulled the cover off a sewer shaft and substituted a home-made container that looked convincingly like a municipal sandbox," the police spokesman informed a crush of journalists the next day. "Once our courier had deposited the money pack in the box, the extortionist approached it from below, opened a trapdoor in its bottom, took the package, and escaped out another sewer entrance. We found a gas mask and some electronic equipment . . ."

"What sort of equipment?"

"A device to detect directional locators . . . and such."

"I don't understand why you even bother with that stuff," a journalist grimaced, exasperated. "He's had you electronically beat since the beginning."

The spokesman looked around for a further question.

"Was there money in the pack?" another journalist wanted to know.

"Ah . . . no, no, I believe there wasn't. Not this time, no."

"Any truth to the rumour that you're considering just giving him the money and being done with it?" one of the boulevard journalists demanded. "I've heard that Karstadt's offered to pay the ransom on several occasions already."

"I've heard that some politicians have demanded the same thing," a television reporter chimed in. "To take the issue off the front pages during the upcoming state elections."

"That's absolutely false," the police spokesman said firmly. "If we give in on this one, he'll be back on our case the minute he's spent the money. He did it after that 1988 job and he'll do it again. Our psychologists are all in agreement about that."

More interesting than its predictably condescending headlines was the enormous amount of space the press gave to this latest handover attempt. Tracking the Dagobert Duck saga had clearly become a national pastime. Many newspapers now dedicated entire pages to an extensive reprise of the story, complete with photos, detailed drawings, and analysis. The police toll-free number experienced another big surge in calls, and a Dagobert rap song by the German rap group Die Panzerknacker, which used Dagobert's voice from the toll-free number as background, enjoyed increasing airplay. A television broadcasting company, SAT-1, announced that it had already begun work on a script for a Dagobert film, and publicly urged Dagobert to get in touch, to "add your input to its content and direction." "The ending," SAT-I spokesman Dieter Zurstrassen assured everyone, "will, of course, remain open."

That may have been a satisfactory arrangement from SAT-I's point of view, but Dagobert obviously saw it differently. In yet another attempt to force his own conclusion to his frustratingly inconclusive saga, he blew up the radio and television section at the Karstadt department store in the city of Bielefeld, about 250 kilometres southwest of Hamburg.

The explosion, which occurred on May 19, shortly after closing time, was one of his most expensive: almost $5-million worth of damage. But again, no one was hurt.

"You guys are really driving me to the limit of my patience," he warned Karstadt executives in his next letter, dated May 25. "If you don't start putting some real money into those packages, I'm going to give you a fireworks that'll make my bombs so far seem like peanuts. Next handover will be July 1. Sincerely, Dagobert."

It wasn't, though. Nor was it on July 8, or August 30, or September 1, or September 15. From mid-May to the end of October, Dagobert scheduled and then cancelled almost a dozen handover attempts, for reasons that ranged from illness to inconvenience to getting stuck in rush-hour traffic.

Or so the police claimed. It had become harder to tell, because on September 3 the police abruptly cancelled its full-disclosure policy with the press, apparently incensed over some speculative articles which had charged that the money packs dangled before Dagobert's nose never contained money, only shredded newspaper, plus a variety of electronic gadgetry, or even, on occasion, a tear-gas or anti-personnel bomb. During one of the handover attempts (the article claimed) a pack with a bomb had accidentally exploded, knocking birds out of nearby trees and afflicting passersby with burning eyes and lungs.

Whatever the facts, by the end of October frustrations between Dagobert and the police had increased to such an extent that an October 27 telephone conversation ended in a shouting match, with the policeman simply refusing to accept Dagobert's date for the next handover attempt, and banging down the phone.

That, too, may have been a psychological ploy.

If so, it failed. Dagobert's response, on November 3, was to set off a fire-bomb in a stockroom of the Karstadt department store in Magdeburg, about 250 kilometres southeast of Hamburg. Designed to produce enough heat to set off the sprinkler system for maximal collateral damage (which it did), the bomb went off after hours, so no one was hurt.

He set off another in an elevator in a Karstadt department store in Berlin's Hermannplatz on December 6. This one exploded during store hours, and might have hurt someone, but the elevator was empty and the bomb had been only loosely packed. It didn't cause much damage.

"I'm fed up with your nonsense and I'm not putting up with it any more," he fumed in a letter several days later. "You're going to give me the money on December 11, and no more fooling around!"

Three days later, at a Conrad Electronics outlet in Berlin's Kreutzberg district, a smallish, well-dressed businessman asked a clerk at the store's special-order department for an electronic programmable switch, product C-44A-49.

The clerk hesitated. Then she said she would check the store's stock. (Product C-44A-49 was one of the items on the Dagobert commission's list.)

There were supposed to be several plainclothes police agents staked out in the store's back room, but she could find only one. He threw a hasty look into the store, then hurried off to get his partner. The two studied the customer through a one-way mirror in the wall behind the cash register.

He *did* bear a faint resemblance to the director of the Dagobert commission.

They discussed strategies. The most important thing was to make sure he didn't leave the store. The next was to check out what else he was buying.

One of the agents hurried over to block the store entrance. He was so eager to get to the door, he climbed right over the turnstile gate. A number of customers – including the smallish businessman – looked up, puzzled at this sudden gymnastics display.

The businessman turned and walked briskly up the stairs to the store's second floor.

The second agent rushed after him, grabbing a shopping basket along the way. At the top of the stairs, he saw his quarry standing in front of a display of remote-control command units, apparently reading the claims on the packaging. The agent turned to a shelf of rheostatic switches and studied them with elaborate interest.

When he looked up seconds later, the businessman was gone.

The policeman looked around frantically. His man seemed to have evaporated. Then he noticed the door to the second-floor stockroom still moving slightly. He rushed down the aisle and burst through the door. He got there just in time to see the businessman ram his way through an armed fire escape, hurtle down the metal staircase with astonishing agility, and leap off its end, some two metres above the ground. Seconds later he had disappeared around the side of the building.

All that remained was the ringing security alarm above the breached fire exit.

Dagobert's escape from the Conrad Electronics store was only one of several botched near-captures the police had decided not to bother the public about. This one, however, apparently rattled the extortionist enough to convince him he needed a Christmas break.

He let the December 11, 1993 date ride and took the rest of the year off.

Even that worked to Dagobert's advantage. The public simply assumed he was repeating his previous year's Christmas amnesty and credited him with an endearing civility and sense of fairness. In an extensive end-of-the-year reprise of the popular extortionist's shenanigans, *Der Spiegel* crowned him "Gangster of the Year" and suggested he had raised the intellectual timbre of the timeless game of cops and robbers to an unprecedented height. Various Berlin commentators credited him with putting Berlin back on the tourist map, and there was talk of trying to have the case transferred to the Berlin police. "After all, those dunderheads in Hamburg have proved beyond a doubt they're incapable of laying a glove on Dagobert," one Berliner was quoted as pointing out. "And anyway, he's one of us, isn't he?"

That had, in fact, become the consensus, both publicly and within the police community. After several months of operating out of Hamburg, the extortionist had used Berlin telephones and Berlin locations for his handover attempts so consistently, one simply had to assume it had been the base of his operations all along. His humour and informality, too, were considered typical Berliner characteristics.

The mood among the police as 1993 came to a close was perversely upbeat. Their luck had been so bad, it was *bound* to improve. Even the odds on Dagobert in England's betting shops, which had risen all year, had reportedly sagged a little toward year's end, based purely on statistical averages. Sooner or later, they felt – and the police could only hope they were right – Dagobert was bound to make a fatal mistake.

This upbeat mood, admittedly, was laced with a good deal of gallows humour. The invitations for the policemen's Christmas bash sported a portrait of Dagobert Duck on the cover, bordered in funereal black. The event itself included several popular water-fowl dances – the Dead Duck Boogie and the Lame Duck Waltz were particular favourites – and the younger officers rapped and stomped up a storm to somebody's borrowed CD version of *Die Panzerknacker*'s "Dagobert Rap Song."

At the other end of the spectrum, a group of German intel-lectuals, calling themselves Donaldists, reportedly anxious to help the police out of their embarrassing predicament, announced that they had finally completed a rigorous study of Disney's Donald Duck comic books and were now in a position to prove that this literary source constituted the origin of many of the extortionist's ingenious handover schemes. "We're not saying he's copying them frame for frame," *Der Spiegel* quoted one Donaldist as saying, "but he's clearly using them as a source of inspiration. We think we should have a representative on the Dagobert commission, so we can provide the police with our invaluable input on this subject."

The Dagobert novelties market also expanded another notch, with a new line of Dagobert garden dwarves (masked and clutching a money pack) selling briskly, alongside the usual Dagobert T-shirts, masks, and ties. The Brandenburg-based East German Radio reported enormous response to its youth-oriented "Catch Dagobert" radio quiz, in which callers were asked a variety of trivia questions in a distorted Dagobert-like voice. Those who answered correctly won a pound of Karstadt department store coffee; those who didn't were condemned to become German policemen. "It's not exactly a high-end concept," a station spokesman admitted, "but the kids are absolutely jamming the phone lines. It's Dagomania out there."

The holidays ended for all Dagobert-chasers on January 4, when his first letter of 1994 arrived at the Karstadt department store in Hamburg. "Okay, people, let's get off on the right foot this time," he urged the store management. "I don't know about you, but I'm more determined and impatient than ever. Be ready on January 15.

"P.S. Remember: if the handover works, you'll never hear from me again."

On January 15 the police got their usual computer-distorted instructions by telephone, but the instructions were intriguing. They were told to pack the money into a cylinder measuring no larger than fourteen centimetres in diameter, and to bring it to the south Berlin district of Steglitz, to a nondescript little park between an autobahn exit and a railway track. There, further instructions directed them to a pile of cement flagstones, where they discovered that Dagobert hadn't yet exhausted his interest in sewer shafts. The flagstones lay beside a sewer-shaft entrance, this one closed with a slightly unusual manhole cover.

The unusual part was a round hole in the middle of the cover, fitted with an inset metallic grate. The hole was fifteen centimetres across.

Dagobert's final note under the top paving stone instructed the couriers to place the money cylinder beside the manhole cover and withdraw. They did that.

Or so the police claimed.

Later on they changed their story. They explained that, because the couriers had failed to bring their flashlights, they had misread the instructions. The instructions had been to place the money cylinder in an upended position *onto* the grate in the manhole cover, not beside it.

The distinction was critical, because the manhole cover turned out to be another intricate Dagobert invention. It had been made out of wood, stained to look like metal, and the inset grate was hinged and controlled by thin ropes from the bottom of the shaft. If the couriers had set the money-filled cylinder on the grate as instructed, Dagobert would have opened the grate from his position in the sewer three metres below, caught the cylinder, and escaped.

As it was, he merely escaped.

By the time the police figured out that they couldn't lever up his manhole cover – it had been wired to the shaft from below – Dagobert had disappeared into the labyrinth of the sewer system.

All they found was his radio microphone under the flagstones. As usual, he'd made sure he could hear everything the couriers and police were saying to each other.

The abuse the police might have expected from the press over this lame start to the new year ("and we're supposed to believe that three policemen forgot their flashlights for a handover attempt at 10:00 at night?") remained at least partly muted by the intriguing rumour, attributed to a variety of sources, that the police had finally given up trying to fool Dagobert with electronic gadgetry and were now putting real money into their money packs.

According to this theory, some commission strategists had decided they might have more overall success by letting the extortionist have his money, which would stop the bombings and get the public and the politicians off the case, while giving the police a chance to catch Dagobert in more conventional ways – like tracing the marked bills or encouraging nosy neighbours to report sudden and unaccounted-for wealth next door. As dull as such methods sounded, they had a very high success record.

And they were cheaper. To date, police attempts to outwit Dagobert had cost the German taxpayer some $30 million – and the bills were still piling up.

This rumour had barely been taken up by the press when a second swept it abruptly off the stage: the police had made an arrest!

The man in question, a retired electrical engineer by the name of Hans-Joachim Thiemen, certainly seemed to fit the bill. He was short, a Berliner, and bore a passable resemblance to the composite drawing the police had finally released. More to the point he was an inventor, a handyman, a model-builder, a robot expert, and an electronics whiz.

Tipped off by nosy neighbours, the Dagobert commission had sent two investigators to check the suspect out. They began by knocking on Thiemen's door, identifying themselves and asking whether "he knew Dagobert."

Thiemen made no effort to deny it.

The investigators' eyes widened.

Thiemen inquired as to the reason for the question. After all, his brother had been dead for over a decade.

The investigators knew nothing about a brother. What did Thiemen's brother have to do with this?

Thiemen explained patiently that it was his brother they were talking about. Dagobert. His brother.

This was getting too deep for the investigators. They called in reinforcements, including several dogs, and searched Thiemen's entire apartment. They found exactly what they had hoped to find: a fully equipped workshop, with all the tools and materials the extortionist would have needed to build his various gadgets.

Hans-Joachim Thiemen was promptly hustled off to commission headquarters.

It took the poor man two full days, and several extra dosages of his stomach medicine, to convince commission interrogators that he was not the extortionist they were looking for. By bizarre coincidence he *had* once worked for the sewer department of Berlin's municipal works, and his dead brother's name really had been Dagobert, and yes, he had just built a robot that could shovel snow and mow lawns. But despite all these suspicious parallels, he had never bombed anyone. Yes, he was quite sure of that. He was prepared to swear it on Dagobert's grave.

After an exhaustive check of all his alibis, the commission let Thiemen go.

It probably helped that, right in the middle of these interrogations, Dagobert telephoned from a public phone in Brandenburg (the police arrived too late) to announce January 22 as the date for the next handover attempt.

On January 22, Dagobert's call at 6:57 p.m. led the three money couriers on a particularly strenuous wild-goose chase all over Berlin. They had to find a key – this time in a phone booth in Klausenerplatz – cross a dangerous railway bridge, and climb a rail embankment so steep they kept slipping back down in the wet clay. Finally they found themselves in the vicinity of the Charlottenburg rail-freight station, stumbling along a line of abandoned tracks after dark. According to their last set of instructions, they were looking for a box of some kind, sitting directly – if Dagobert's sketch was to be believed – on the left-hand rail, somewhere ahead.

It was. A black plywood box, notched out at both ends, so that the rail ran straight through it. The lid of the box was locked. The couriers unlocked the box and shone their flashlights inside.

"Now what in the hell is that?"

Inside the box, already affixed to the rail and ready to roll, was a tiny homemade railroad speeder.

It was about sixty centimetres long, fifteen centimetres wide, and looked like an electrified skateboard. It was propelled by a matched set of rubber-coated traction wheels, which were driven by a cogged belt attached to a powerful electric motor. Two heavy rechargeable battery packs flanked the speeder on either side, making it bottom-heavy and more stable. On its top was an empty metal freight-box and another sealed metal box, presumably containing the unit's electronics. There was a large red button on the side of the sealed box.

PUT THE MONEY IN THE FREIGHT-BOX AND PUSH THE RED BUTTON, the instructions taped to the speeder read. THEN STAND BACK. DO NOT ATTEMPT TO FOLLOW.

"It's some sort of little monorail thing," the courier reported into his radio. "He wants us to pack the money into the top of it and push a start button."

"Where's it going to go?" headquarters wanted to know.

The courier stood up and shone his flashlight up the tracks. "Hard to say. There's a sharp bend not too far ahead, and I don't know where it goes after that."

There was a pause from headquarters. "All right. Put in the money and start it up. But try to follow it from a safe distance."

"Will do."

The courier removed the protective plywood box from the speeder and dropped the money pack into its freight-box. Then he straightened up and secured his flashlight and radio.

"You guys ready to roll?"

He pushed down on the big red button.

There was a loud hum, and a bright red light lit up on the side of the sealed metal box. Then, with a screech of protesting rubber and the high whine of spinning wheels, the little speeder rocketed off.

All three couriers were caught off guard by how quickly it disappeared into the night.

"Quick! After it!"

Which was easier said than done. In the dark, they stumbled over unexpected rocks, uneven ties, unseen holes.

Suddenly a flash of light cut through the dark, followed by a loud bang, like a rifleshot. Then another, and another.

"Look out! The bastard's shooting!"

All three flung themselves to the ground, searching for cover.

The shooting stopped. Silence returned. A faint smell of cordite wafted through the air.

The little railroad speeder had disappeared around the bend.

"Man! He really *has* got his knickers in a knot, hasn't he!"

"Maybe it's just as well he finally got his money."

One of the couriers was already back on his feet and searching around with his flashlight. Suddenly he stopped, played the light back and forth on a spot beside the tracks, and began to laugh.

"Trigger wires!" he said.

"Trigger what?"

He stood back slightly and swung his foot forward, as if kicking a soccer ball. There was another flash of light and a loud rifleshot.

The two others hit the dirt. "What the hell?"

The soccer-ball-kicker, still standing, snorted. "Trigger wires, you morons. They're all over the place. When you step on them they blow off some sort of firecracker. Obviously meant to slow us down."

"Or tell him we're on our way. Damn! Let's move it!"

They resumed their chase, triggering a few more flashes and bangs, and then there were no more wires.

Half a kilometre farther up the tracks, having encountered nothing of further interest, they stopped to report to headquarters. Suddenly one of the couriers held up his hand.

"Hey, shut up a minute. Don't make a sound."

Out in the darkness they could hear a clearly distinguishable buzzing sound. As they stared towards the sound, they made out a pinpoint of red.

"Is that the speeder?"

It was. A hundred metres farther along they found it, derailed and upended, its drive wheels still spinning furiously. It must have hit a rail spike or similar protrusion at a very high speed, because the impact had hurled the money package right out of the freight-box and at least four metres farther down the track. It lay in a small mud-filled depression, otherwise untouched.

One of the couriers pushed down on the speeder's start button and the buzzing stopped.

Only five minutes later they came across the buffer that Dagobert had fastened across the track to catch his money-delivering machine. In nearby bushes they also found a cotton sack and a roll of aluminum foil. Obviously Dagobert hadn't believed the rumour about the police giving up on direction locators.

Though they moved in quickly, the police found no further trace of Dagobert.

Even the police had to admit they were impressed with this latest Dagobert invention. "Unquestionably ingenious," a police spokesman acknowledged. Hamburg police director of operations Michael Daleki – while pointing out that this also proved how dangerous Dagobert could be – judged him "without equal in the history of German crime. If his speeder hadn't derailed, our people wouldn't have stood a chance."

"The man's an artist!" publisher Bernd Kramer of Kramer Verlag enthused. "An artist without equal. Show me anyone who's ever delivered such an enduro-performance before – and without a sponsor!" He announced that his publishing house had already contracted with respected crime reporter Werner Schmidt for a book on the master extortionist.

Germany's filmmakers were similarly intrigued. Film director Wolfgang Petersen (*Das Boot*) acknowledged he was planning a Dagobert film, and so did veteran crime filmmaker Juergen Roland. SAT-1 announced it was adding a fourth scriptwriter to its team, and repeated its invitation to Dagobert to "get in on the ground floor."

Two weeks later, the police received further evidence of Dagobert's ingenuity – and their first big break.

An alert municipal worker called the Dagobert commission hotline to report an unusual discovery. The alarm system protecting a steel-door emergency exit from an S-train tunnel (with connections to the city's sewer system) had been cut, and a false wooden wall had been built in front of it, leaving a thirty-centimetre space between wall and door. The wall had been fitted with a fifteen-centimetre-square hinged flap, just large enough to drop a money pack through, with a box set down behind it to catch the package. It had all the hallmarks of another Dagobert construction: the couriers would be instructed to drop the money pack through the slot, it would fall into the box, Dagobert (who would be waiting in the tunnel) would open the steel door (unseen and protected by the false wall), grab the money, and retreat into the tunnel, locking the steel door behind him. By the time the police figured out how to get into the tunnel, he would be long gone.

The discovery sent a surge of excitement through the commission. After almost two years of maddeningly futile effort, this was their first opportunity to be proactive rather than constantly reactive. The emergency exit was promptly put under twenty-four-hour observation, both from inside and out. The alarm cable was left unrepaired, and municipal workers were ordered to stay clear of the tunnel.

On February 12, Dagobert contacted Hamburg with another letter. In it he accepted his speeder's derailment on the January 22 handover attempt as his own failure, and promised not to plant another bomb "if this next handover works." He scheduled it for February 19.

By February 18, the police had covered every imaginable eventuality in Dagobert's false-wall gambit. They had put together a complete map of all contiguous tunnels and exits – an enormous undertaking in itself, since many emergency exits weren't even marked on the city's sewer maps – and planned to place agents in every one of them. The surrounding area would be "hermetically sealed" and absolutely crawling with plain-clothes officers and unmarked cars.

But on the evening of February 18 the temperature dropped, and by next morning freezing rain had turned the highway between Hamburg and Berlin into an ice rink. The police decision to push ahead regardless proved an expensive mistake; more than half a dozen police cars ended up in collisions or ditches. When Dagobert telephoned to pass on his next instructions, most of the headquarters brass hadn't even reached Berlin. Using the weather as their excuse, the police cancelled the handover.

Dagobert rescheduled for February 26, but on the day before got cold feet and rescheduled for March 12. Seeing little point in keeping the emergency exit under observation in the meantime, the police withdrew their stakeouts.

When they returned, on March 8, the fake wall was gone. It had been disassembled and neatly stored, along with some paints and paint thinners, in a nearby tunnel.

Dagobert, it appeared, had decided to put this plan on hold.

For the next six weeks, the police and the extortionist reverted to their old accustomed tussle of wills and wiles, with Dagobert's repeated cancellations apparently related to the unseasonably wet weather. The fact that he always seemed to cancel when it rained made the police suspect he was planning another attempt through the sewers, where rising water levels would cause him problems. Berlin's sewer workers were once again put on city-wide alert.

Then an investigator reported he had found a truck that might have some connection to the extortionist.

Since all the evidence indicated that Dagobert probably lived in southeast Berlin, the police had stepped up patrols in that area, and one of the patrols had noticed a Phoenix collapsible mountain-bike – exactly the kind Dagobert had used on several earlier handover attempts – folded up behind the driver's seat of a white Daihatsu pickup truck.

A check of the truck's licence plates showed it to be a rental, with a return date that happened to coincide with Dagobert's next scheduled handover date: April 19. When that handover failed again (the couriers got stuck in traffic) and Dagobert rescheduled for April 22, an investigator called the rental agency and discovered that the truck's rental period had been extended to April 22 as well.

Furthermore, nobody in the immediate area knew anything about the truck, and the documents with which it had been rented proved untraceable.

Not exactly earth-shattering leads, and there were a dozen innocent explanations that could have accounted for them, but promising leads in this case had been so hard to come by that the commission decided to take no chances. The truck was put under twenty-four-hour observation.

On April 20, in what was eventually determined to be his sixtieth letter to the Karstadt department store, Dagobert told store executives to expect his next phone call on April 22, around 10:00 a.m.

On April 22, at 9:44 a.m., a man approached the pickup truck, unlocked it, and climbed inside. He was short, blond, and sported a clipped moustache. He drove off in a northerly direction, then turned west. Fifteen minutes later he was in Treptow, a working-class Berlin district of mostly duplex and row housing, bordering on the east side of the former Berlin Wall. The man parked the truck on a side street about half a block from two adjoining telephone booths at 77 Hagedorn Street, which he spent a further fifteen minutes watching. Then he went into one of the booths.

From their own parked car, two mobile-unit policemen could see their man lift the telephone receiver and begin punching telephone buttons. Then he turned away and spoke into the receiver.

Seconds later the police radio crackled an all-points bulletin. "Suspect telephone caller traced to public telephone booth 1467, at 77 Hagedorn St. All units in the Treptow area please acknowledge."

"My god," one of the policemen almost sighed. "That's really him in there."

"Should we wait until he's finished talking?"

"Are you crazy?" The first policeman was already yanking open his door. "With this guy's luck, he'll turn into air before we cross the street!"

It was a prescient remark. As the two policemen crossed the street at a dead run, the man in the phone booth slipped out the door and was already halfway down the block before the policemen managed to catch up with him. Even then he might have disappeared into one of the apartment doors lining the sidewalk, or jumped into a passing car for a quick getaway.

Instead, he simply turned to face the approaching policemen and gave them a tired grin.

"Oh, what the hell," he shrugged. "You guys win."

◆

The mysterious extortionist whom eighty-four million Germans knew only as "Dagobert" turned out not to be a disgruntled policeman, or a Secret Service operative, or an unemployed Stasi agent, or a KGB operative.

He proved to be nothing more exotic than an unemployed automobile painter.

His name was Arno Funke, age forty-four, and he lived with his Filipino wife, Edna, and their three-year-old son, Christian, in a three-room attic apartment in the modest Berlin suburb of Marienfeld.

His motive for blackmailing two of Germany's most profitable department stores had simply been to kickstart his life back to what it had been before he'd become unable to work due to ten years of inhaling automotive spray paint carcinogens. He'd envisioned using the money to finance a hotdog stand in Berlin.

In court he proved to be everything the public had hoped for: charming, amusing, and artlessly candid. He made no attempt to play to the audience, and admitted everything readily and even helpfully. He apologized to anyone he had unintentionally inconvenienced, and he seemed to genuinely mean it. At the same time, as the judge led him patiently through the details of his two years of jousting with the police, he couldn't suppress the occasional flash of satisfaction at the ingenious ways he had repeatedly outwitted them. (Neither could his courtroom audience – including the three judges.)

Though Funke had completed only seven years of formal schooling ("nobody thought I had enough birdfeed between the ears, your honour – including me"), court psychologists rated his general IQ at 120 (high) and his technical IQ at an impressive 145. The police reported that, when they raided Funke's rented workshop in the Berlin suburb of Bohnsdorf following his arrest, they found a nearly completed miniature remote-controlled submarine that Funke admitted he'd designed and built for use in an upcoming handover attempt. He'd planned to direct the money couriers to the dock of a local lake and have them fit the money into the waiting submarine, which he'd intended to navigate underwater by remote control to an undisclosed destination. There, the submarine would have surfaced and sent out a radio signal, enabling Funke to retrieve it in the dark.

Dagobert's trial proved so popular that Germany's two largest television networks, ZDF and ARD, repeatedly interrupted regular national programming to provide updates and details of his testimony. Naturally, they also dedicated entire programs to the proceedings. *Bild* magazine and *Super-Illu* slugged it out for magazine rights to Funke's story (plus exclusive access to his family photo albums), which *Super-Illu* eventually won for a reported $91,000. SAT-1 bought the television rights for a reported $1.5 million – by bizarre coincidence the exact amount that Funke had attempted to extort from Karstadt. Funke's wife, Edna, also found eager buyers for her collection of Super-8 family home movies.

Little, if any, of the money was expected to end up in Funke's pockets, since Karstadt executives had already given notice of a multimillion-dollar civil damage suit. Asked how he felt about this, Funke's shrug was placid. "I can't argue with that. They've got a right to it."

On March 14, 1995, Arno Funke was sentenced to seven years and nine months in prison, well short of the fifteen years the judges could have handed down by precedent. Fifteen months later, on appeal, Germany's supreme court increased that sentence to nine years. With good behaviour, Funke could be out by the time this book is published.

If so, it's unlikely the formerly unemployed automobile painter will be unemployed for long. He's already been over-whelmed with job offers from a variety of industrial and elec-tronics companies – jobs that will finally allow him to use his remarkable technical knowledge and abilities for *lawful* purposes.

Sources

1. THE LADIES SOCK IT TO THE FRANC

Stuart Gordon, *The Book of Hoaxes*, Headline Books, London, 1995.

Alexander Klein, *Grand Deception*, J. B. Lippincott, New York, 1955.

Egon Larsen, *The Deceivers*, John Baker, London, 1966.

Carl Sifakis, *Hoaxes and Scams*, Facts on File, New York, 1993.

Carlson Wade, *Great Hoaxes and Famous Impostors*, Jonathan David Publishers, New York, 1976.

2. AROUND THE WORLD IN EIGHTY MEGAHERTZ

Stuart Gordon, *The Book of Hoaxes*, Headline Books, London, 1995.

David Roberts, *Great Exploration Hoaxes*, Sierra Club Books, San Francisco, 1982.

Nicholas Tomalin and Ron Hall, *The Strange Last Voyage of Donald Crowhurst*, International Marine/Ragged Mountain Press, Camden, Maine, 1970.

3. THE MAD MONARCH OF AMERICA

John Cech, *A Rush of Dreamers: Being the Remarkable Story of Norton, Emperor of the United States and Protector of Mexico.* Marlowe, New York, 1997.

Robert Cowan, "Norton I, Emperor of the United States and Protector of Mexico," *California Historical Society Quarterly*, 2, 1923.

Richard Dillon, *Humbugs and Heroes*, Doubleday, New York, 1970.

Albert Dressler, *Emperor Norton of United States*, Dressler, Sacramento, 1927.

William Drury, *Norton I, Emperor of the United States*, Dodd, Mead, New York, 1986.

Isobel Field, *This Life I've Loved*, Longmans, Green, London, 1937.

William Kramer, *Emperor Norton of San Francisco*, Norton Stern, Santa Monica, 1974.

4. ANOTHER DAY, ANOTHER PICASSO

Stuart Gordon, *The Book of Hoaxes*, Headline Books, London, 1995.

Clifford Irving, *Fake!*, McGraw-Hill, New York, 1969.

Carl Sifakis, *Hoaxes and Scams*, Facts on File, New York, 1993.

5. CALLING ALL DRAKES – YOUR INHERITANCE IS WAITING!

Stuart Gordon, *The Book of Hoaxes*, Headline Books, London, 1995.

Alexander Klein, *Grand Deception*, J. B. Lippincott, New York, 1955.

Egon Larsen, *The Deceivers*, John Baker, London, 1966.

Alfred E. W. Mason, *Life of Francis Drake*, Hodder and Stoughton, London, 1941.

Norman Moss, *The Pleasures of Deception*, Reader's Digest Press, New York, 1977.

Zelia Nuttall, *New Light On Drake*, Hakluyt Society, London, 1914.

Scoundrels & Scalawags, Reader's Digest Association, New York, 1968.

Carl Sifakis, *Hoaxes and Scams*, Facts on File, New York, 1993.

Carlson Wade, *Great Hoaxes and Famous Impostors*, Jonathan David, New York, 1976.

6. MAU–MAUING THE MILITARY

1. Wilhelm Voigt, Notorious Captain of Koepenick

Egon Larsen, *The Deceivers*, John Baker, London, 1966.

Carl Sifakis, *Hoaxes and Scams*, Facts on File, New York, 1993.

Carl Zuckmayer, *Der Hauptman von Koepenick* (1930), Fischer Buecherei, Frankfurt am Main, Germany, 1961.

2. The Preposterous Escapades of Kanonier Schmidt

Alexander Klein, *Grand Deception*, J. B. Lippincott, New York, 1955.

7. MAKING HAY IN CATHAY

Henri Cordier, *Ser Marco Polo; Notes and Addenda to Sir Henry Yule's Edition, containing the results of recent research and discovery*, J. Murray, London, 1920.

Marco Polo, *The Book of Ser Marco Polo, the Venetian, concerning the Kingdom and Marvels of the East, translated and edited, with notes, by Colonel Sir Henry Yule, 3rd edition, revised throughout in the light of recent discoveries by Henri Cordier. With a Memoir of Henry Yule by his daughter Amy Frances Yule*. J. Murray, London, 1929.

Marco Polo, *The Travels of Marco Polo (1254–1323)*, J. M. Dent, New York, 1939.

Jerome Prescott, *One Hundred Explorers Who Shaped World History*, Bluewood Books, San Mateo, California, 1996.

Jean Bowie Shor, *After You, Marco Polo: The Experiences of the Author and Her Husband Following the Trail of Marco Polo from Venice to Peiping*. McGraw-Hill, New York, 1955.

Frances Wood, *Did Marco Polo Go To China?*, Secker & Warburg, London, 1995.

8. SUPREME NAUGHTINESS IN THE FORBIDDEN CITY

Stuart Gordon, *The Book of Hoaxes*, Headline Books, London, 1995.

Hugh Trevor-Roper, *The Hermit of Peking*, Fromm International, New York, 1986.

9. POWER TO THE PEOPLE

1. John Keely's Bargain-Basement Atomic Energy

Alexander Klein, *Grand Deception*, J. B. Lippincott, New York, 1955.

Curtis McDougal, *Hoaxes*, Macmillan, London, 1941.

Carl Sifakis, *Hoaxes and Scams*, Facts on File, New York, 1993.

Robin L. Sommer, *Great Cons & Con Artists*, Bison Books, London, 1994.

2. Louis Enricht's Gas from a Garden Hose

Scoundrels & Scalawags, Reader's Digest Association, New York, 1968.

10. GANGS THAT COULDN'T LOOT STRAIGHT

Stephen Pile, *Cannibals in the Cafeteria*, Harper & Row, New York, 1988.

11. EXTORTION BY REMOTE CONTROL

"Braten in der Luft," *Der Spiegel*, no. 5, 1994.

Paula Chin and Joanne Fowler, "Misducken Identity," *People* magazine, vol. 41, no. 12, April 4, 1994.

Gisela Friedrichsen, "Viele Mäuse – der Katze Tod," *Der Spiegel*, no. 4, 1995.

"Gewisse Erleichterung," *Der Spiegel*, no. 17, 1994.

Helmut Hoege, "Als Wäre Ich Auf Arbeit," *Die Zeit*, June 14, 1996.

Helmut Hoege, "Eher Nur Ein Donald," *Die Zeit*, January 20, 1995.

Helmut Hoege, "IQ Von 145," *Die Zeit*, March 17, 1995.

Helmut Hoege, "Vorbild Hasenmaschine," *Die Zeit*, February 3, 1995.

"Höhere Strafe," *Hamburger Abendblatt*, June 15, 1996.

Olaf Jahn, "Die Geladene Waffe an der Schläfe," *Hamburger Abendblatt*, January 21, 1995.

Olaf Jahn, "Geständnis Mit Augenzwinkern," *Hamburger Abendblatt*, January 18, 1995.

"Kaufhaus-Erpresser Dagobert Vermindert Schuldfähig?" *Hamburger Abendblatt*, March 8, 1995.

Dieter Krause, "Ich Hab's Für Euch Gemacht," *Der Stern*, April 28, 1994.

Dieter Krause, "Was Macht Eigentlich Arno Funke?" *Der Stern*, April 3, 1997.

Kuno Kruse, "Der Schrullige Typ Im Alten Mercedes," *Die Zeit*, April 29, 1994.

"Mal in Talern Schwimmen," *Der Spiegel*, no. 21, 1994.

Gerhard Mauz, "Sprengkörper im Gefuege," *Der Spiegel*, no. 12, 1995.

Klemens Polatschek, "Die Dagomanie," *Die Zeit*, March 11, 1994.

Werner Schmidt, *Achtung! Hier Spricht Der Erpresser Dagobert*, Karin Kramer Verlag, Berlin, 1994.

"Sieben Jahre Für Dagobert," *Hamburger Abendblatt*, March 15, 1995.

Saskia Tants, "Dagobert War Bewaffnet," *Hamburger Abendblatt*, April 25, 1994.

Sibylle Togotzes, "Dagobert Strahlt Nicht Mehr: Die Zwei Gesichter des Angeklagten Arno Funke," *Hamburger Abendblatt*, January 29, 1995.

Dietmar Treiber, "Beim Richterspruch Wurde Er Blass," *Berliner Allgemeine*, March 15, 1995.

Dietmar Treiber, "Ich Wollte Mal Im Geld Schwimmen," *Berliner Allgemeine*, January 18, 1995.

"Wer Ist Dagobert Wirklich?" *Magdeburger Zeit*, January 17, 1995.

Günter Werz, "Hundehaufen War Nur Nasses Laub," *Hamburger Abendblatt*, February 8, 1995.

Sharon Brown

Born in 1946, Andreas Schroeder grew up in British Columbia and attended U.B.C. A well-known figure in the literary community, he has served as literary critic of the Vancouver *Province*, co-founder/director of the *Canadian Fiction Magazine*, and co-founder/editor of *Contemporary Literature in Translation*. He has taught Creative Writing at Simon Fraser University, the University of Victoria, and the University of Winnipeg. He currently shares the Maclean-Hunter Chair in Creative Non-fiction at the University of British Columbia.

He has published over a dozen books, including *File of Uncertainties* (poetry), *The Late Man* (short fiction), *Dust Ship Glory* (novel), and *The Eleventh Commandment* (translation). His memoir, *Shaking It Rough*, was nominated for the Governor General's Award in 1976. His fiction and poetry have been included in over forty anthologies, and his byline has appeared in most Canadian magazines and newspapers. In 1991 he was awarded the Canadian Association of Journalists' Best Investigative Journalism Award. The second volume of his famous scam series, *Cheats, Charlatans, and Chicanery*, was shortlisted for an Arthur Ellis Award in 1997.

In addition to his writing, he has been a regular broadcaster for CBC-Radio – most notably on "Basic Black" – and a tireless crusader for writers' benefits in Canada. He served as Chairman of the Writers' Union of Canada in 1975-76, and as the founding Chair of Canada's Public Lending Right Commission in 1986-88.

Andreas Schroeder lives in Mission, B.C., with his wife, Sharon Brown, and their two daughters, Sabrina and Vanessa.